The Co-Regulation Revolution

Tap the Power of Embodied Connection

for Trauma Healing & Anti-Oppression Work

By Beth Dennison

M.Ed., M.A. in M.F.T., L.M.T., S.E.P.

ISBN- eBook- 979-8-9883192-1-4

ISBN- Paperback- 979-8-9883192-0-7

Published by:

The Center For Body Up Co-Regulation

5 Goffe Street, Hadley MA, 01035

Cover Design: Beth Dennison

The Center For Body Up Co-Regulation

www.WeCoregulate.com

Dedicated to:

My Mother,

Frances Isabel Ferry Dennison,

a fabulous co-regulator.

All my co-regulation partners,

the friends, colleagues, students, clients and

dance buddies who keep me sane and regulated.

Acknowledgments

I am deeply grateful for all the people who help me build and develop this work. Thank you for sharing your vitality, your vulnerability, and your new ideas.

To my committed and enthusiastic students and clients, thank you for using me well, co-regulating regularly and valuing this work.

I am grateful for the hope and inspiration of the brave and brilliant people whose work I am honored to build upon, especially Stephen Porges, Peter Levine, Lisbeth Marcher, and Ditte Marcher.

Shayna Hesselgrave, thank you for years of support, encouragement and modeling of co-regulatory behavior.

I am especially grateful to Sia Ivone Blaser for her endless hours of support and engagement wiith me and this work, her reliable co-regulation and her myriad insightful suggestions and useful criticisms.

Hunter Flournoy, without your wise personal counsel and broad editing skills, this project might never have been completed.

Table of Contents

Preface

Do you want meaningful, manageable ways to build a more just and sustainable culture?

Would you like to enliven your professional practice while working remotely?

Do you want to feel more connected with folks you see online?

This book and this work are devoted to building healthy co-regulatory relationships and healthy culture. Even if you do not think of yourself as an activist, building healthy relationships, especially healthy peer relationships, makes a difference in dismantling oppression.

Even online, it really is possible to feel deeply connected. In this book, I am going to show you how. Embodied connection is enlivening! It is good for us, prevents burnout, and does not need to take a lot of time.

For energy, getting present, connecting, calming down, getting to know your nervous system, and much more, Body Up Co-Regulation (BCR) works, online and in person.

This book is for anyone who wants to cultivate deeper connections, personally and professionally. BCR is especially useful for practitioners such as therapists of all kinds, coaches, yoga teachers, somatic practitioners, and educators. You can certainly read the book cover to cover. You can also go directly to the BCR Exercises List (p. 157) with video page QR code), or dive into a Basic Practice Session (p. 221).

Reading will orient you to BCR. Practicing BCR will rewire your nervous system for co-regulation.

Practice, Practice Practice!

Co-regulation is experiential and relational. We learn by doing it. We strongly encourage you to take a leap and practice the exercises with colleagues and peers, or friends and family.

Co-regulators, empower yourselves. Be sure you enter freely into any co-regulation sessions. Also, be sure that you ask and negotiate for what works for you. Remember that you are free to end the session at any time for any reason, and without giving a reason.

> This book is for anyone who wants to cultivate deeper connections, personally and professionally.

There are Three Levels of Practice in BCR.

Peer Practice: Peer Practice is how we rewire our nervous systems for peer relating, which is key to countering oppression. BCR, as a peer practice, is intended for folks who are generally stable enough to build regulation skills and rich, enlivening, embodied, relationships. We can support each other to grow and heal in profound ways. When in crisis, please get professional support.

Practitioners (including psychotherapists): All practitioners need the foundational peer experience as a basis for using BCR professionally. Then, when working, we can hold our professional frame while sometimes taking a peer role. This takes clarity of intention and careful consideration. Further training is in order.

It is important that your intentions for your client line up with your scope of practice. Be sure you know your scope of practice and the code of ethics for your field and/or license.

If you are not trained in psychotherapy, work with regulatory intent and avoid therapeutic interventions. Before co-regulating with clients, practice with peers to get to know your nervous system and the exercises.

Read Chapter 1, on Orienting to Body Up Co-Regulation, Chapter 4, about Safety, and Chapter 5, on Intention. Especially, get familiar with the sections on Safety and Contraindications (p.94).

Psychotherapists: This book offers basic practices to develop skills for embodied co-regulation, nervous system to nervous system. BCR builds safety, connection, and trust quickly. It offers clients useful tools for understanding and regulating their nervous systems, and for creating co-regulatory peer relationships. For in-depth guidance on the application of BCR in therapy, keep an eye out for my next book "The Dance of Co-Regulation in Therapy," or seek supervision in BCR. (The book release date will be announced on WeCoregulate.com)

Anti-Oppression Work

Wiring our nervous systems for collaborative, peer relationships is a necessity for getting off of the hierarchical ladder of white supremacy culture. That ladder has us stepping on each other to climb it and trashing our planet with greed and war as we go up.

All forms of oppression play out on the ladder of white supremacy culture. It is not just about racism. Western culture has shaped our institutions to favor white people, but you do not have to be white to get caught on that ladder.

Learning to cultivate collaborative peer relationships offers us a way off of the ladder, and we all need one! Collaborative peer relating is for interacting with people like ourselves and people who are less like ourselves.

Co-regulation, online or in person, wires our nervous systems for collaborative peer relating. When we trust our peer relationships we do not need to rely solely on climbing the competitive ladder of white supremacy culture to survive and to feel safe.

Let's replace oppressive dynamics with co-regulation, collaboration, and an expectation of connection and belonging.

Our egos will let go of familiar, hierarchical habits but only when there is something else to grasp onto. I am proposing we all find more of our safety in strong, co-regulatory peer relationships. Co-regulation may not be all that is needed to end oppression, but it is an essential ingredient.

Co-Regulation: A Friendly Revolution!

I hope that this work serves as a cornerstone in a friendly but powerful cultural revolution. We can all start relating from warm-hearted, well-regulated states. When we get stuck in unnecessary threat responses, we can use co-regulation to shift back into collaborative states and cooperative behavior. We can take action that builds deeper connections, and kinder and more sustainable social and environmental practices. I want to share this knowledge and these practices with you.

Co-regulation feeds our health and vitality and allows us to avoid burnout while staying engaged and caring. Emotional resource does not have to be finite! Co-regulation shows us how to be there for others in a way that feeds us. We can nourish ourselves and nurture others at the same time. Access to co-regulation means we do not have to go numb or get hard-hearted because we can stop the constant competion for attention, emotional resources and status. Co-regulatory peer relating offers an antidote to oppression.

The Co-Regulation Revolution is a continual turning toward mutuality and toward embodied relating. Exploitation in the mind/body relationship is an internal blueprint for racism, sexism and all forms of oppression. As long as we are dismissing our own bodies as shameful and beneath our attention, it is easy to dismiss and look down on others. Running an oppressive dynamic in our internal world quickly blinds us to oppression in the external world. It just seems normal. When we start attending respectfully to our bodies, it is much harder to buy into dismissing and demeaning others.

Let's replace oppressive dynamics with co-regulation, collaboration, and an expectation of connection and belonging. Let's learn these tools for genuine collaboration across differences.

Let's cultivate this rewarding, hopeful way of relating.

> Co-regulation may not be all that is needed to end oppression, but it is an essential ingredient.

Introduction

We all need co-regulation now - personally and for our collective survival. And we need to be able to do it online.

Global wake-up calls are blaring: war, the pandemic, climate change, and the current movements for social change and justice (BLM, #metoo, etc). Our world is changing fast. There are threats to our health, our rights, our relationships, and our survival.

These large-scale issues play out in our personal lives. Oppression and polarization breed anxiety, depression, and competition for survival. Isolation fuels addiction and poor health. War and climate change threaten our safety, finances, and way of life. It is easy to end up in a downward spiral of emotional dysregulation and primitive behavior.

Those of us with a cushion of money and social privilege suffer, too. We end up numb as we close our ears and our hearts to those less privileged. In the face of current upheavals, our sense of safety is a house of cards. The deck may be stacked in our favor, but it is balanced on an untenable, oppressive system. The storm is rising!

None of us need to lose our humanity in the face of life's increasing challenges. We all need authentic connection, emotionally and physically, and, to step up and meet life's challenges. We need to know that we can connect and help each other. We also need to be able to stay regulated enough to collaborate on complex issues.

Co-regulation offers that help and connection. Co-regulation pulls us out of apathy and overwhelm, settles us down when we are reactive, and helps us hold steady and kind under pressure. Sometimes good connection seems to crumble too easily. Body Up Co-Regulation (BCR) practices are quick and reliable. They build sturdy connections. The practices are simple to learn and quickly become useful - personally and professionally.

BCR draws on important research, theory, and practice:

Neurobiological Research - Neuroplasticity teaches us that behavior and physiological responses can be rewired throughout our lifetimes. The Elements of Attunement create connection, nervous system to nervous system. Mirror neurons support our capacity for co-regulation.

Polyvagal Theory - Our autonomic nervous system evolved in three layers, the newest being the Social Engagement System. Neuroception, our unconscious sense of threat and safety, determines whether we default to primitive behavior or more prosocial behavior. Getting stuck in unnecessary threat responses is bad for our health, our relationships, and our ability to think and cooperate. We first learn autonomic regulation and emotional habits from our early caregivers, and then from those we mirror closely.

Somatic Psychotherapy - A solid psychological sense of self is rooted in a solid physical sense of self. The body is core to perception, health, healing, identity, and relationships, whether we are aware of it or not. Sensing our bodies gives us a chance to make healthy choices based on present-time reality.

How can we feed our often fragile sense of hope and give others hope?

Feeling ourselves gives us a chance to make healthy choices based on present-time reality.

Trauma Work - Decades of study and clinical work with trauma clients have shown me that what is good for trauma clients helps us all to thrive and cooperate. Most of us do better when we have safe connection with others, when we slow down, include body awareness, and have reliable antidotes to shame. Trauma clients are our canaries in the coal mine. We all need what they need, they just show it sooner.

When we are dysregulated, in threat responses, we react defensively. Our behavior turns primitive. Our thinking gets simplistic and polarized: us against them. Bullying and power plays seem reasonable. When we get caught in dysregulation, we cause damage on many fronts. BCR gets us out of unnecessary threat responses – what a relief. This is why I remain hopeful.

When we are well-regulated, we have more bandwidth to listen to and understand other people's positions and concerns. We also have more capacity to stay present and think clearly about complex problems and issues.

In doing BCR we cooperate with our own nervous systems and with one another. We work in harmony with our neurological wiring, which evolved in service of connection and co-regulation. Before the pandemic, I had no idea people could get so engaged, embodied, and connected - so fast and online.

Necessity being the mother of invention, the pandemic fired my creative juices. Coming at the end of my career, the pandemic demanded that I take everything I have learned about connection, nervous system to nervous system, and apply it to working online. My career in trauma work taught me about the human nervous system, and what kinds of relationships help us heal and thrive. The BCR practices come from a lifetime of exploring how to build safe, embodied relationships.

Anti-oppression work has motivated me and my development of BCR from the very beginning. I have been cultivating Body Up Co-Regulation as a therapeutic tool for a decade. I have been seeking anti-oppression tools for 45 years. BCR integrates the most effective elements that I have found for building meaningful connections across differences, with efficient ways to support each other in regulating our nervous systems.

Healthy peer relating is essential to ending oppression. In my experience, racism, sexism and all forms of oppression happen in the context of abuse of power in hierarchical relationships. When we humans do not know how to trust peer relationships, we over-rely on roles and hierarchy to feel safe. That keeps us striving for power and leaves us more likely to misuse it.

"Gather together a large group of unsettled bodies - or assemble a group of bodies and then unsettle them - and you get a mob or a riot. But bring a large group of settled bodies together and you have a potential movement - and a potential force for tremendous good in the world."

-Resmaa Menakem, *My Grandmother's Hands*

Co-Regulation is Revolutionary!

White supremacy culture is killing people and our planet - and has been, for centuries. BCR is revolutionary because it builds collaborative relationships that allow us to get off the ladder of white supremacy culture.

Together, we are stronger and more capable of facing the moment. The Co-Regulation Revolution means we are all rewiring our nervous systems for collaboration, despite global catastrophe, might makes right politics, personal stress, and past traumas. BCR bolsters a can-do attitude and the will to act. In a time of hopelessness, overwhelm and addiction, such agency is revolutionary.

> BCR is revolutionary because it counters our habits of competition and compulsive ranking. It offers a pathway out of hierarchy and out of performative, role-based relating. It builds connection across differences including age, gender, class, and race.

It is a Co-Regulation Revolution because you and I, and those we share this practice with, plant seeds for hope.

BCR is revolutionary because the practices require and cultivate safety, especially social and emotional safety. Co-regulation depends on safety, as do learning and collaboration. Attending to safety around others, at a nervous system level, is revolutionary.

BCR is revolutionary because it offers interactive practices for shifting out of threat responses when they are no longer needed.

BCR is revolutionary because it reverses our western cultural tendency to separate the body from the mind. In a world that prizes thinking over feeling, to acknowledge our *body up* experience and communicate about it, is revolutionary.

BCR cuts through the social isolation of the digital age and pandemic restrictions. BCR provides real social, meaningful relating even online.

It is a Co-Regulation Revolution because you and I, and those we share this practice with, plant seeds for hope. It is anti-oppression because it is always good for both people or it is not co-regulation. My choice and your choice to co-regulate expand our capacity for presence, connection, and clear thinking. These qualities make a difference in our world. I invite you to co-regulate, see how it feels, and share it.

What Does This Book Offer?

Read on for ...

What does co-regulation have to do with Anti-Oppression work? (Chapter II)

Strategies to enliven your work and Avoid Burnout. (p. 119)

Safe structures for building Authentic Peer Relationships. (Chapter IV)

Focus your Intention In Body Up Co-Regulation (BCR) for changing nervous system states, building capacity, and working your emotional edges. (Chapter V)

Foundations of BCR. (p. 43)

The Pratice Pie - A map of BCR practices organized by intention. (p. 149)

Alphabetical list of Practice Pages - Free access to demo videos and written instructions for BCR Practices.

CHAPTER I
Orienting to Body Up Co-Regulation

Life changed for most of us when the pandemic hit. I had been seeing therapy clients and teaching Body Up Co-Regulation (BCR) in person. All of a sudden, I was starved for connection. I knew I had to find a way to co-regulate online or I was going to go flat and dysfunctional. I did find a way, and here it is. It has made a huge difference for me, my students, and my clients.

I am driven by more than my own need for connection. Hope and joy and aliveness call me to stand up for what is best in us. Living our best lives depends on our collaborative social fabric.

We humans thrive in embodied peer relationships. Body Up Co-Regulation weaves that social fabric quickly and efficiently.

Even when you hold a baby, there is an element of recognition of our being human peers. Yes, the infant requires our care and we make many of the decisions. However, they offer us a mirror of safe vulnerability that often opens our hearts. Co-regulation with peers opens our hearts and enlivens us in a similar way. It is the warp and weft of our social fabric.

When that social fabric unravels, we begin to feel isolated, alone, flat, numb, and burnt out.

Increasingly, many of us experience attuned human connection and cooperation as scarce commodities. Luckily, they do not have to be. We can avoid burnout as we connect and help each other! We are wired to nurture one another while nourishing ourselves. We can show up for others without depleting ourselves. It feeds us to connect, learn, and collaborate. Co-regulation works!

To go fast, go alone. To go far, we must go together.
- African Proverb

Without a supportive social fabric that nourishes us,

- It's easier for any of us to feel separate, hopeless, greedy, and competitive.
- We can become silent, and grow numb. It is easy to grow blind to our own privilege.
- We don't have much hope for stopping others who abuse power.

The more we nourish hope in the power and goodness of human connection the harder it is for authoritarian bullies thrive at home and abroad.

Co-regulation and healthy peer relationships are key ingredients in the fight to end oppression. Co-regulation gives us resiliency. Peer relationships give us a way off the ladder, a place to stand and belong without having to compete for status on the ladder of oppression.

1. Embodied Connection Online is Possible and Powerful!

It is easy to lose touch with body awareness, especially online! Most of us have logged hundreds of hours watching TV and sitting at a computer where we trained our nervous systems to ignore our bodies. Life is full of distraction, overwhelm, hurts, mental efforts, and entertainment - so many possibilities (and reasons) to leave bodily sensation and awareness in the dust.

Working and relating online does not typically engage our bodies. We forget to adjust our posture for comfort. We may neglect a sore neck until the pain is very loud. We seldom take a full, deep breath. Our voices can get tense and loud with others on zoom. We also may feel like the other person or people are distant and not available for good connection.

Is it hard for you to imagine feeling connected, embodied, and engaged online?

Is it an experience you've touched and want to amplify and maintain on purpose?

The good news is that our bodies give potent cues for connection that work, even at a distance.

Cues for Connection and Safety Online

To survive and thrive, we need to feel a sense of connection, a nervous system to nervous system. Our brains look for and sense specific connection and safety cues. We can create meaningful connection online, or in person at a physical distance.

By tracking the cues that evolution has given us, we can get connected and make adjustments for even more connection and safety in our relationships.

Our nervous systems track these cues at an unconscious level all the time. There are useful cues to pay attention to:

Internal Cues: Breath rhythm and depth, body relaxation and tension, eye contact preferences, our own facial expression, posture, physical pleasure and pain, emotions, thoughts, and thought patterns.

Social Cues: The other person's eye contact patterns, facial expression, posture, movements, tone of voice, breath patterns, distance, emotions, words, and ideas. (Yes, distance from the camera matters!)

Environmental Cues: Lighting, camera angle, background colors, sounds, and images.

"Co-regulation has created a whole new positive dynamic, a happier and more beautiful and connected dynamic, between me and my son... Something to help calm down his nervous system so that the doorway to thinking about the real issue and how to solve it can be wide open."

– M.S., mother and co-regulator

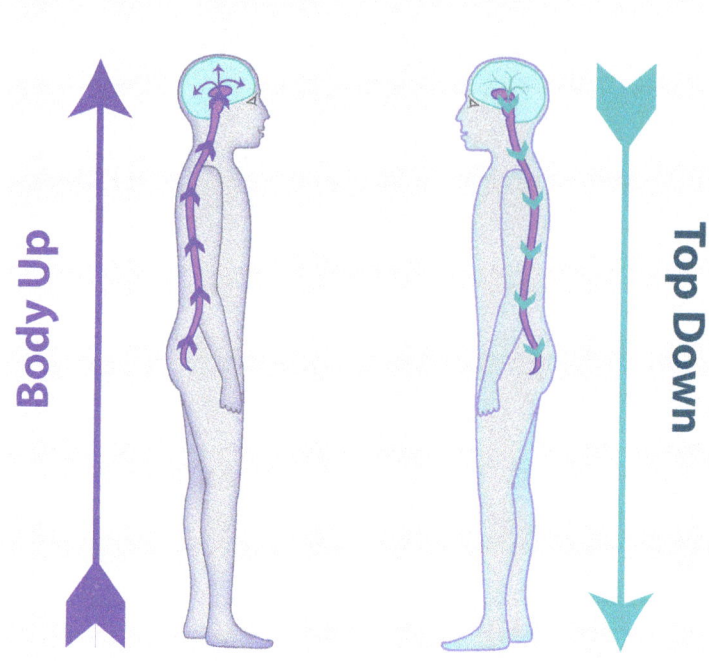

Body Up and Top Down

Body Up
Unconscious
Involuntary

Some internal experiences arise from the body, hence the term *"body up."* For example, this can be true of sensual pleasure, physical pain, or a simple need to urinate.

Threat responses in the ANS arise *body up*. When the *body up* experience is a threat response, it usually trumps any conflicting *top down* agenda.

Top Down
Mind Over Body
Conscious
Voluntary Control

Some internal experiences come from the *"top down."* For example, our thoughts and beliefs can generate emotions or even an upset stomach. Problems in our brain can result in out-of-control emotions.

At times, we want and need *top down* control over our *body up* responses. However, when there is a strong sense of threat, *body up* responses will claim priority.

2. What is Body Up Co-Regulation?

To regulate means to shift gears as needed in your nervous system. Solo Regulation means regulating your nervous system by yourself. Co-Regulation means regulating yourself with another person.

Body Up Co-Regulation (BCR) means sensing our bodies to know what state we are in and working with our bodies to shift states as needed. By leading with *body up* awareness, Body Up Co-Regulation taps the innate systems for regulation that evolution has given us.

BCR is a set of effective, embodied practices that can be done online and in person:

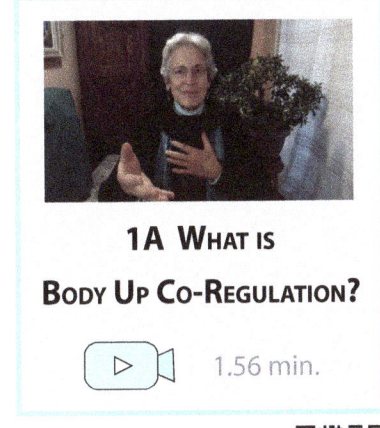

1A WHAT IS BODY UP CO-REGULATION?

 1.56 min.

QR for Video

- Practices for down-regulation when we want to rest, sleep or dispel anxiety.

- Practices for up-regulation when we want to wake up, get going, or get things done.

- Practices that support connection when we want clear communication, emotional engagement or both.

- Practices that create potent opportunities for people to touch their dysregulated, emotional edges, heal, and reregulate.

- Practices that reduce burnout and support pain management by diminishing unnecessary threat responses.

The practices are relational, regulatory, therapeutic, and diagnostic. They arise from principles, research, and experience including interpersonal neurobiology, Somatic Experiencing, Bodynamics, and yoga. (See Foundations of Body Up Co-Regulation, P.43).

Start Now!

Before reading onward, and at points throughout the book, we invite you to cultivate embodiment and *body up* co-regulation. Embodied relating grows with practice.

We learn better when we are well-regulated. Learning the theory in this book and how to do the practices, can be easier when you drop into body awareness with the suggested demo videos.

Just watching people co-regulate can be regulatory!

What Do You Notice as You Watch?

Right now, before reading onwards, take five minutes to get a feel for what Body Up Co-regulation can be like online. Watch or join in with Sitz Bones Rock (4:13 minutes).

Do you notice any sensations in your body?

Any changes in the state of your nervous system?

Do you feel calmer, energized, settled, present?

Do you feel less present, more anxious, physical discomfort?

Are you aware of mental distractions?

Are your emotions available?

It can be very useful to take a few minutes afterwards to journal. Reflect on what you noticed before the practice, during, and after.

If you like, invite someone to do the practice with you, online or in person. Practicing embodiment throughout your day builds the habit of staying present. Practicing with others (online or in-person) wires our system to expect that co-regulation is possible, even online.

As you read onwards, consider pausing to sway your torso at any point, and notice how you feel.

1B INTENTION IN SITZ BONES ROCK

▷ 0:35 min.

Video
QR

Sitz Bones Rock

 4.13 min.

 Video QR

- **For Arriving in Your Body**
- **For Ease and Soothing**
- **For Finding Home in Our Core**

Allow your body to gently sway along with the demo video.

3. What is Embodiment and Why Does It Matter?

I'm going to offer my five reasons why embodiment really does matter. But first, let's get clear about embodiment and dissociation.

A simple definition of embodiment is being alive, in a body, and sensing that body.

Dissociation means shifting our attention away from something, especially away from the body or present time reality.

Of course, there are many reasons that we dissociate from our bodies. We may be tired or in pain. We may be afraid to remember something traumatic or unpleasant. We can dissociate from present time, from other people, and from parts of our bodies. There is no simple linear scale.

> A simple definition of embodiment is being alive, in a body, and sensing that body.

Furthermore, we shift in and out of connection with our bodies from hour to hour and decade to decade. For instance, we may get very embodied as we exercise or do yoga, but drop body awareness in social space. Relating online, for work or social life, can feel disconnected and disconcerting, or simply unsatisfying, partly because we forget to include our bodies.

Evolution has wired us to connect and to experience that connection *body up*. I know I am connected when my body smiles or laughs with you, or when tears prick my eyes at hearing about your grief. We are wired to give and receive nourishment via embodied connection and attunement. The balm of attunement to each other's rhythms depends heavily on our embodied experience. *Top down* we can think, believe and remember that we are connected. *Body up*, through our physical senses, we can have a real-time experience of connection and attunement, even online.

1C WHAT IS EMBODIMENT? WHY DOES IT MATTER?

 3:02 min.

QR for Video

Five Reasons Why Embodiment Matters

1. Reality Checks for Safety

Our bodily senses give us cues and clues about safety. Seeing, hearing, smelling, feeling, tasting, and touching all inform our moment-to-moment reality. Memories from the past or assumptions about the future and the present do not give us reliable information about the current situation. We can respond best to current circumstances when we are present enough to track physical and social reality in real time. Being aware of our bodies is essential for assessing threat and safety.

2. A Solid Sense of Self

A solid psychological sense of self is grounded in a solid physical sense of self. So in Body Up Co-Regulation (BCR), we start with finding an embodied sense of self, and keep coming back to Finding Home in Your Core. It is hard to have good relationships if we can not stay connected with our sense of self around other people.

3. Reduce Loneliness and Shame

Real-time embodied connection is the best antidote to loneliness and shame because it tell us that we belong and we matter. Believing we are all connected may or may not help. The embodied experience of feeling real-time attunement and connection does dissolve shame and loneliness.

4. Physical Health

When we sense our bodies, we can take better care of ourselves. Taking better care of ourselves means dropping out of unnecessary threat responses that wear out our autonomic nervous system. It also means catching health issues early, which minimizes suffering and saves us money in medical bills.

5. Minimizing Oppression

Embodiment helps us diminish oppressive behavior and expand our capacity for empathy. When we disconnect from our bodies, we can do nasty things to other people without it bothering us. If I am awake in my body (and heart) and I hurt you, I will probably still feel it, even if I turn away. If I am not connected with my body (including my heart), I can forget your pain as soon as I look away or change the subject. Without embodiment, it is easy to misuse power and be oppressive and not even notice.

Without embodiment, it is easy to misuse power and be oppressive and not even notice.

4. Understanding Regulation and Co-Regulation

Our survival depends on regulating our nervous systems to adjust our physiology to meet the demands of life.

For example, when a bicyclist is bearing down on me, I need a quick surge of energy (a threat response) to move me out of harm's way.

Once I am safely to the side, I had better down-regulate, the sooner the better. If I stay revved up, I wear out my nervous system and compromise my capacity for clear thinking, healthy digestion, and respectful relating.

Threat responses limit our capacity for play, relaxation, clear thinking, and collaborative interaction. Staying stuck in unnecessary threat responses shortens our life expectancy. So, shifting out of them is essential for physical and relational health.

Being Well-Regulated is not a Static State.

Being well-regulated means being able to adjust our energy for the situation at hand, and the kind of engagement we want to have with that situation. Our nervous systems adjust very differently for physical work, rest, emotional connection, intellectual pursuits, play, or navigating a complex or dangerous environment.

Regulation can happen in various ways, some alone and some collaborative. Conversation, exercise, breath awareness, sex, dance, sleep, hugs, sports, doing something you love (art, music, gardening), and laughter can all be regulating.

Co-regulation means regulating yourself with another person. It is especially efficient because our nervous systems are wired by evolution to shift gears together. We are social beings who can learn (or re-learn) to rely on each other to survive and thrive.

Co-Regulation is Efficient.

When we know how to reregulate fast, we dare to take more risks, tackle bigger projects and build relationships with people who are different from us.

Solo regulation is essential, but co-regulation is more efficient. Solo regulators often avoid intimacy and conflict because it is harder for them to rergulate after intense interactions.

Life is a Regulation Game.

When we make co-regulation part of our life and stay well-regulated, we are more likely to:

• **Live longer and happier lives** - because we do not wear out our bodies.

• **Stay more present and engaged** - because we are organized around a less reactive core, and adjusted for the task at hand.

• **Have more satisfying relationships** - because we are less easily overwhelmed, can weather conflict, and know how to help each other reregulate and come back toward our best selves.

• **Avoid Burnout** - because we know how to stay present under stress and find support quickly.

• **Heal from Trauma** - because we do not get stuck in dysregulated states.

• **Take on big issues more productively** - like racism, sexism, and climate change, because of our expanded capacity to handle complexity and intensity.

• **Trust ourselves to respond well in complex or intense situations** - because we know we have the capacity to stay present and engaged.

• **Get off of the ladder of white supremacy culture** - because we know how to build co-regulatory peer relationships.

• **Have more fun** - because we dare to take more risks.

• **Feel less lonely** - because we know how to build connection and more co-regulation.

QR for Video

1D LIFE IS A REGULATION GAME

▷ 2:07 min.

5. Expression, Reflection, Response

The Three Pillars of BCR

Co-regulation is our birthright. It is a biological imperative. You do not have to be an expert to start co-regulating, nervous system to nervous system, you already do it. Mothers and infants do it. Friends and lovers do it. Co-regulation means shifting emotional gears in our nervous system in connection with others. By definition, co-regulation means good for you and good for me, too.

Co-regulation depends on expression, reflection, and response.

Expression is about showing ourselves, our feelings, our vulnerability, our autonomic state. Showing who we are and how we feel is the basic first step in co-regulation. Expression in Body Up Co-Regulation (BCR) can be body language, facial expression, movement, words, etc. Without expression, there is no reflection or response.

Reflection from others is how we know we are seen. Knowing that we are seen and how we are seen are essential to developing a sense of self. Reflection can be mirroring the other's gestures and words as accurately as possible. It can be speaking as clearly as possible what you witnessed or heard from the other. Part of being present is about seeing others as they are.

QR for Video

Responses from others let us know how our self expression affects our communication partner. Like reflections, responses can come in words or sounds or body language, etc. In Body Up Co-Regulation, recognizing and sharing how we have been affected by the other can build connection and be even more co-regulatory than the reflected movements.

1E THE THREE PILLARS OF BODY UP CO-REGULATION

 2:00 min.

Differentiating between reflection and response helps us navigate the sometimes rocky landscape around what a person did or said (expressed) and what we think it means.

Expressions, reflections, and responses are the core of communication. In day-to-day life, they weave together organically. They all depend on the neurological elements of attunement. We read each other nonverbally all the time through eye contact, tone of voice, posture, gesture, movement, rhythm, timing, and intensity. (See the Elements of Attunement, P. 81).

An Example

Scene: A pair of friends, Julie and August, practice BCR. Julie senses herself and leads the swaying movement of Sitz Bones Rock for a few minutes.

Expression - Julie, as Leader, sways slowly left and right.

Reflection - August mirrors her. They come to stillness and talk about the experience.

Expression - Julie: I liked the slow swaying and the stretching. It helped me feel more present.

Reflection - August: I noticed you started slow and dropped into taking a stretch on each side. I noticed you made eye contact several times.

Response - August: It was easy and relaxing to mirror you. Thanks for helping me slow down.

As we co-regulate with Body Up Co-Regulation (BCR) exercises, we have many opportunities to practice expression, reflection, and response, both as the Leader and as the Mirror. You may enjoy noticing what is especially comfortable or uncomfortable for you, and how that may change from moment to moment and week to week as you practice more.

TALK!

Putting words to our *body up* experience allows us to share, digest, and make sense of it. This is essential. When we cannot talk about it, anything difficult tends to get stuck and shame-bound.

QR for Video

**1F
TALK!**

▷◁ 2:36 min.

In BCR, **TALK!** means give words to your body awareness and share about it. Many of us learned not to share our *body up* truth or any vulnerability in our families. Maybe it was not safe. Maybe it upset people and was more trouble than it was worth. Or maybe we just never learned to put words on our feelings and sensations because our families did not know how to do that.

Give Words to Body Awareness

We all do better when we can name and share our experience. Putting words on our *body up* experience helps us:

- Understand what is happening to us
- Ask for what we want
- Get help when we are stuck, uncomfortable or confused
- Talk about things we may feel alone with or ashamed of
- Build trust and intimacy

We all do better when we can name and share our experience.

Freeing up our capacity to TALK! about our *body up* experience is a key part of BCR. We note our baseline as we start each practice. Then after each practice, we share with each other, about how it went and what changed from our baseline.

Co-Regulation can be almost magical!

The big deal is that it changes how we feel, quickly. Here is what people say about it:

"I go from stuck in grumpy to finding a big smile on my face."

"I get engaged and enlivened."

"I find the bandwidth to face the next challenge."

"So much can shift in such a short amount of time!"

"I get kinder and more loving towards myself."

"It can feel like hope, joy, integration, aliveness, expansion or determination."

6. The Benefits of Mirror and Leader Roles

Monkey see, monkey do! Many of the Body Up Co-Regulation (BCR) practices involve taking turns as Leader and Mirror, and sharing what we each notice in the experience. Primates and people learn by observing and doing. We connect by expressing ourselves, noticing one another, and choosing to share an experience.

These roles are ancient, evolutionary learning and communication strategies. They reach a primitive part of our brains. Leading and mirroring are especially important for embodied learning and developing a sense of self.

In BCR, we deliberately exchange roles every peer practice session. This is necessary to support each person in building skills for regulation and for peer relating. Practicing both roles is a part of weaving the fabric of peer relationships and social justice.

Mirroring

In BCR, mirroring means doing what the other person is doing, as accurately as you comfortably can. The purpose of mirroring is to be with someone where they are in the moment. Accurate reflection of rhythm is a particularly strong way to build a sense of attunement and belonging. As Mirror, reflect your partner's nonverbal expression. If mirroring is uncomfortable for you, you can always witness without moving.

Benefits for the Person Serving as Mirror:

- You can relax into being present with a simple job to do.

- Mirroring a regulated system can be very regulatory.

- Mirroring builds connection and reduces loneliness.

- Explore how others embody and express emotions, boundaries, and presence.

- Practice tracking and empathy.

- Practice tracking self and other at the same time.

Mirroring can antidote shame - It can be wonderful to notice that just by being present we make a difference. We do not even have to do or initiate anything.

Leading

In BCR, leading means sensing yourself and doing the exercise as you feel like doing it. The purpose of leading is to explore your nervous system so you can feel yourself and learn about what regulates you. Leading gives us a chance to take in connection and attunement and how people respond to us.

Benefits for the Person in the Leader Role:

- Get support for exploring your embodied experience.
- Learn to talk about sensations and normalize feelings and emotions.
- Notice what is regulating for you and ask for it.
- Feel ourselves being seen and reflected.
- Enjoy being touched by a reflected sense of self and knowing you matter.
- Feeling attunement can increase safety and connection and reduce loneliness.
- Learn to lean into connection and to regulate fast!

Leader and Mirror roles provide a useful structure for getting regulated and embodied and reducing shame. Even more important is that switching back and forth between Leader and Mirror roles lays the groundwork in the nervous system for healthy peer relating. Switching roles in the co-regulation exercises also helps us show and see our differences without going one-up or one-down.

7. Why is Co-Regulatory Peer Relating Important?

The word *peer* comes from the Latin *par*, which means equal. The peer relating we are interested in assumes that both people deserve equal respect and agency. They may not be equal in some areas (role power, financial resources, physical abilities, etc.) but they relate to one another as deserving, fellow human beings with dignity. In healthy peer relating, we each have the agency to make suggestions and changes. Together, we share responsibility for what we create. It becomes co-regulatory when it is good for both people at a nervous system level.

Let's differentiate between healthy peer relating and oppressive relating. Healthy peer relating is cooperative and supportive. It means sharing power, skills, and vulnerability.

Oppression is always about misuse of privilege and power. "Peer" implies that there is no power imbalance. However, peers can, and often do, compete for status and relate oppresively using any advantage they can find. For example, classmates or office mates of equal rank, can, in fact, be compulsively competitive or bully one another.

> Together, we share responsibility for what we create.

Healthy Peer Relating and Oppressive Relating

Peer Relating: Cooperative, supportive, sharing power, skills, and vulnerability.

Healthy peer relating means we expect equal dignity and agency. It means we are self-reflective about power dynamics and take concrete action to repair any misuse of power.

Oppressive Relating: Exploitive, dismissive, coercive, abusive, bullying.

Misuse of power in hierarchical relationships is opressive. The oppressor benefits, the oppressed are exploited and forced to suffer and accommodate.

You might think that healthy peer relating is common, easy, and organic. However, there are very real challenges to relating as equals. Even when we want connection, intimacy, and collaboration, many of us in western culture expect connection to cause more stress and anxiety than it is worth.

We may dread showing need and vulnerability. We may fear rejection and potential loss of status. This pattern in the nervous system affects our entire lives.

19

Western culture teaches compulsive ranking. Our tendency is to judge and rank each other, especially when we feel the least bit unsafe. Our brains evolved to assess rank and social status fast, before we are even conscious of what we are doing. We learn to orient to power hierarchies whether they are subtle or obvious. We learn to placate the people in power and cling to our position or role for safety and stability.

In my own life, I learned to track status from a young age. Without a conscious thought, I know who I can order around, and who I had better obey. I bet you do, too.

What we are really interested in here is how to shift our culture towards healthy, collaborative, co-regulatory relating and away from oppressive relating.

> Without a conscious thought, I know who I can order around, and who I had better obey. I bet you do, too.

- We can tolerate and even celebrate our differences - we do not have to compete, judge, and rank each other all the time.

- We can stop wasting time and energy on power struggles, and one-upmanship.

- In healthy peer relating, there is an assumption that both people have strengths and skills that can be a resource for both people.

As we get better at healthy peer relating, we develop trust in our ability to assess safety and navigate the vulnerability of reaching out to share needs and emotions. We begin feeling more generous and confident about offering our resources. We start expecting that safe connection will bring nourishment, support, and collaboration.

When we know how to function well in co-regulatory peer relationships, we have a place to land, so we can step off of the ladder of white supremacy culture and oppression. This is important for all of us, not just people of color. Mutuality and respect cultivate acceptance, safety, presence, and an ability to generate new ideas and collaborate.

In healthy peer relating, we share the agency to suggest, create, have boundaries, and take responsibility for the reality at hand. Then it gets far easier to take risks, try new things, ask for help when we need it and collaborate on challenges, local and global.

Co-regulation is the is at the core of healthy coperative relationships because it rewires our nervous systems to expect nourishment, respect, and cooperative problem solving when we go for connection. Our individual health and our survival as a species depend on the collaborative capacity of our social fabric. The point of this book is to offer tools for healthy peer relating. In Chapter II, we explore the anti-oppression power of peer relating.

"The most significant threat to our health and relationships is staying caught in unnecessary threat responses. So, shifting quickly out of threat responses, once they are not needed, is the key to long-term physical and relational health."

— Stephen Porges, PhD, *The Polyvagal Theory*

Highlights from this Chapter

- We are wired for co-regulation. It is our birthright, and we need it to survive and thrive.

- Cultivating embodiment makes a huge difference in our health and relationships.

- Embodied connection is surprisingly accessible online, and is useful both professionally and personally.

- Co-regulation helps us heal, learn, and cooperate on problems big and small.

- BCR builds authentic, Co-regulatory, peer relationships, a key element of anti-oppression work.

- BCR highlights the basics of good communication: expression, reflection, and response.

CHAPTER II
Confronting White Supremacy Culture:
The Anti-Oppression Power of Co-Regulatory Peer Relating

QR for Video

**2A
OPPRESSION, EMBODIMENT
AND CO-REGULATION**

▷🎥 2:21 min.

In my experience, racism, sexism, and all forms of oppression arise and play out as abuse of power in hierarchical relationships.

We humans, have been oppressing each other for millennia and we all suffer as a result. Currently, the Movement for Black Lives (#BLM) and #metoo movements are in response to this oppression. The power hierarchy with unfair access to power and resources on The Ladder of Oppression continues.

When we don't know how to thrive in peer relationships, we avoid them. That leaves us perpetually on a ladder of hierarchical thinking and hierarchical relating. When our experience is limited to a status ladder, we tend to try to climb it.

Climbing the ladder contributes to oppression. The more engaged everyone is in climbing the ladder of power and privilege, the easier it is to condone small abuses of power. Soon it is not just the small ones but bigger and bigger ones. Our unconscious justification is likely to be, "It is my safety and my children's future that I am serving by this small misuse of my power and privilege. Everybody does it."

Racism, Sexism, and all forms of oppression are based in hierarchy. The pervasive culture of white supremacy trains all of us to be status conscious, no matter the color of our skin. Hierarchy is natural and useful. Systemic abuse of power is not.

Oppression causes deep harm, pain, trauma, and suffering for people. Physical, material, social and emotional disadvantage are the direct result of oppression on the oppressed. It is happening now and has been for generations. When we are willing to see it, oppression is pervasive, heartbreaking and unconscionable.

The Ladder of Oppression vs. Culture of Collaboration

© 2020 Elizabeth Dennison wecoregulate.com

We can shift out of compulsive climbing and into collaborative peer relating. Body Up Co-Regulation (BCR) gives us real hope for a kinder way to live. My perspective is that safe, rewarding, peer relationships are essential to ending oppression, otherwise, there is no reason to get off the hierarchical ladder of power.

1. Oppression is Bad for the Oppressors, Too!

I have known for decades about what I call the "down-side of one-up". Oppression not only dehumanizes the oppressed, but it also forces those with systemic power to harden their hearts against feeling or seeing the pain they cause or benefit from.

For (us) white folks (I am white and grew up with privilege), white supremacy culture reduces our connection with others and with ourselves. It can constrict our access to body wisdom, creativity, intuition, and empathy.

Academia, corporate America, and current politics are infamous for cultivating competitive, backstabbing environments where people cut each other down and cannot afford to "look soft."

One-up roles, above the other folks, usually look way better than one-down, victim roles. Without a positive experience of co-regulation in peer relationships, there is little possibility or motivation to get off the ladder of hierarchy and oppression.

Some Down Sides of One-Up

Emptiness - Greed does not fill the emptiness inside, heartfelt connection does that.

Compulsive Competition - Judgments of self and others, and status consciousness can take over our lives and our nervous systems.

Isolation - Compulsive ranking isolates us. We cheat ourselves out of any meaningful relationship with most of the human race.

Strategizing without Connecting - We manage people and situations rather than trusting and being nourished by our connections with others.

Denial and Shame - We often cut off from our bodies and our hearts to avoid feeling responsible for the repercussions of our privilege.

One-up roles, above the other folks, usually look way better than one-down, victim roles.

Poor Physical Health - When we are disconnected from our bodies, we do not notice the care they need. Illness and stress levels rise.

Disproportionate Guilt/Responsibility - We can take on more responsibility than is sustainable, and face burnout.

White Savior Complex - To see ourselves as good, we assume we know what is best for those "lower on the ladder" and take action without listening for what is needed.

Rat Race and Overwork - We go obsessively for money, power, and success and do not cultivate relationships that deepen and nourish us over time.

Loss of Multiculturalism - If I am always climbing the ladder, I do not allow my life to be enriched by other ways of being (cultures, languages, arts, ways of connecting, etc.).

We do not even see the disadvantages of going one-up. Most of us have no clue how much one-up oppressor roles deaden our lives. If you are anything like me, this is a pretty startling and upsetting insight and you want to do something about it.

If you find this disturbing, you are fairly healthy. If you want to work with this, BCR has some profoundly useful tools for building nourishing peer relationships and getting off the ladder.

2. Useful Definitions

White Supremacy Culture - The idea and expectation that specific attitudes and concepts ought to dominate individuals and groups. These include better than/worse than (compulsive ranking), productivity over sustainability, and all the -isms (racism, classism, ageism, elitism, sexism, etc.). You do not have to be white to be a participant in white supremacy culture. Anyone who habitually engages in one-up relating is participating, even when it is unconscious.

The Ladder of Oppression - A conscious and/or unconscious model of relating that says, "My status (place on the ladder) determines my access to power, safety, and resources." The ladder has us caught in a habit of ranking everyone in power roles (potentially in the abusive dynamic of oppressor and victim). A person who is oriented to the ladder (as white supremacy culture requires) is often both an oppressor and a victim at the same time. You know who you can step on and where you better be careful.

Healthy Peer Relating - People treating each other with dignity and respect and avoiding unnecessary power dynamics. In healthy peer relating, our common humanity is prioritized over ranking. When we can acknowledge both vulnerability and strengths each person has responsibility and agency in what we create together. Peer relating is non-hierarchical.

Hierarchical Relating - (Authoritative, dominant/submissive, competitive, caretaking...). Hierarchical relating means one person has more power, authority, or responsibility than the other. They may use their power for the common good or fall into oppressive misuse of power.

Hierarchy - Ranking individuals or groups and assigning them power based on any number of indices. Hierarchy based on skill level, experience, or training is natural and makes good sense. Hierarchy based on class, gender, and skin color usually leads to misuse of power and oppression. (See p. 38 for more on peer relating and hierarchy and antidotes to oppression).

Oppression - Where one person or group serves their own agenda to the detriment of another. Oppressor behavior is characterized by exploitation and denial. The oppressed are often forced to learn to accommodate.

Exploitation - Appropriating the resources of others for one's own gain.

Denial - Willful or unconscious blindness to painful, uncomfortable, or inconvenient truths. This psychological mechanism for protection against emotional or neurological overwhelm can become self-serving and oppressive.

Shame - A highly aversive emotional and physiological experience. It is easily provoked by fear of rejection or

Shame is the blade that splits our wholeness into a presented self and a held-back, hidden self.

loss of status because we humans need to belong and to matter. Shame is a social emotion that gets laid in and clears in relational space. Shame is the blade that splits our wholeness into a presented self and a held-back, hidden self.

3. The Dynamics of Oppression and The Internal Blueprint for It

Exploitation and **Denial** are the fundamental cornerstones of oppression. In racism, sexism, classism, etc. the oppressor's agenda and timing prevail. That agenda may be money, or social status, or sexual pleasure. It may be avoidance of shame or work or unpleasant tasks. Whatever the agenda, the oppressor uses their power to see that the oppressed people serve the oppressor's agenda. This is exploitation.

In denial, we steer away from noticing things that are uncomfortable or overwhelming. In the oppressor role, we get good at enforcing our agenda and ignoring any objections from the oppressed.

In particular, we deny any evidence of wrongdoing on our own part. We also tend to go into denial of our own feelings and end up going emotionally numb. This numbness is an unconscious but pervasive part of hanging on to privilege.

The Internal Blueprint for Oppression

The mind/body relationship is our internal blueprint for oppression. It is the internal pattern of relating to our bodies that we export as a pattern of relating to other people. This is not to imply that the mind-body relationship is the source of oppression. It simply serves as an internal blueprint where the dynamics of oppression get encoded and perpetuated.

The mind tends to exploit the body to carry out the mind's agenda all day long. Denial shows up when the mind does not want to deal with our bodily reality. (E.g. we spend billions of dollars on over-the-counter drugs and addictions to maintain that denial and avoid feeling.)

Understand that Oppression is All Around Us AND Within Us.

White supremacy culture teaches that the mind is superior to the body - that mental intelligence and awareness are superior to body wisdom and emotional intelligence. This is the internal blueprint for oppression. How we treat our own bodies becomes the unconscious blueprint for how we treat other people.

We get wired to do it to ourselves, and insulate ourselves from knowing how damaging oppressive dynamics are. We lose our capacity to feel! Generations of trauma, on and in bodies of all colors and genders, have generated this cultural dynamic.

The Dynamics of Oppression

Built on the Internal Blueprint for Oppression

The Internal Blueprint for Oppression

Mind over Body

White Supremacy Culture

over

Sustainability and Mother Earth

Ranking Mind-Oriented as Better Than

Slavery — Master over Slave

Racism — White over BIPOC

Sexism — Male over Female

Adultism — Adults over Children

Classism — Higher-Class over Lower-Class

Ranking Body-Oriented as Lesser Than

©1989 Elizabeth Dennison

These Dynamics Play Out Externally in Many Ways.

Slavery is a huge traumatic reality and an iconic example of all oppression. The master (oppressor) exploits the slave (victim) on the master's agenda. Denial shows up when the slave objects and the master does not want to hear about it.

Social/Interpersonal Forms of Oppression include racism, sexism, adultism, and classism. White bodies, males, adults, and members of higher classes (ranked as mind-oriented and superior), oppress non-whites, females, children, and members of lower classes (ranked as more body-oriented and inferior).

Culture over Planet: White supremacy culture grabs any opportunity to exploit the earth's resources and ignore sustainability. This is a serious error. The effects of climate change, mega-storms, wildfires, air pollution, and loss of essential biodiversity are getting hard to deny.

Oppression should be shocking but it isn't. When we live with an internal blueprint for oppression, the external social forms of oppression may not surprise us or even get our attention, especially if we are the oppressors. It is easy to relate to the environment as a resource that we have the right to exploit and deplete.

> Oppression should be shocking but it isn't.

4. BCR Dismantles The Internal Blueprint for Oppression

Oppressive dynamics are seated within us. They are pervasive, not only in our social reality but in our relationships with our own bodies and hearts (and with planet earth). Western culture trains the mind to exploit the body and avoid noticing the body's needs and objections.

We routinely deprive ourselves of sleep, ignore thirst, and avoid showing any strong emotions. We spend billions of dollars on addictions, drugs (recreational, over-the-counter, or prescription), and other distractions that help us change the way we feel and ignore our bodies.

Enlivenment with *Breath Wings*

One of the most insidious ways the mind oppresses the body is to suppress our breathing! Looking squarely at big, challenging issues and confronting shame can be overwhelming and nudge us in a freezy direction.

Before reading on, watch or join in with
Breath Wings.

Breath Wings is a great way to come back to enlivenment and easy breathing.

- Do it at a pace that feels right for you or follow along with the demo video.

- Just watching people co-regulate can be co-regulatory.

- What happens for you as you deepen your breathing with a few rounds of Breath Wings, or as you watch the video?

If you do some faster, more robust breathing and movement, be sure to do some rhythmic movement afterward to ground ad integrate any expanded bandwidth. Walk, letting your arms swing, or do some *Cross Crawl* (p. 170).

Breath Wings

 5:44 min.

 Video QR

- **For Arriving, Heart Opening, Expanding Breath**
- **For Building Capacity in Relational Space**

To Begin: Sit comfortably upright, in front of your co-regulation partner. If online, be sure they can see your arms and head.

Leader - *Inhale,* and open your chest, raise your chin towards the sky. (Take your head back only as far as is comfortable).

Exhale, curling head and arms inwards towards your chest. Repeat the gesture, breath, and stretch in a comfortable rhythm. Eyes can open or close at will.

Mirror - Match your partner's gestures and pacing, eyes open.
Be available to offer a smile when they make eye contact.

Timing: Continue fast or slow for 1 - 3 minutes - or as much as you like.

To End: Pause, eyes closed, hands flat on your chest. To integrate expanded bandwidth, sense your feet on the ground, gently feeling your heels reach forward and down for connection to mother earth.

Both TALK! 1 - 2 min: Share about your experience. Leader starts.

Switch Roles, and Repeat.

The Internal Blueprint for Oppression

Vs.

Internalized Oppression

These are two distinct but related concepts. The Internal Blueprint for Oppression provides the embodied circuitry for various forms of Internalized Oppression.

The Internal Blueprint for Oppression:

We feel free to victimize our bodies and find it normal to sacrifice them to the mind's agenda.

Our nervous system gets wired to prioritize the mind's agenda and ignore bodily health, comfort, and wisdom. The social agenda often trumps bodily needs and *body up* knowing. I can work for hours and forget to eat or drink. Women routinely wear painful high-heeled shoes because the mind cares more about what they look like than how they feel. I can forget my heart for days!

Internalized Oppression:

We take in and believe oppressive messages from society and use them to judge, limit, control, and harm ourselves.

Internalized sexism may have a woman believing she is ugly if she does not match the fashion industry's current standard of beauty. Internalized sexism may lead a man to believe he is weak and unmanly if he shows vulnerability. Internalized racism may have a person of color believing they have no chance to succeed in a white-dominated world. Internalized racism may lead a white person to feel shame and outrage if a person of color succeeds where the white person has failed.

Dismantling the Internal Blueprint for Oppression

As long as we are running oppressive dynamics internally, in the mind-body relationship, it seems normal to run them in our social environment, and in our relationship with Mother Earth.

Body Up Co-Regulation (BCR) helps build collaboration into the mind-body relationship: In other words, embodiment practices strengthen our awareness of body sensation, bodily wisdom, and bodily needs. As we attend to *body up* awareness and prioritize authentic sharing in real time, we rewire our nervous systems for cooperation with our bodies and each other.

When the communication channels between body and mind become more sturdy and reliable, we trust ourselves more and become more trustworthy because we are not dismissing (oppressing) our bodies. As we bring this integration into our lives, we have access to more integrity in our relationships with other people and with the environment. BCR does this in a variety of ways:

TALK! In BCR, we share our *body up* experiences during the TALK! portion of each practice. In verbal sharing about our physical and emotional reactions, we strengthen the communication channels between body and mind. Speaking about what we notice in our body and mind brings our bodies into social space in a simple, organic way. Doing so relieves shame and affirms to ourselves and to our practice partners that bodies matter.

Mirroring and Body-Oriented Presence: Serving as Mirror, witnessing another's embodiment, and noticing when they are including their body in their experience, affirms that mind-body collaboration is OK and even desirable. Mirroring gives us a simple, potentially low-thought job. Mirroring allows us to be with another person without having to strategize for safety, status, and connection, and without having to pass judgment on the situation.

As long as we are running oppressive dynamics internally, in the mind-body relationship, it seems normal to run them in our social environment, and in our relationship with Mother Earth.

Even beyond that is the gift of "no mind" presence that can come with mirroring. The necessity for mind-over-body dominance dissolves in the face of the experience that our mere presence, without thought, can be richly nourishing to others. The simple mirroring we do in BCR is often deeply healing for both the Leader and the Mirror.

Swapping Roles Cultivates Safety: As we swap Leader and Mirror roles in BCR, we are practicing moving in and out of control very deliberately. We maintain each person's dignity, responsibility, and agency throughout the exchange. This fosters a relational space where it is safer to include our bodies in collaboration with another person. The mind can release control of the body when it can drop its need for control of social dynamics. Then, we can afford to drop the oppressive dynamic in the mind-body relationship and really pay attention to our body awareness.

Including and Valuing the Body: "Othering" is a key mechanism that makes systemic oppression possible: Us vs. Them (Other). The Other is often seen as a threat, or as insignificant, and certainly not deserving of resources. When the mind is habitually dominant, the body is "other," foreign, untenable, undeserving, and chronically overlooked. Through BCR, we build intimacy with our bodies as we include and choose to honor what we notice. As we welcome our body awareness, we weave it into our identity – no longer "other" but now indispensable. As we witness our BCR partners and hold space for their embodiment and expression, we build bandwidth for safe inclusive relating with our own bodies.

It is essential to experience that including our bodies can be safe and nourishing. Neither the social ego nor the mind need to maintain constant dominance in order for us to stay safe.

> The simple mirroring we do in BCR is often deeply healing for both the Leader and the Mirror.

5. We Keep Climbing the Ladder to Avoid Feeling Shame

If denial is a cornerstone of oppression, shame is the cement that holds it in place.

Shame is powerful because it threatens to take us down the ladder. Shame threatens us with not mattering and not belonging, and we humans need to belong and to matter. Evolutionarily, being banished from the tribe was often a death sentence.

We climb the ladder to gain status and security and avoid shame. Personally, my need to avoid shame and believe that I am one of the "good white people" keeps me in denial of my racism and the impacts of my privilege. Meanwhile, I hold on to my place and perpetuate the ladder.

Shame is an incredibly durable shaper of behavior because we don't just avoid shame, we avoid the mere expectation of shame. To think about the effects of shame, imagine finding yourself naked in public, or being exposed as a pedophile. How do you feel? Do you want to repeat that experience - ever?

"Shaming is one of the deepest tools of imperialist, white supremacist, capitalist patriarchy because shame produces trauma and trauma often produces paralysis."

— bell hooks, PhD, scholar and activist

Shame keeps us from doing the reality checks that prompt us to change our behavior.

If I want to swim in April, I put my foot in and test the water. If it is too cold, I come back and try again in May or June. I do the reality check. I decide based on the present situation, and eventually, I do go swimming.

However, if I expect to get shamed for something, I never want to feel that again, so I avoid the behavior. That means I never do the reality check, and I never even consider the risk of trying new behaviors and getting off of the ladder.

- Co-regulation offers authentic connection and belonging, which makes shame more tolerable.

- Shame freezes us in old unconscious habits. Co-regulatory relating opens our hearts and awareness to new ways of relating to others.

- Building resilience to shame helps us face the ways that we orient ourselves to the white supremacy ladder. Then, we can make our choices consciously.

Denial or Self-Confrontation?
How Do We Deal with our Privilege?

How do you handle passing homeless folks on the sidewalk?

Often, I walk by, mentally suppress what I've seen, and forget about it. But, in that moment, when I look away and walk on, I distance myself from another person and their experience. I deny my humanity and theirs. Do I need to?

I can justify many small misuses of my power or privilege. Or, I can make a conscious decision to choose between denial and self-confrontation. I could argue that I have to turn away: "I can't save everyone," "I have a right to my little world, I have enough to do, handling what is already on my plate." "After all," I may tell myself, "safety first," or "my children's future first."

In **denial**, I may employ a little willful blindness about what I just did. I may tell myself I do not care and go numb to my emotions. The consequence of denying my humanity and theirs is an increasingly numb life and an increasingly dangerous world.

6. Embodied Peer Relating

For me, **self-confrontation** is about noticing where I go numb and dismiss others, and make a conscious choice about reaching for connection and aliveness. In order to choose self-confrontation, I have to face my shame about having privilege and misusing power. Usually, that takes both courage and support. Honest self-assessment with resilience around shame is necessary if we are to shift oppressive beliefs, change our behavior, and hold on to our hearts and our humanity.

In Body Up Co-Regulation (BCR) and healthy peer relating, shared humanity is acknowledged. We cultivate authentic connection with ourselves and others. We honor individual agency. We respect choice and negotiate boundaries. Everyone's needs are legitimate, and empathy grows. "Better than/worse than" dynamics recede as everyone engages with internal and external safety.

Safety in embodied peer relating. Feeling safer in one's own body helps us stay present for healthy peer relating, and peer relating helps us learn to feel safer in our own body.

Safer means more capable of defending ourselves and negotiating comfortable boundaries. The supposed securities of hierarchical relating ("knowing where I stand in relation to the other") can transform into knowing that we can stand together. We do not need to cling to hierarchical roles or reactive misuses of power, just in order to feel safe. In fact, once we can feel our bodies and trust our peer relationships, we may discover that we feel safer than we ever did on the ladder. (For more on Safety, see Chapter IV.)

Embodied peer relating is complex. It requires a lot of capacity because there are several agendas to track, at least four - *body up* and *top down* for both people. If we want to be more fully present and embodied around others, we need to develop more bandwidth for complexity. BCR is extraordinarily efficient at helping us develop our capacity for navigating embodiment and complexity.

> The supposed securities of hierarchical relating ("knowing where I stand in relation to the other") can transform into knowing that we can stand together.

Hierarchies of skill, knowledge, and resources are important. Let's not overlook how crucial it is to have an experienced captain in a storm, a midwife at a birth, or a well-rested parent on duty while the exhausted one naps. Resources, expertise and leadership matter. However, we tend to abuse power if we cling to our roles when they are no longer necessary for the situation. This is especially true if we are unconsciously habituated to power and privilege. In BCR practice, we routinely switch roles from Leader to Mirror and back. This equips us to lay down power roles and find our safety in peer relating.

Modeling healthy peer relating in therapy. As a master therapist, I hold different knowledge, skill, and perspective from my clients. That is why they come to me. However, there is another essential reason they return for subsequent sessions: I invite and practice collaborative peer relating with them, when and as appropriate. I like to say that one of the best gifts we therapists can give our clients is skills for healthy peer relating. Embodied, real-life modeling is the obvious way to transmit those skills.

7. BCR Antidotes Oppression in Our Lives

There is a basic sense of dignity and respect for all life that comes with embodied presence. We become more attuned to others and reluctant to perpetuate harm.

Our world seems to be devolving into increasingly autocratic, exploitive, abusive "might makes right," hierarchical, cultural dynamics. Oppression means people are not safe from exploitation, abuse, and the temptation to abuse power. Body Up Co-Regulation (BCR) offers an alternative. We can reverse this pervasive loss of safety and lack of heartful peer relating. Practicing BCR antidotes oppression in important ways:

First, BCR teaches us how to be safe and feel safe in non-hierarchical, collaborative relationships. The experience of safe, nourishing peer relationships gives us motivation and support to find alternatives to the ladder of white supremacy culture. Without this experience of beneficial peer relating, it can seem like there is no safe alternative to compulsive ranking and striving.

Second, BCR provides tools and practices for negotiating safety with embodied boundaries instead of hierarchical role boundaries. In BCR, switching between Leader and Mirror roles gives us practice in sharing power. That means we do not have to resort to power dynamics to feel safe.

Third, BCR builds the complex neurological wiring we need for embodied peer relating. This means we can maintain connection with our hearts and our humanity and enjoy more nourishing relationships. As we welcome our own *body up* experience, we increase our sensitivity to others' experience.

Fourth, BCR helps us relate across differences and the more sturdy our relationships with people are, the less likely we are to oppress them. Relating to people with different resources, beliefs, education, and cultures is more complex than relating to people like us, whoever we may be. In building our capacity to stay present with complexity, BCR helps us bridge diversity.

Fifth, BCR allows us to reregulate our nervous systems fast, so we do not have to shy away from difficult situations, emotions, and challenges. When we have tools to reregulate quickly, we can take action for the common good instead of reactively pursuing power, control, and greed out of primitive threat responses. *Re-regulating quickly is an essential tool for everyone who is committed to dismantling racism or standing against oppression on a regular basis.*

> Embodied peer relating offers insurance against oppression because we can not hurt others without feeling it in our own bodies and nervous systems.

Nourishing peer relationships are necessary motivation if we are to drop hierarchical relating and get off of the ladder of white supremacy culture.

As we practice swapping Leader and Mirror roles, we learn mutuality and flexibility in power dynamics. We learn that collaboration with another person can be safe and nourishing.

39

8. Chapter Conclusion

BCR shows us that we can find safety in connection and collaboration, instead of seeking safety in dominance and hierarchical habits of relating.

Co-regulation shifts us out of oppressive dynamics, internal and external. Try it, you'll like it!

BCR offers many essential ingredients for dismantling white supremacy culture. The revolution we need takes motivation and perseverance. BCR nourishes us and equips us to pursue what we value and believe in, without getting burnt out or losing heart.

There is a basic sense of dignity and respect for all life that comes with embodied presence. We become tuned to others and reluctant to perpetuate harm.

Embodied peer relating offers insurance against oppression because we can not hurt others without feeling it in our own bodies and nervous systems.

Relationships that leave the body out often blind us to the effects our decisions and behavior have on other people's bodies and emotions. If we hold the body split off and in denial, we can do nasty things to other people without noticing or caring. Peer relating that is primarily cerebral or social and not embodied offers no insurance against oppressive behavior.

The Co-Regulation Revolution lies in our practice of embodied peer relating. It depends on each of us addressing our own one-up habits. It also depends on our dedication to shifting the internal blueprint for oppression we carry in our own mind/body relationship. Our choices here matter, and we thank you for any and all courageous steps you take.

Highlights from this Chapter

- Deepening our wiring for co-regulatory peer relationships paves a way out of white supremacy culture.

- Oppression is bad for people, people who are oppresed and people who are in the oppressor role.

- Internalized oppression and an internal blueprint for oppression (mind over body) live in the vast majority of us.

- As we learn to feel safer in our bodies and trust our peer relationships, we often discover that we feel safer with peers than we ever did climbing the Ladder of Oppression.

CHAPTER III
The Roots and Science of Body Up Co-Regulation

Body Up Co-Regulation (BCR) is first and foremost about safe relationships. This lines right up with Polyvagal Theory. These practices emerged from my lifetime of inquiry about how to build safe, nourishing relationships in life and as a trauma therapist.

The BCR practices give us a chance to practice four basic developmental tasks: Finding Home in our Core, Exploring Boundaries, Giving the Body a Voice, and Tracking Self and Other. The work is rooted in embodiment practices, co-regulatory peer relating, somatic psychotherapy, and neuroscience.

BCR is a set of practices that offers people connection with their own bodies and each other in real time. For me, being alive in a body and connected to other people makes life worth living. Healthy relationships feel good. They are good for us. They are good for our health and longevity. They are good for our nervous systems. They are necessary for healing trauma. This chapter highlights some of the disciplines that BCR draws from, and the neuroscience it is based on.

1. The Foundations of BCR

Working with trauma shows me what makes us fall apart and what works to pull us back together and heal. Body Up Co-Regulation (BCR) is built on the modalities listed here because they are the most efficient things I have found for helping us humans heal and thrive. I am ever grateful and inspired by the work of the giants who generated these approaches:

Polyvagal Theory

Stephen Porges' far-reaching work with the autonomic nervous system highlights the importance of threat and safety in connecting with our bodies and each other.

Porges' Polyvagal Theory emphasizes safety and organizes what we know about relating nervous system to nervous system. Porges' discovery of the social nervous system and his understanding of the evolutionary ladder offer us an invaluable paradigm shift in understanding the relationship between our physical and social behavior.

Interpersonal Neurobiology

We are wired to relate nervous system to nervous system. We are organized to shift autonomic states and moods together. We know this thanks to the research and inquiries of Dan Siegel, Alan Schore, Antonio Damasio, Mark Solms, and many more...

Somatic Experiencing

SE teaches us that PTSD is in the autonomic nervous system, not in the event. Peter Levine's breakthrough work on trauma in our nervous systems offers profound tools for healing and resiliency. Knowing that trauma lives in the nervous system allows us to work with it there, from the body up.

Internal Family Systems

In IFS, we recognize that we all have a capital "S" self and various parts which are sometimes at odds with each other. Richard Schwartz's wise, kind, effective work with parts and how they often show up in the body offers us tools for embodiment and therapeutic relationships that are non-hierarchical.

Bodynamics

I am ever grateful and inspired by the work of the giants who generated these approaches.

This pioneering work of Lisbeth Marcher and Sonja Fich focuses on which muscles support which developmental tasks, ego functions, and psychological functions. The BCR exercises capitalize on their discoveries.

Re-Evaluation Co-Counseling

Harvey Jackins' wonderful contribution to humanity builds healthy peer relationships and supports the process of dismantling oppression. BCR builds on RC by offering a rare opportunity to engage intentionally, at our emotional edges, with titration strategies and solid, social support.

Physical Practices

Several practices that I have studied cultivate embodiment in relational space and inform BCR.

- Hatha and Kundalini Yoga draw us into our bodies and build our capacity for embodied presence.

- Aikido creates embodied connection and the capacity to remain regulated and compassionate even in close contact and under attack.

- Contact Improvisation offers broad opportunities for safe, embodied relationships, sharing rhythm and weight, negotiating boundaries, and collaborative risk-taking.

2. Polyvagal Theory and Co-Regulation

You do not need to know any science to practice or experience the benefits of co-regulation. Parents and infants do it all the time. The good news is we can track and change our nervous systems on purpose. Polyvagal theory and neuroplasticity show us that we can actually rewire our brains for cooperative connection. We can learn to nourish ourselves as we nurture each other. Polyvagal Theory reminds us that we can actually be nourished, rather than stressed, by helping others regulate themselves.

Together, we can help each other shift into states that are optimal for the task at hand. All of this is especially important because co-regulation is more efficient than solo regulation. Co-regulation shifts us into and out of threat responses faster than we shift alone. It allows us to face and digest things that we cannot cope with alone. Together we can navigate more complexity and intensity than we can alone. Our capacity to collaborate and co-regulate gives me hope.

> Co-regulation allows us to face and digest things that we cannot cope with alone.

Overview of the Six Key Concepts

These six keys are useful for understanding ourselves and our behavior at our best and our worst. Following this overview, each key is described in more depth.

1) Safety, Safety, Safety

When we feel threatened, our neuromodulators have us orienting to danger. We are not available for relaxed relationship building, for healing from trauma, for complex problem solving, for learning, or for taking on big cultural issues like racism, sexism, global warming, or the pandemic. As we rewire our nervous systems for collaborative peer relationships, we need to assess for safety and feel safe enough.

2) The Evolutionary Ladder

The social nervous system is the newest rung on the evolutionary ladder. Different steps on the ladder have given us different options for responding to threats and surviving. We can help each other shift into the autonomic state that is appropriate for the task at hand, be it sleep, physical protection, or inclusive problem-solving about dicey issues.

3) A Social Threat Response Hypothesis

We are highly motivated to defend our social status. This need gives rise to compulsive competition, greed, oppressive behavior, workaholic habits, strategizing for war, and codependent behavior like fawning and accommodation.

4) Neuroception - Faster Than Perception

Our autonomic nervous system (ANS) responds to threats before we consciously perceive them. We call this neuroception. It can be triggered by an external experience, or by internal reactivity.

5) The Visceral Afferents

The dorsal and ventral segments of the vagus nerve make up the polyvagal nervous system. The dorsal vagus fibers are mostly visceral afferents. They bring information from the visceral organs to the brain. *Body up* awareness means listening to the visceral afferents. The ventral vagus fibers are a major component of the social nervous system.

6) Co-Regulation

When we can access it, co-regulation is a highly efficient way to shift out of unnecessary threat responses. It also helps us stay steady under threat, shift into a state that is adaptive for the task at hand, and avoid burnout.

3. Six Key Concepts of Polyvagal Theory, In-Depth

1) Safety, Safety, Safety

We need two green lights from our nervous system to feel safe, and to be in our bodies around other people: *top down* safety and *body up* safety.

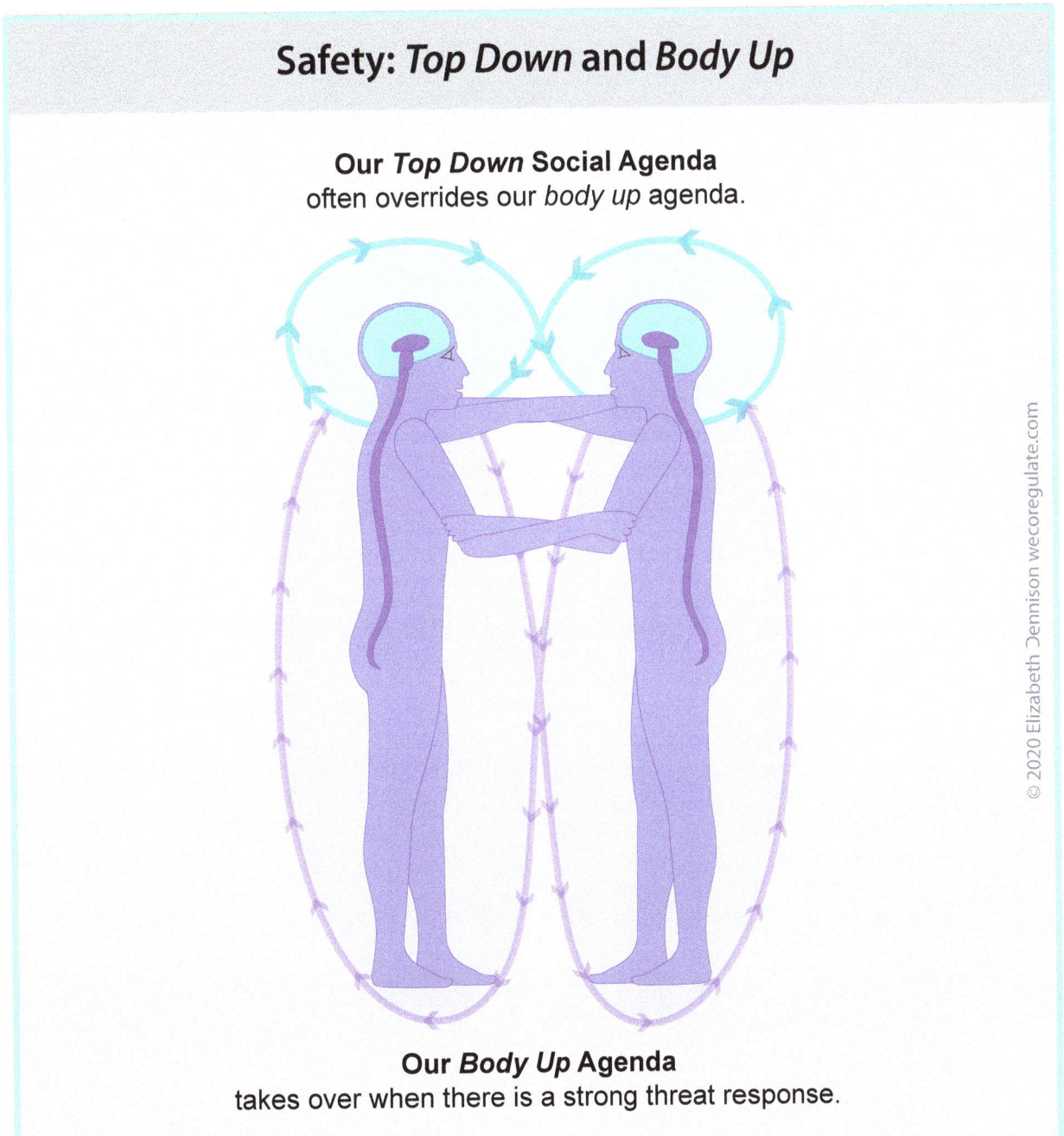

Safety: *Top Down* and *Body Up*

Our *Top Down* Social Agenda
often overrides our *body up* agenda.

Our *Body Up* Agenda
takes over when there is a strong threat response.

3A SAFETY:
TWO GREEN LIGHTS

 1:43 min.

QR for
Video

There is a *top down*, conscious perception of safety and there is a *body up*, unconscious experience of safety (meaning our nervous system registers safety at an unconscious level). In order to bring our best self forward (i.e. to engage our social nervous system), we need both, but they can often work at cross purposes.

Top Down Safety

Our *top down* sense of safety drops when we worry that we will be judged, shamed, or humiliated for showing weakness or for doing something unusual or unacceptable. Ensuring that we belong and we matter is often a very high priority and can override or dismiss our *body up* needs.

Body Up Safety

Our *body up* sense of safety drops when our social priorities interfere with attending to our body up needs. (Even something as simple as not taking a break to rest or pee can put us on edge.) For us to feel safe, our nervous system (including our amygdala), needs to know that we can and will speak up for ourselves, and take physical action to protect and care for ourselves.

When our *body up* sense of safety is seriously threatened, we can get triggered. That means strong *body up* threat responses will override any *top down* social agenda. We may get scared stiff and unable to move, or so angry and reactive that we yell unreasonably at people we love.

QR for
Video

Safety with Intensity and Complexity

Intensity and complexity are the two things that overwhelm the nervous system. When we are overwhelmed, we do not feel safe. Social situations can be intense and complicated even without the added intensity and complexity of body awareness.

3B
COMPLEXITY AND INTENSITY

 1:12 min.

So, in Body Up Co-Regulation (BCR), because we combine social engagement and body awareness, it is essential to track and adjust the exercises to avoid overwhelming the nervous system. To adjust the practices for avoiding overwhelm, see Chapter 4 on Titration (p. 90).

2) The Evolutionary Ladder

Understanding the evolution of our human nervous system and its present-day capacities gives us important insight into our behaviors and reactions. Our best chances for healthy cooperation and survival depend on this.

The autonomic nervous system (ANS) governs the delivery of oxygen and energy to the body and brain. Porges has made it clear that the ANS has three layers, the three rungs on the ladder. They can calm the body down, rev it up, or adjust it for effective communication.

3C THREE STEPS ON THE EVOLUTIONARY LADDER

 ▷◁ 1:13 min.

QR for Video

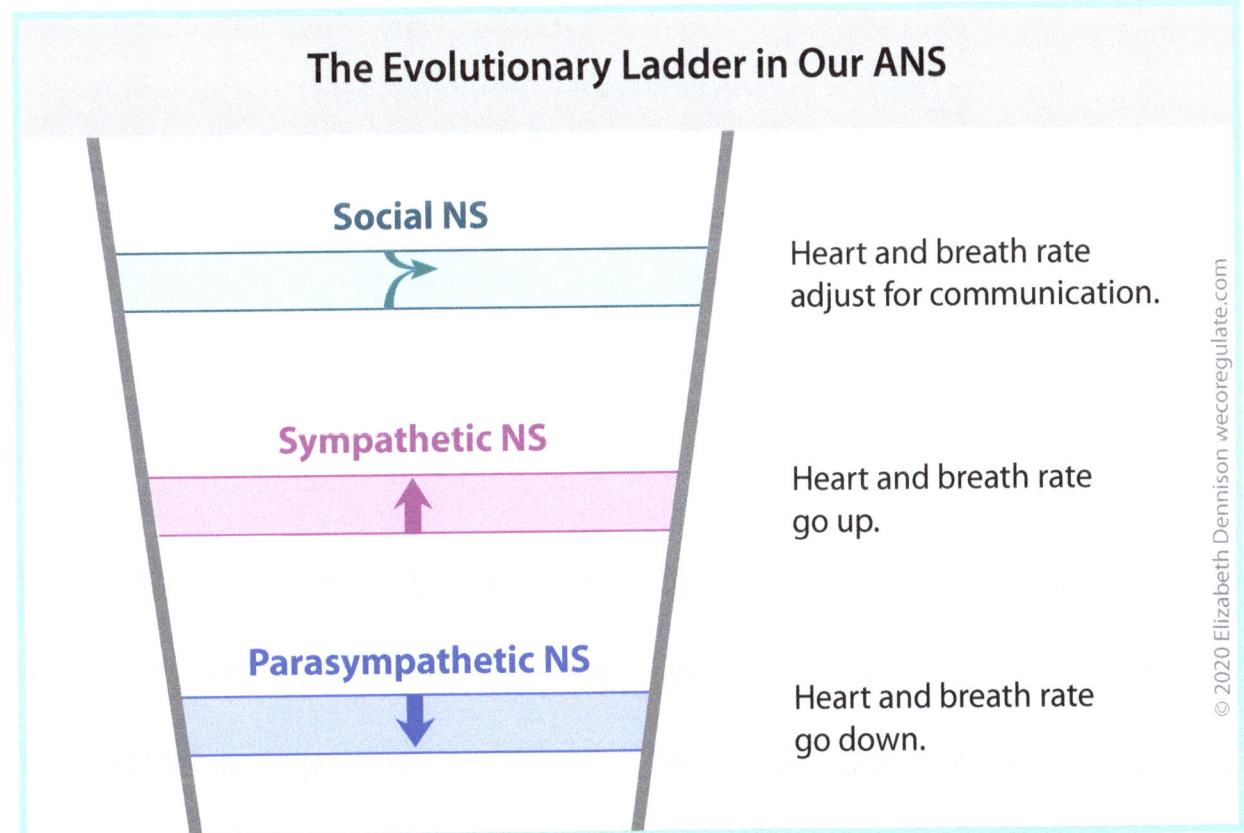

The Evolutionary Ladder in Our ANS

Social NS — Heart and breath rate adjust for communication.

Sympathetic NS — Heart and breath rate go up.

Parasympathetic NS — Heart and breath rate go down.

© 2020 Elizabeth Dennison wecoregulate.com

49

Tapping into the Social NS

Hands Show Breath is a simple way to explore our social nervous system and how we feel about connection in the present moment.

Before reading on, watch or join in with

Hands Show Breath.

- Do you want to be more connected or do you want to close your eyes and stay with yourself?

- Do you like mirroring someone else's rhythm or does it feel better to track your own rhythm?

- How do you feel after engaging with this practice?

- Who in your life would you like to do this with?

Hands Show Breath

 6:14 min.

- **For Getting Connected with Self, Other, and Breath**

 Video QR

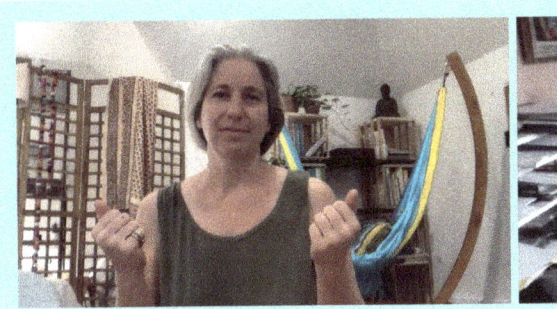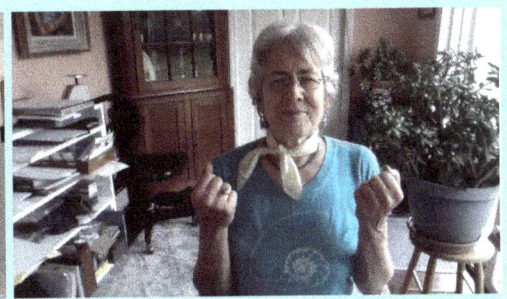

To Begin: Sit or stand comfortably, facing your partner.
If online, be sure you can see each other's torso, hands, and face.

Leader - Elbows bent so hands are near shoulder/chest height yet relaxed.
Palms on your chest or in relaxed, gentle fists in front of your chest.
Open your hands wide as you inhale. Eyes open and close at will.
Return your hands and fingers to the original position as you exhale.
You set the pace and rhythm. Do what feels good to you.

Mirror - Eyes open, so you can track your partner.
Mirror their motion and rhythm. When they make eye contact, offer a smile.

Timing: - First Leader: 1- 2 minutes.
TALK! 1- 2 min. Leader starts.
Switch Roles, and Repeat.

The Evolutionary Ladder in Our ANS

Let's look at our autonomic nervous system in terms of its evolution. Each new layer on the evolutionary ladder gives us creatures an evolutionary advantage.

The parasympathetic nervous system evolved first. It is designed to preserve energy by down-regulating the system. It evolved with bony fish, amphibians, and reptiles. They can scuttle into a hole with a quick burst of energy, but they cannot sustain a chase or keep themselves warm in a cold environment like mammals.

The sympathetic nervous system evolved with mammals. It revs us up with adrenal glands that can maintain a steady body temperature and sustain high arousal in fight or flight.

The social nervous system, AKA our social engagement system, is designed to send blood to the brain to adjust for the complex task of communication. All mammals also have a primitive social nervous system, but primates and humans have a much more developed and complex social nervous system.

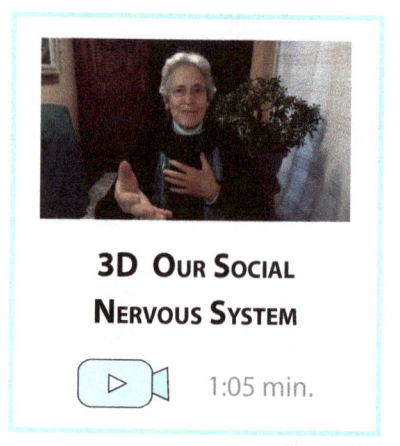

3D OUR SOCIAL NERVOUS SYSTEM

▷ ◻ 1:05 min.

QR for Video

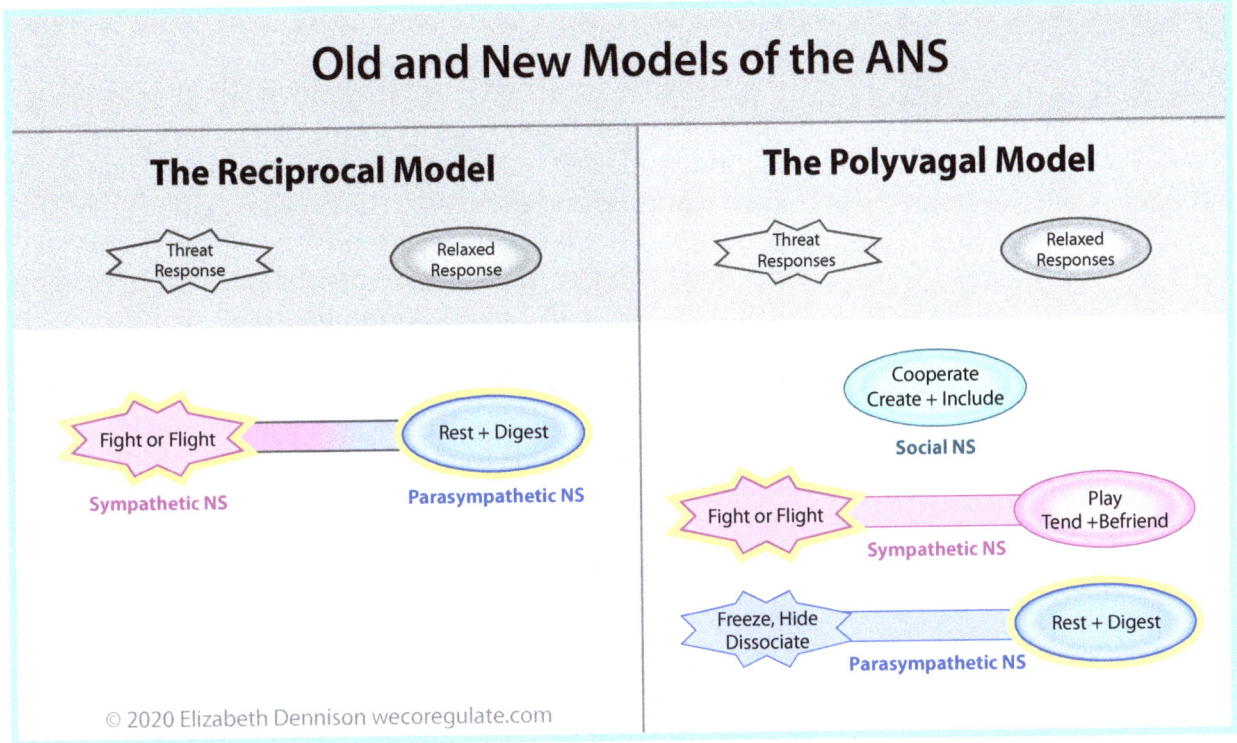

Let's consider two models of the ANS: The Reciprocal Model (the familiar root model of the ANS) and Porges's Polyvagal Model (with the three layers of the evolutionary ladder). Both include the familiar "fight or flight" and "rest and digest" responses.

Each model offers a framework for understanding our nervous systems and our human behavior. Nothing in Porges' Polyvagal Model contradicts anything in the root paradigm. It simply offers a more nuanced map, especially of what happens when we get overwhelmed, and how we can heal.

The root or Reciprocal Model is familiar to many and very useful, especially in healthy nervous systems. The Polyvagal Model offers invaluable tools for working with PTSD and people with neurodiversity. It builds on the older, Reciprocal Model to include Porges' discovery of the social nervous system.

The Reciprocal Model

In high school, I learned the well-known Reciprocal Model of the autonomic nervous system, where more fight or flight means less rest and digest and vice versa. This root model is simple and contrasts the down-regulation of the parasympathetic nervous system with the up-regulatory effects of the sympathetic nervous system. It is very helpful and broadly relied on medically.

The Reciprocal Model paints a simple, useful picture. However, it has some serious deficits when used as a model to understand deep dysregulation, trauma, and co-regulation.

The Reciprocal Model had us looking for psychological explanations and remedies for problems of neurological dysregulation. In particular, the frozen, speechless, shutdown, hopeless, dissociative states (so common in people with post-traumatic stress reactions) have been poorly understood and ineffectively treated in the past.

The Reciprocal Model also ignores the relaxing, playful, and therapeutic aspects of the sympathetic nervous system and the tremendous resource of the social engagement system.

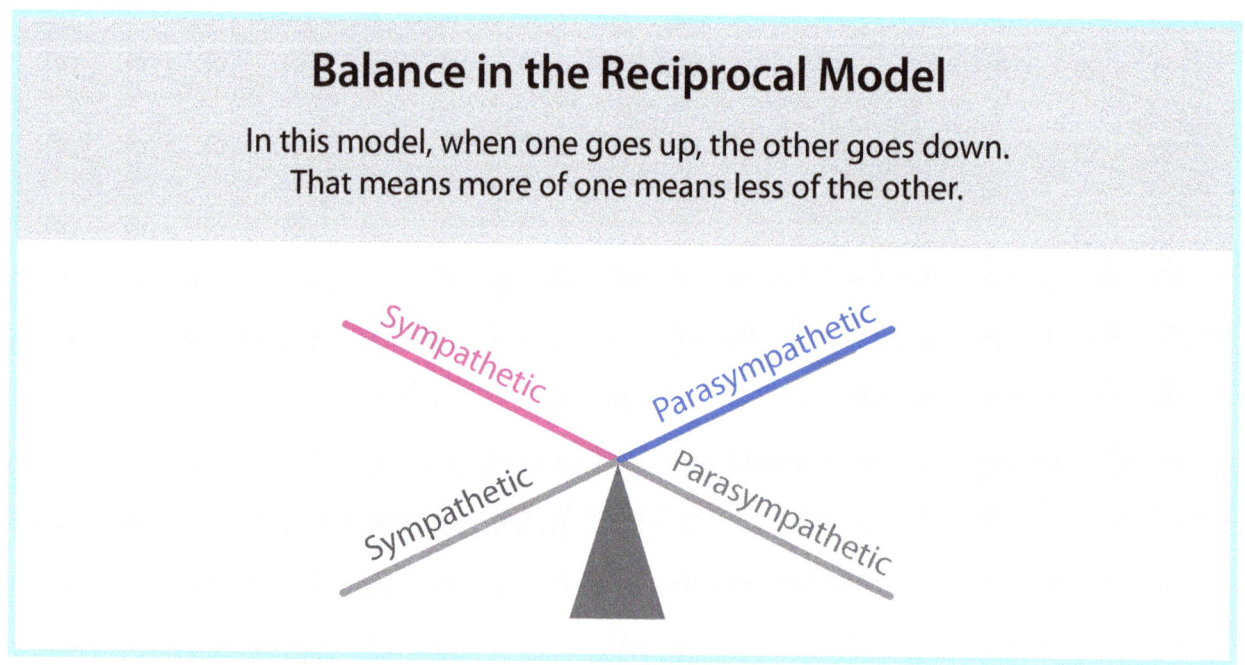

Balance in the Reciprocal Model

In this model, when one goes up, the other goes down.
That means more of one means less of the other.

The Polyvagal Model

Stephen Porges has given us paradigm-shifting research and a model of the ANS that accounts for many of our previous challenges in understanding and healing from PTSD and developmental PTSD. This model shows how evolution gave us new physiological threat responses with significant advantages for survival as we evolved up the ladder.

The Polyvagal Model is hierarchical. It has three layers that govern the allocation of energy and oxygen in our bodies. Porges emphasizes the importance of safety, highlighting the threat responses of the lower two layers and the safety in the social nervous system.

The first layer is the parasympathetic nervous system, the oldest, lowest layer. (It is also called the old parasympathetic nervous system). It is about down-regulation. It is designed to conserve energy and minimize all oxygen

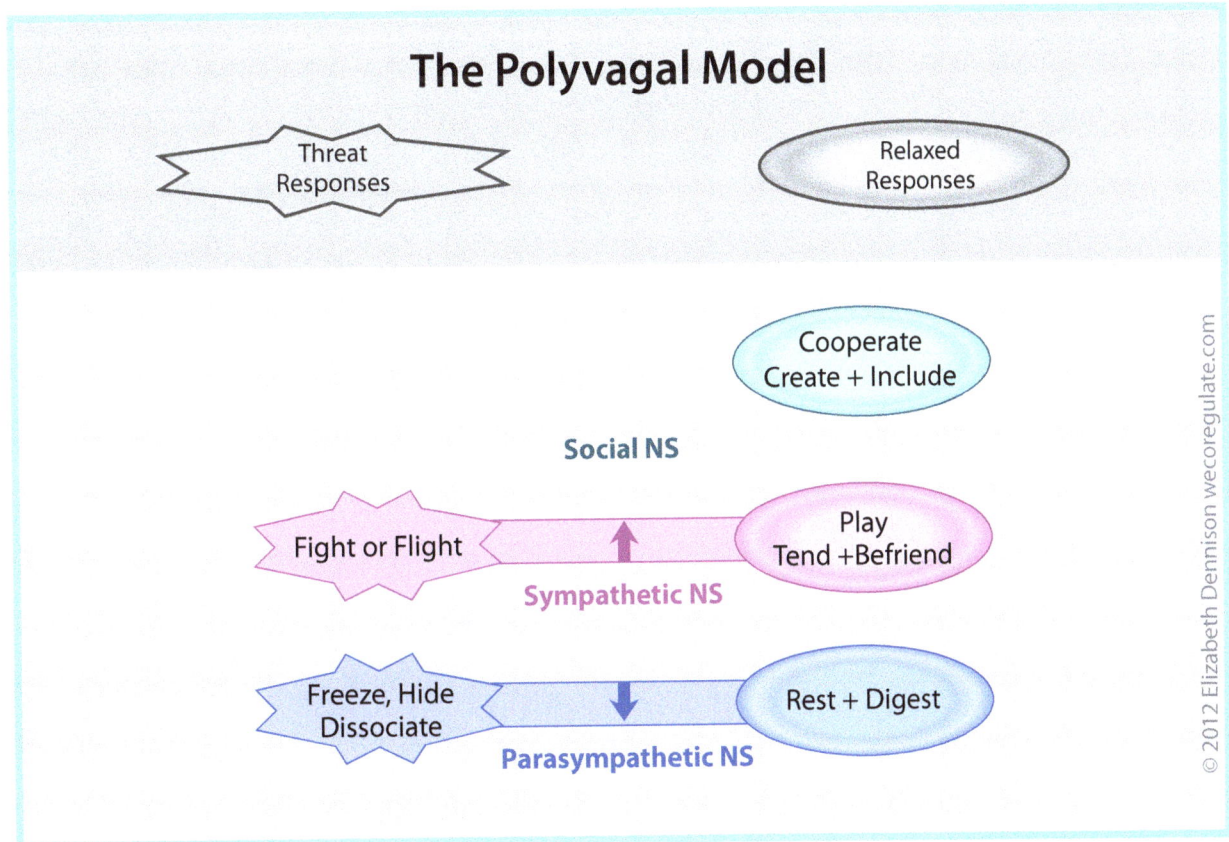

use. The threat responses include freezing, hiding, and shutting down in fear, dissociation, and depression. The relaxed responses are the familiar rest, digest, and relax.

The second layer is the sympathetic nervous system. It produces up-regulation. It sends lots of oxygen to the muscles for activity. The threat responses are the familiar "fight or flight." The relaxed responses include "tend and befriend," sexual arousal, and active play, like roughhousing. I like to call it "happy puppy": no fear and lots of energy and curiosity.

The third layer is the social nervous system (AKA the social engagement system and the new parasympathetic nervous system). It sends blood to the brain to supply the complex, energy-demanding activity of the social nervous system. It takes a lot of oxygen and brain power to read, track, and respond to social interaction. The relaxed social nervous system response is inclusive, cooperative, and creative. It organizes our nervous systems for doing things together: communication, socializing, learning language, complex thinking, healing from dysregulation, and taking on problems big and small.

The Polyvagal Model matches people's lived experiences, making it useful and easy to relate to. It explains and predicts symptoms and healing mechanisms. It points towards breakthrough clinical strategies especially for working with sensitive nervous systems, avoiding retraumatization, and working with frozen states. The Polyvagal Model focuses me on utilizing the social engagement system and reducing shame, which supports co-regulation and improves my life!

"The most significant threat to our health and relationships is staying caught in unnecessary threat responses. So, shifting quickly out of threat responses, once they are not needed, is the key to long-term physical and relational health."

- Stephen Porges PhD, *The Polyvagal Theory*

Up and Down the Evolutionary Ladder in the ANS

Co-regulation is a highly efficient way to shift out of threat responses.

The nervous system is a responsive and elegant system that constantly adjusts to the perceived needs of the moment. We tend to drop down the ladder when we feel threatened or overwhelmed. Ideally, we rise back up to our best, relaxed social functioning as soon as possible.

What might it look like to slide down the ladder under serious threat? Consider war. You are socially engaged - with a scouting group on a mission with a plan. Suddenly you are under attack by a much larger force. It is every man for himself, fight or flight. Then, you take a bullet that hits an artery, your blood is pumping hard. You will bleed out fast if you stay revved up. Your nervous system shuts you down into a dorsal vagal freeze. You may even survive because your pursuers take you for dead.

What does it look like to shift up the ladder? Waking in the morning from sleep we shift from parasympathetic rest and digest into intentional movement. Perhaps we reach out for a cuddle or a relaxed stretch, gently activating the sympathetic nervous system. As we wake up more, our thinking gets organized and we may be happy to be invited into some collaborative social engagement on a complex and important project.

Threat responses tend to move us down the ladder into more primitive behaviors and black-and-white thinking.

Co-regulation helps us move up the ladder into collaborative, inclusive behaviors and flexible thinking.

3E Up and Down the Evolutionary Ladder

▷ 🎥 1:38 min.

QR for Video

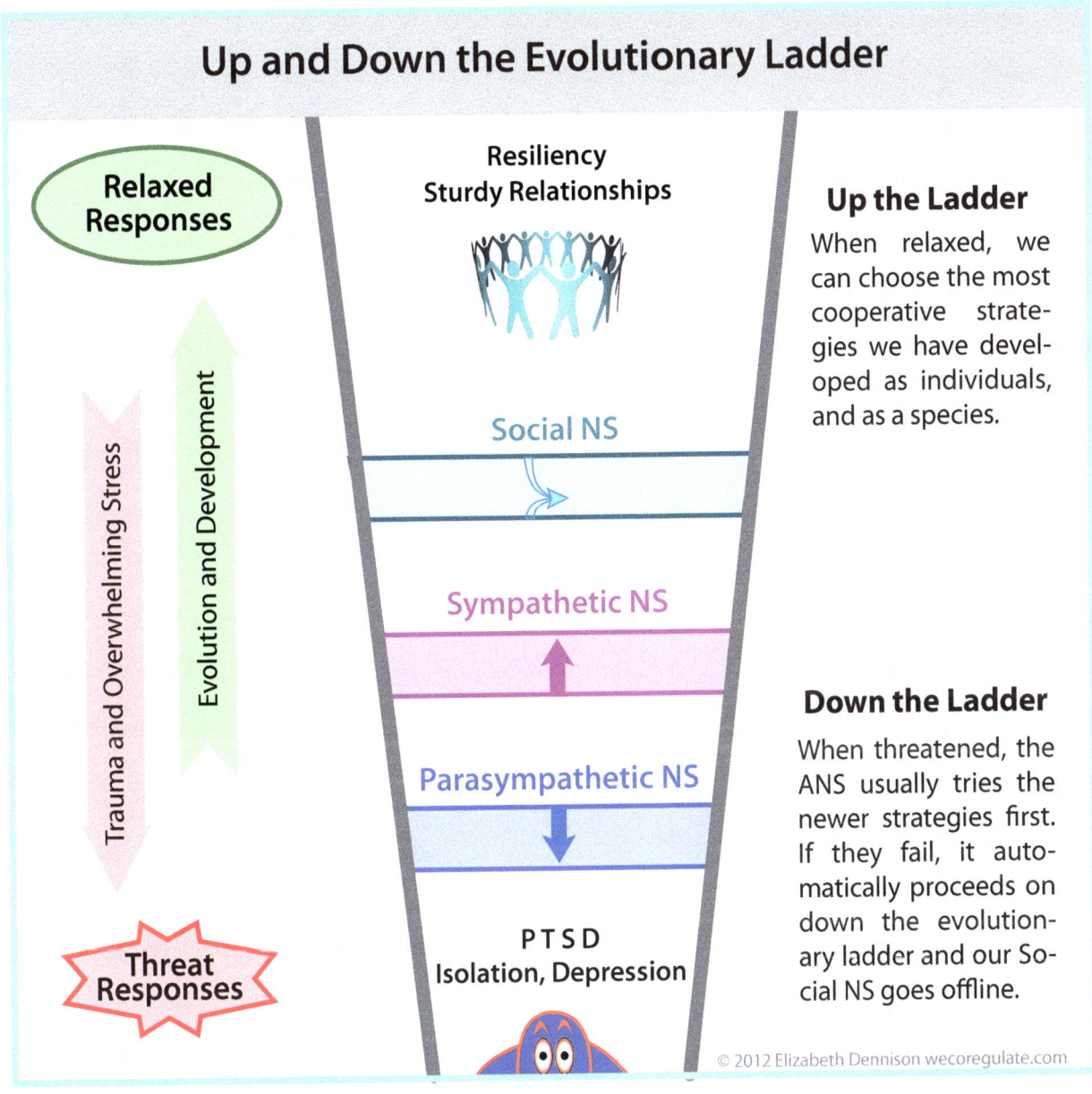

Up and Down the Evolutionary Ladder

Relaxed Responses

Trauma and Overwhelming Stress

Evolution and Development

Threat Responses

Resiliency
Sturdy Relationships

Social NS

Sympathetic NS

Parasympathetic NS

P T S D
Isolation, Depression

Up the Ladder

When relaxed, we can choose the most cooperative strategies we have developed as individuals, and as a species.

Down the Ladder

When threatened, the ANS usually tries the newer strategies first. If they fail, it automatically proceeds on down the evolutionary ladder and our Social NS goes offline.

© 2012 Elizabeth Dennison wecoregulate.com

Life is a Regulation Game!

Managing Overwhelm

Prayer Push is often empowering. It can help us find our competence. It can help us embody the boundaries and safety we need to avoid sliding down the evolutionary ladder into primitive, defensive behavior.

Before reading on, watch or join in with Prayer Push and feel for your response.

- Which breath pattern do you prefer?

- What do you like about it?

- What speed feels best to you?

- Do you like mirroring someone else's rhythm or does it feel better to track your own rhythm?

- How do you feel after engaging with this practice?

- Who in your life would you like to do this with?

Prayer Push

 7:48 min.

- **For Embodying Empowerment and Boundaries**
- **For Getting Energized**
- **For Exploring Breath, Movement, and Your** *Body Up* **Preferences**

 Video QR

Start with your hands in prayer pose, at your heart. Blow out through the mouth and extend arms out straight to the side from the shoulders, palms facing away, and fingertips extending back toward the ears. Inhale as the hands return to prayer. Repeat 3 - 5 times.

Next, reverse the breath pattern: Inhale as your hands push away. Exhale as you return to prayer hands. Do you prefer one breath pattern? If you like, practice whichever breath pattern you like, at your own rhythm.

To End: Pause, eyes closed, spine tall, chin slightly tucked, hands flat on your chest. Sense your feet on the ground. Connect with yourself.

3) A Social Threat Response Hypothesis

My hypothesis is that there is a threat response in the social nervous system. I show this in The Three Layer Model (p. 64), which has three threat responses and three relaxed responses. This integrates my decades of clinical experience with social threat behavior.

The Social Threat Response

Communication for Safety

Social threat responses include compulsive competition, oppressive behavior, greed, workaholic habits, strategizing for war, and adaptive or codependent behavior like fawning or accommodation.

© 2012 Elizabeth Dennison wecoregulate.com

As a clinician, I need to be able to recognize and work with the social nervous system state that drives social threat behavior. As social beings, we can get nasty and abusive when our social status is threatened. The ventral vagal threat response I hypothesize is complex, nuanced, and draws heavily on the circuitry of Porges' social nervous system.

Social threat responses include compulsive competition, oppressive behavior, greed, workaholic habits, strategizing for war, and codependent behavior like fawning. For me, any useful model of the ANS must locate and account for these ubiquitous and problematic behaviors.

Babies do not make war, practice oppression, or get caught in compulsive competition. So, as an infant researcher, Porges would naturally lack data for a social threat response. The Polyvagal Theory focuses on threat and safety and the evolutionary ladder. I have added the social threat response to illustrate that communicating to defend or enhance our social status is a complex safety and survival issue with powerful motivation.

My hypothesis is that our social threat responses organize our social behavior around threat and safety. At a social level, we perceive and respond to threats in diverse and complex ways. We engage in compulsive competition, greed, bullying, and oppression. We plan for war. We may cope with social threats by fawning, over-accommodation, and codependent behavior.

As a species, having three different threat responses increases our chances of short-term survival. Having three different relaxation responses expands our capacity for healing, cooperation, and long-term survival. The Three Layer Model helps us understand and utilize these options consciously. This means that each layer of the nervous system slides along a continuum from a protective response to a relaxed or growth-oriented response.

As therapists, parents, and people who care about relationships, thinking in terms of these six nervous system states gives us valuable understanding that cuts shame and suggests rich, new options for healing from the body up.

Like The Polyvagal Model (p. 55), The Three Layer Model gives us clear strategies to work with fragile nervous systems without retraumatizing them. It describes, explains, and predicts frozen states and viable healing mechanisms. It guides us in designing therapeutic social engagement strategies for therapy, family, and community. The Three Layer Model also points to new approaches for handling aggression, working with attachment issues, and building cooperation, even online.

> Having three different relaxation responses expands our capacity for healing, cooperation, and long-term survival.

Unlike Polyvagal theory, The Three Layer Model includes complex defensive social behavior. This validates people's lived experiences, especially by highlighting our strong need to achieve and defend our social status and sense of belonging.

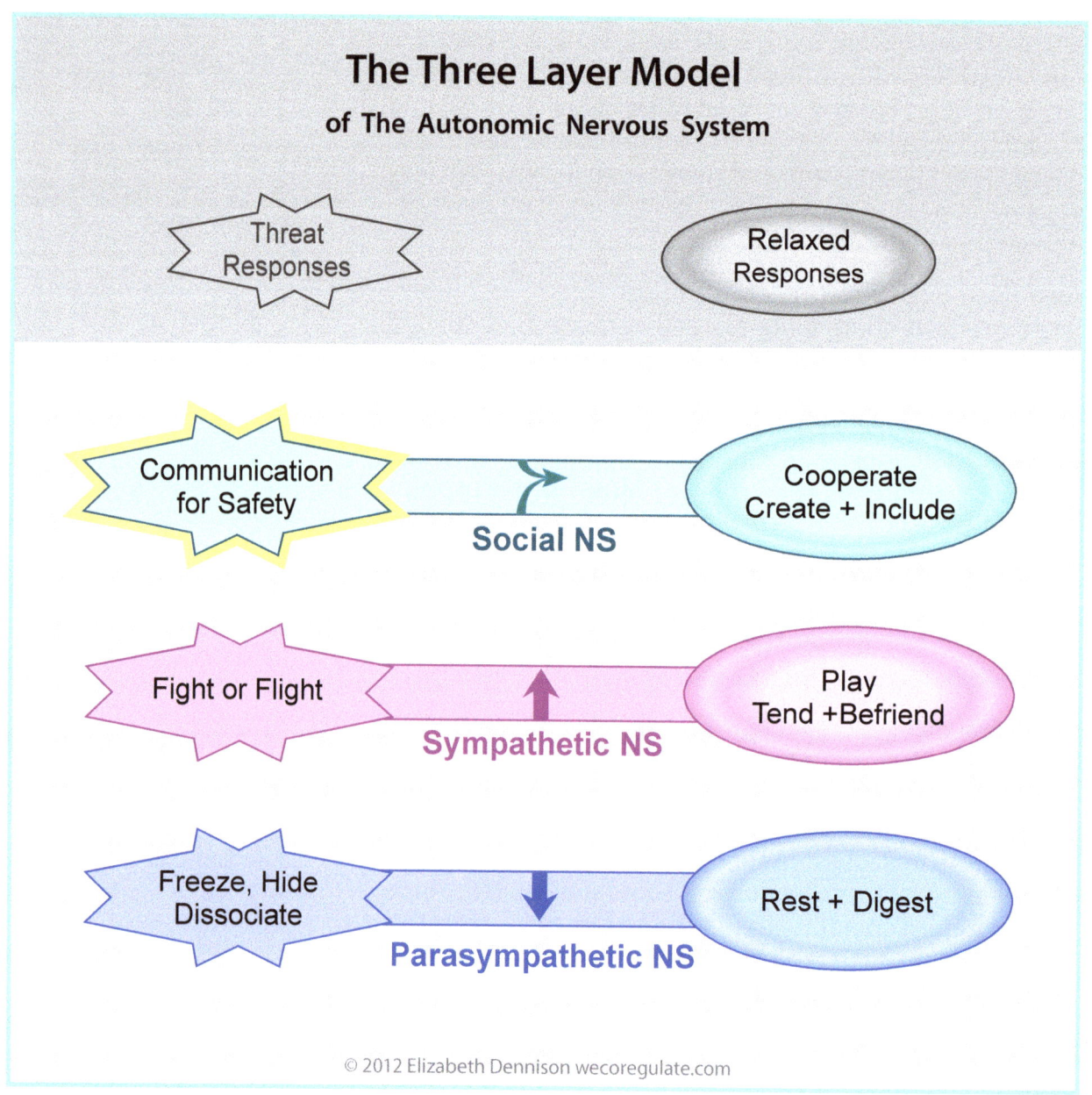

Mixed States - Because Humans Are Complex

The Three Layer Model also draws attention to the idea that each layer of the nervous system can slide along a continuum from a protective response to a relaxed or growth-oriented response.

The different layers of our nervous system can carry different combinations of relaxation and threat responses at the same time. For instance, I can have a background worry (minor sympathetic arousal) about a follow-up mammogram and still enjoy dinner with friends (social engagement and healthy digestion).

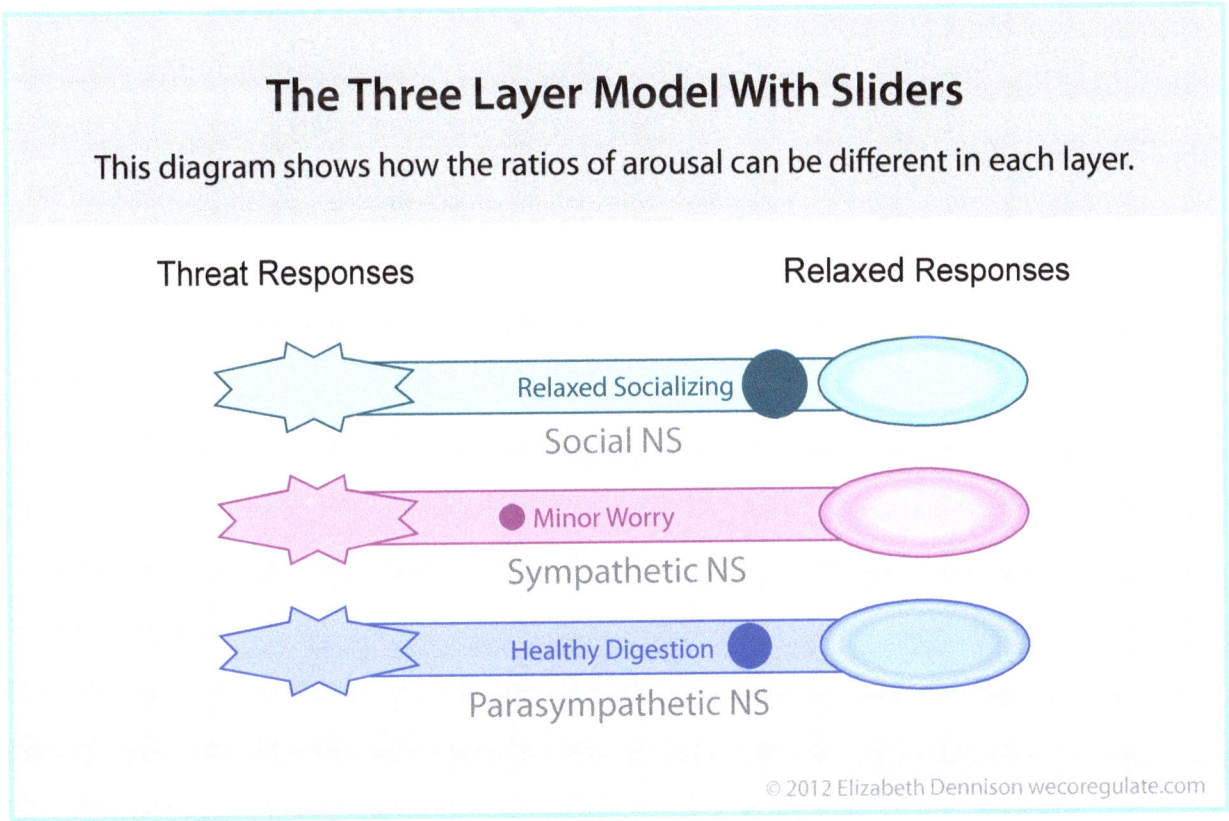

The Three Layer Model With Sliders

This diagram shows how the ratios of arousal can be different in each layer.

Threat Responses   Relaxed Responses

Relaxed Socializing
Social NS

Minor Worry
Sympathetic NS

Healthy Digestion
Parasympathetic NS

© 2012 Elizabeth Dennison wecoregulate.com

The Mood Map and Some Useful Questions

QR for Video

3F
THE MOOD MAP

▷◻ 0:49 min.

Our moods ride the waves of our ANS. The Mood Map graphic helps us recognize ourselves in the ANS states that underlie our moods. Once we can notice and name where we are, and which states we like, avoid, and get stuck in, we start to have much more choice about our moods and behavior. Choice and intention are important in regulation. This is because only when the prefrontal cortex is engaged, can it quiet the reactivity of the amygdala in threat response.

We can learn how to shift states. When we recognize our autonomic state, we can strategize about what states will serve us best and how we can get to where we want to be. We can explore other options for responding to threats. We can discover and reach for different relaxed responses. This is the work and play of BCR.

Choice and intention are important in regulation, because once the prefrontal cortex is engaged, it can quiet the reactivity of threat responses in the amygdala.

The Three Layer Model as a Mood Map

3 Threat Responses

3 Relaxed States

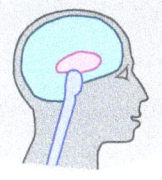

Communication for Survival

Looks Like: Us against them/it, verbal strategies for competition + war
Feels Like: In this together
Healthy: Depending on the team, tuned for communication, responsible, competitive
Stuck: Compulsive competition, greed, driven by $, relationship & power issues, status, workaholism, codependence, compulsive accommodation or fawning

Social NS
→
Fine Tunes

Interactive
Cooperative Attunement

Verbal communication, socializing, tThinking, learning language, creativity, problem-solving
Feels Like: Securely connected, cooperative, inclusive, supported, creative, clear, big thinking, competent to take things on, understood, hopeful, iInspiration in relationship

Fight or Flight

Looks Like: Defensive orienting, hypervigilance, save yourself, compulsive competition
Feels Like: Scared, angry
Healthy: Determined to survive, competing for survival
Stuck: Panicky, anxious, alone, unprotected, unbidden defensiveness, hypervigilance, rigid all-or-nothing reactions

Sympathetic NS
↑
Activates

Active: Tend and Befriend
Happy Puppy

Curiosity, play, grooming behavior, sex, emotional awareness, bonding in relationship
Feels Like: Safe to express and explore, loving, included, part of the herd, glad, sad, flexible, curious, playful, trusting, sensual, intimate, appreciative of life and others

Freeze, Hide, Dissociate
The Trauma Cave

Looks Like: Bracing, shut-down, dissociation, dorsal dive, apnea
Feels Like: Numb, depressed, disconnected
Healthy: Hidden, safely dissociated
Stuck: Frozen, braced, hopeless, helpless, hard to think, desperate, ashamed, needy, fuzzy, foggy, spinning

Parasympathetic NS
↓
Down Regulates

Vegetative
Rest, Digest, and Recover

Well-regulated digestion, sleep, temperature, immune and inflammatory systems, wound healing and recovery
Feels Like: Safe to rest, at ease, calm, meditative, able to let go, sleep, collapse, recover

67

The Mood Map (p. 67) helps us recognize ourselves. To get to know your nervous system, try tracking yourself. Ideally, we can access all the states as needed, without getting stuck in any of them. In life, they blend and over-lap, except for strong fight/flight and freeze responses which can completely take over.

Questions for Tracking Yourself on The Mood Map

The following questions help us understand ourselves and where we get stuck. Knowing why we get caught in primitive behavior reduces our self-judgment. It also lends us more compassion for others when they get withdrawn or irrational.

For instance, in a threat response, we humans often shut down and feel stupid, or go volatile and yell at people we love. Now we know that it is usually not a deficit in intel-ligence or a personality defect. It is likely to be reactivity in our nervous system.

In my practice, I use the following questions:

In which states do you like to hang out?

Where are you now?

Where do you get stuck or where are you afraid of getting stuck?

Are there states you have trouble getting to that would serve you if you could get there?

BCR helps us be aware of our NS states, and adjust intentionally to meet the demands of the moment. Re-regulating out of threat responses is especially important for our long-term health. Co-regulation evolved as a mechanism that is particularly well-suited to shifting out of threat responses as pairs or a group.

Whether you are a peer co-regulator or a practitioner, you can also use this Mood Map to be strategic in responding to others who are stuck in maladaptive states.

Take a little time to look at the Mood Map and answer the questions for yourself and maybe for a friend, family member, or client.

4) Neuroception: Faster Than Perception

Our neurology is exquisitely tuned for our survival. The instant a threat registers in the nervous system, we respond neurologically and physically, well before we have time to consciously notice and consider the situation.

Something drops out of a tree. Do I eat it or does it eat me? This is not a moment for careful consideration. It is useful that neuroception takes over!

When you see a snake, you probably jump away first and think about it later. Neuroception is fast. We respond before we even perceive things consciously.

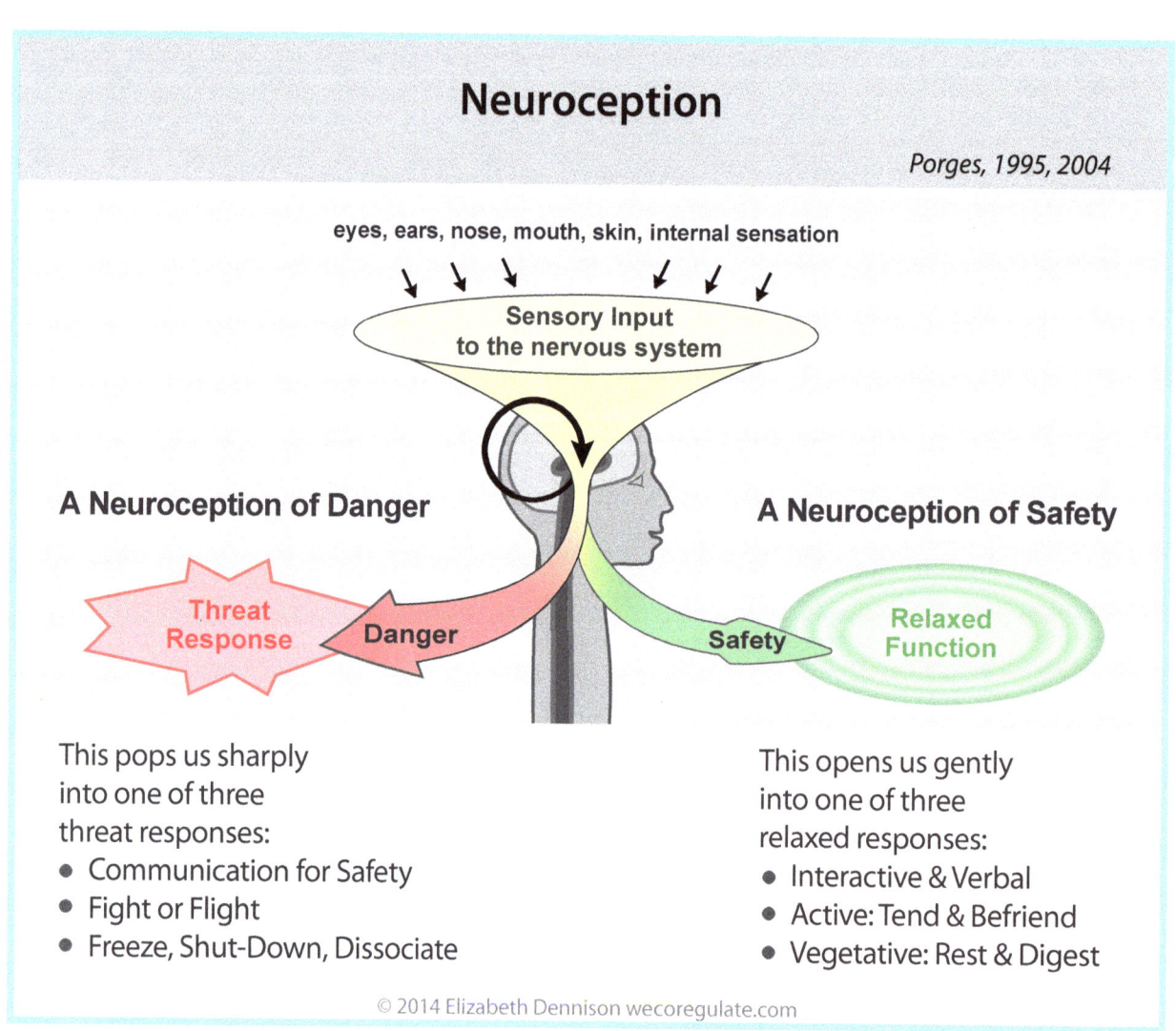

Neuroception

Porges, 1995, 2004

eyes, ears, nose, mouth, skin, internal sensation

Sensory Input to the nervous system

A Neuroception of Danger

Threat Response — Danger

This pops us sharply into one of three threat responses:
- Communication for Safety
- Fight or Flight
- Freeze, Shut-Down, Dissociate

A Neuroception of Safety

Safety — Relaxed Function

This opens us gently into one of three relaxed responses:
- Interactive & Verbal
- Active: Tend & Befriend
- Vegetative: Rest & Digest

"Neuroception is a fast, unconscious assessment process in which neural circuits distinguish whether situations or people are safe, dangerous, or life-threatening," writes researcher Stephen Porges in The Polyvagal Theory (2010).

Neuroception happens in the amygdala. Sensory input from the external world comes directly to the amygdala for threat evaluation. A neuroception of safety allows a relaxed response and further conscious consideration. A neuroception of social threat, physical danger, or life threat activates the amygdala in a threat response.

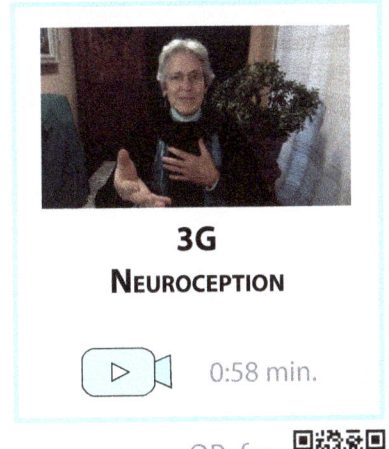

3G
NEUROCEPTION

 0:58 min.

QR for
Video

Neuroception and Perception

Neuroception is strong and it is faster and more primitive than perception. Perception is more accurate and informed. Neuroception is what our neural circuits pick up below conscious awareness.

Perception is what we notice consciously, once we are relaxed enough to think and consider. The two do not always agree. When you are in a noisy, industrial environment, you may feel on edge, even though you are physically and emotionally safe.

In addition, there is another important factor at work here that affects our sense of safety. We are wired to interpret our own internal activation as a sign of external danger. The black circular arrow, in the diagram above, illustrates this.

Our internal state can influence both our neuroception and perception of the external world. Internal agitation makes us more reactive, defensive, more easily triggered, and more hypervigilant. An internal sense of safety allows us to be spacious and creative and less primitive in our response to our world.

We are wired to interpret our own internal activation as a sign of external danger.

With neuroception, our nervous system picks a threat or relaxed response that seems best adapted to the situation at hand, based on our prior history of responding to threats and surviving. We can sometimes mask and deny these reactions. We can learn, over time, to change the basis for these reactions. But, we can not just stop them when they are happening.

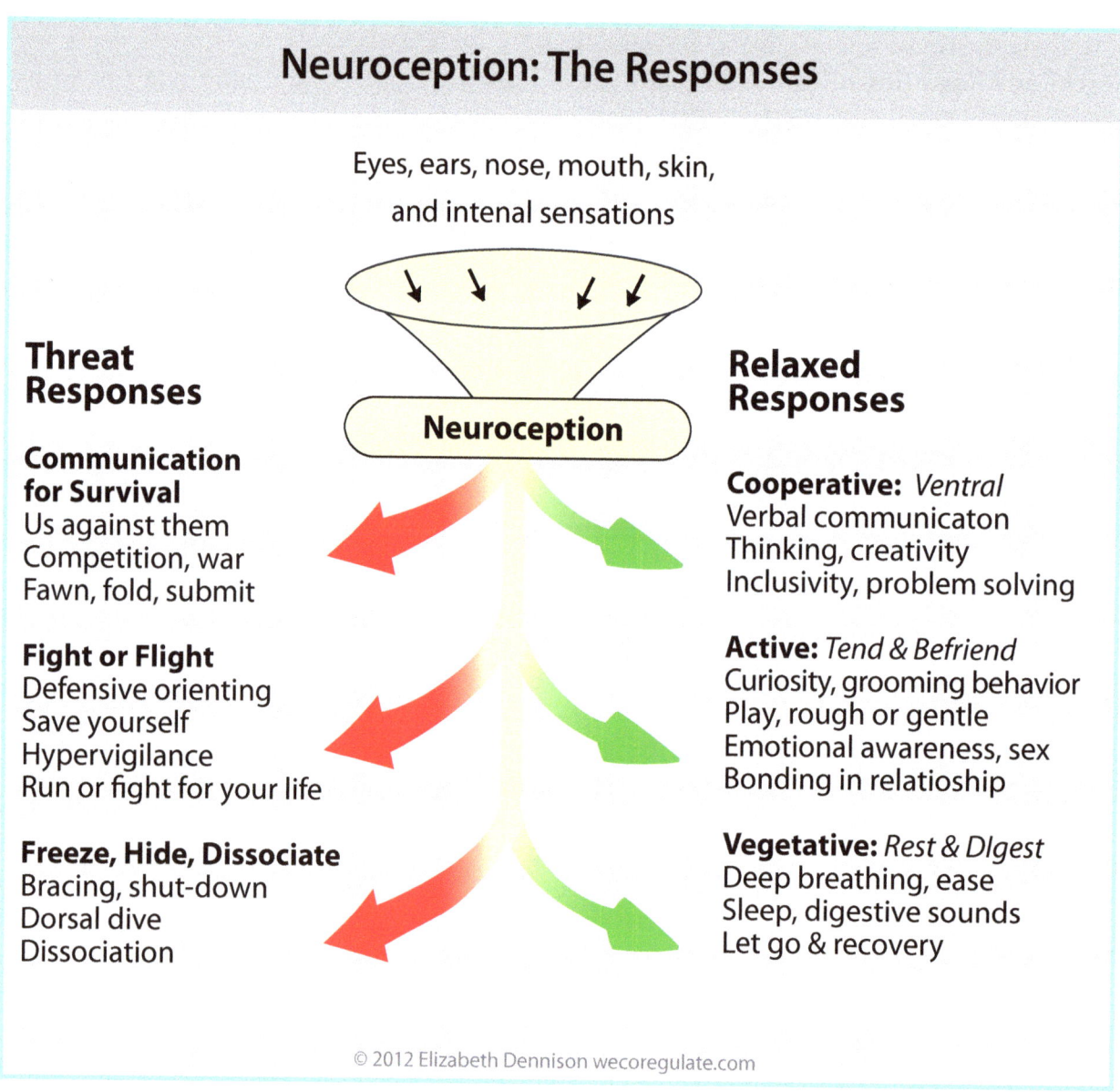

Neuroception: The Responses

Eyes, ears, nose, mouth, skin, and intenal sensations

Neuroception

Threat Responses

Communication for Survival
Us against them
Competition, war
Fawn, fold, submit

Fight or Flight
Defensive orienting
Save yourself
Hypervigilance
Run or fight for your life

Freeze, Hide, Dissociate
Bracing, shut-down
Dorsal dive
Dissociation

Relaxed Responses

Cooperative: *Ventral*
Verbal communicaton
Thinking, creativity
Inclusivity, problem solving

Active: *Tend & Befriend*
Curiosity, grooming behavior
Play, rough or gentle
Emotional awareness, sex
Bonding in relatioship

Vegetative: *Rest & Dlgest*
Deep breathing, ease
Sleep, digestive sounds
Let go & recovery

© 2012 Elizabeth Dennison wecoregulate.com

Why Neuroception Matters

Understanding neuroception is important for several reasons. It can relieve shame about feeling stupid when we are just frozen. It can help us understand why we do not feel safe when we have every reason to believe we are safe. It is an important early warning system.

When we are immobilized in fear and can not think, talk or move, it helps to realize that we are not stupid, just dysregulated by a strong sense of threat.

When we come back into a more regulated state and have enough oxygen going to our brains, we will be able to think, talk and move again. Understanding this cuts our shame about feeling stupid or that there is something wrong with us.

Feeling unsafe even though other people assure us that there is nothing to worry about, is very unsettling. It can make us pretend we are fine just to fit in and save face. Choosing to go with the crowd here is a typical example of the social nervous system overriding our *body up* experience!

Once we understand neuroception, we can honor what we feel and stop pretending to be fine when we are not. We can pay conscious attention to what our nervous system may be reacting to and make a conscious decision about it. Understanding neuroception gives us a chance to make sense of why we do not feel safe. Then, we can do something about it.

Our *body up* neuroception of threat is an important early alert system. We do not have to know what is going on to know that something feels wrong and to pay attention to that. When we trust ourselves to make sense of our *body up* awareness, we get important information about our world. Then, we can consciously assess the reality of the situation. When we trust ourselves to react quickly when something feels wrong, we do not have to be hypervigilant all the time.

Threat Responses Deprive the Brain of Oxygen

Our social nervous system is complex and requires lots of oxygen to function fully. When a strong neuroception of danger pops us into a strong threat response, we cannot override it. Social engagement loses priority, and oxygen is shunted away from the brain. In freeze, the whole system down-regulates and takes in a bare minimum of oxygen. In fight/flight, we may breathe hard, but most of the oxygen goes to the muscles, with just enough oxygen going to the brain to decide what to use for a weapon or where to run to.

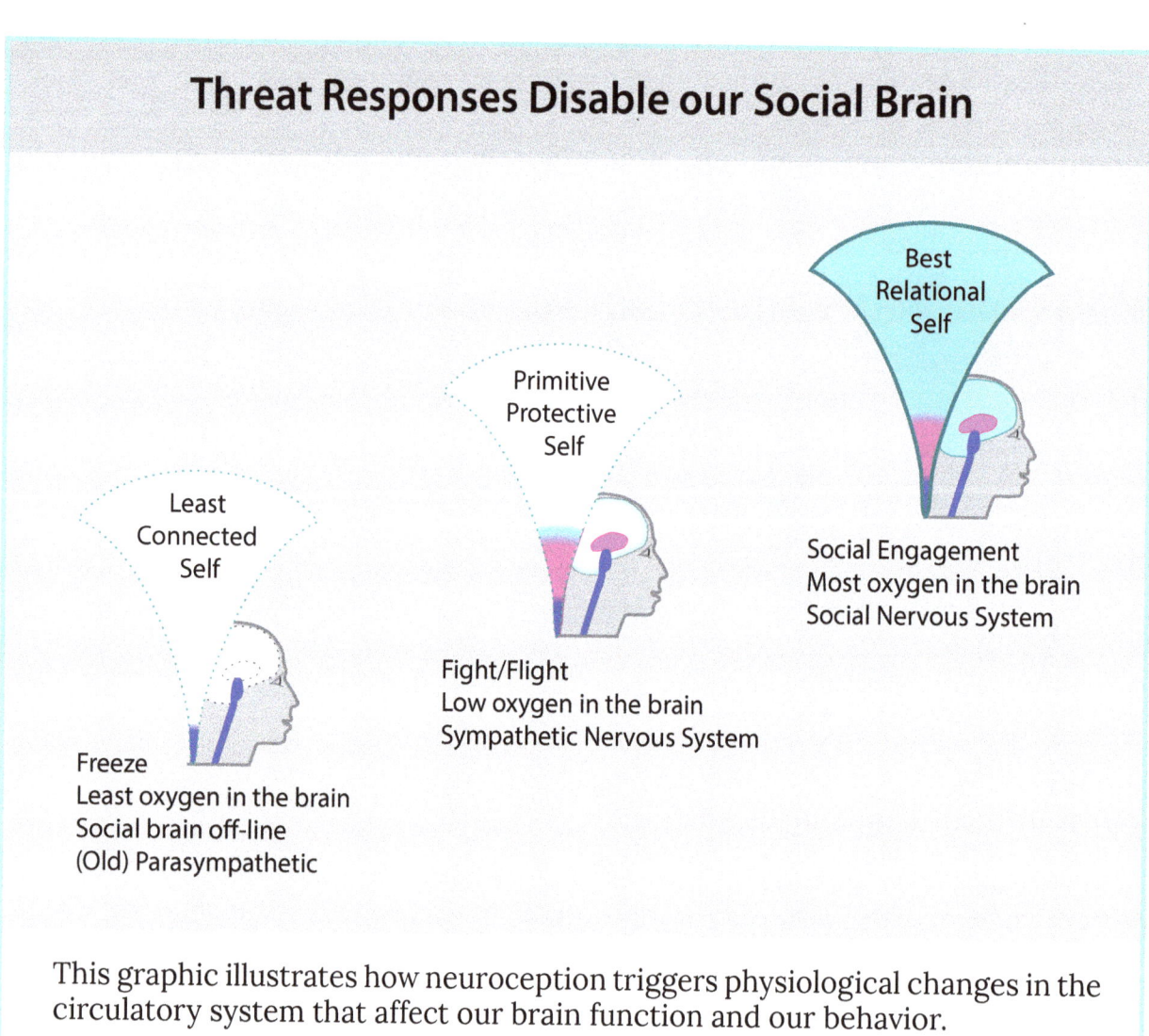

Threat Responses Disable our Social Brain

Best
Relational
Self

Social Engagement
Most oxygen in the brain
Social Nervous System

Primitive
Protective
Self

Least
Connected
Self

Fight/Flight
Low oxygen in the brain
Sympathetic Nervous System

Freeze
Least oxygen in the brain
Social brain off-line
(Old) Parasympathetic

This graphic illustrates how neuroception triggers physiological changes in the circulatory system that affect our brain function and our behavior.

It is not only physical danger and life-threat that can trip us into a threat response. Even a complex or intense social situation can trigger a threat response that drains the brain of oxygen.

When we get overwhelmed or triggered, we are likely to default into a primitive, protective mode or a frozen, shut-down mode. A neuroception of safety is necessary if we are to reregulate for social engagement and keep our best relational self available.

Neuroception is fast, but it is unconscious and does not always make good decisions about new situations. That is why we often need to do some conscious reassessment when there is time and safety. We can consciously override our threat response behavior in the moment. (However, it does take some time to clear the arousal from our system.) With time and attention, we can rewire our system to drop its reactivity to old triggers that no longer signify current danger.

3H
THREAT RESPONSES

▷🎥 1:00 min.

QR for Video

Neuroception - What to Remember

Neuroception is fast and unconscious, whereas perception is slower and more conscious. Neuroception can instantaneously produce three distinct threat responses. These responses can rev us up, shut us down, or turn our social behavior defensive or primitive. In addition to responding to threats, neuroception informs our sense of relaxed safety in social engagement, spontaneous play, and deep rest. We are unlikely to feel truly safe, or accurately know when we feel threatened, without listening to our *body up* circuitry.

The afferent fibers of the vagus nerve (see below) are the key to tracking our visceral, sense of threat and safety. I find it very hopeful that we can deliberately attend to our *body up* awareness and use it to find safety and respond accurately to the tides of life in the present moment.

A neuroception of safety is necessary if we are to re-regulate for social engagement and keep our best relational self available.

Finding Safety

Back Stack can pull us out of our *top down* social agenda and get us listening to our *body up* truth. Slowing down to body time often helps us find a neuroception of safety at a deep level.

Before reading on, explore Back Stack and find how it affects you.

- How does your body tell you it is time to come up or did your mind make the call?

- Did this practice shift how present you feel in your own skin?

- Was the practice a welcome break or an annoying interruption?

Back Stack

 6:32 min.

 Video QR

- **For Arriving in Your Body**
- **For Feeling a Sense of Identity/Dignity**
- **For Finding Home in Your Core**
- **For Finding Readiness to Connect**

Sit up straight with feet flat on the floor, palms on thighs. Check in about physical contraindications (below).

Curl down toward the ground. If you like, take some of the weight through your arms to your thighs. Be sure to curl down only as far as is comfortable. Hang there as long as it feels good. Your arms can hang down if you like.

Wait until your body wants to come up.

Then, slowly, (assisting with your arms if you like), curl up again, stacking your vertebrae till you sit tall.

Repeat 2 or 3 times.

PHYSICAL CONTRAINDICATIONS: Dizziness, glaucoma, unmedicated high blood pressure (if so bend forward only from the neck).

5) The Visceral Afferents

Afferents are nerve fibers that bring information from the body tissue to the brain. Viscera are internal organs that live in a body cavity, especially the abdomen and chest. These include the heart, lungs, digestive organs, and internal reproductive organs.

The Vagus nerve is a huge complicated nerve that is an important part of the parasympathetic nervous system. Because it has two distinct parts, Porges named his theory Polyvagal Theory, "poly" meaning "many." The two parts are the evolutionarily older dorsal vagal fibers and the newer ventral vagal fibers. They have very different functions.

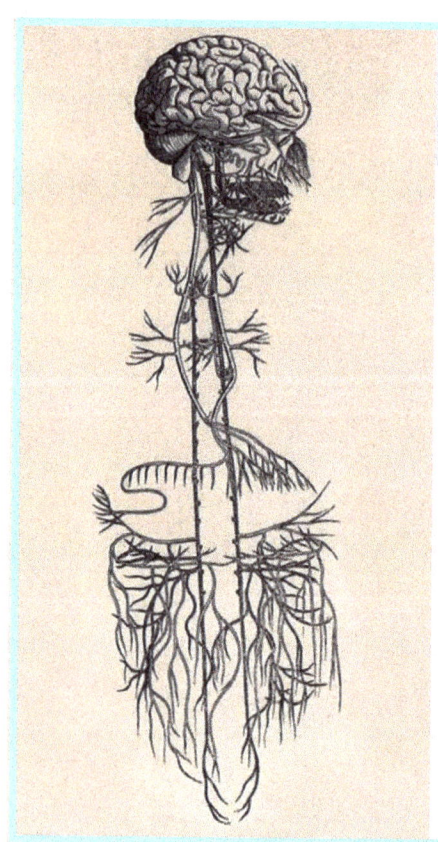

The Vagus Nerve

The fibers of the ventral vagal nerve, with other cranial nerves, constitute the social engagement system (AKA new parasympathetic nervous system or social nervous system p. 52). This is Porges' discovery and delineates a whole new step on the evolutionary ladder.

The older, dorsal vagal fibers make up a significant part of the parasympathetic nervous system (AKA the old parasympathetic nervous system). Eighty percent of the dorsal vagal fibers are visceral afferents, devoted to how we sense ourselves.

It is the visceral afferents that let us know, from the body up, how we feel. They inform our neuroception of threat or safety. They shape our more nuanced perception of how we are feeling physically and emotionally. And they generate strong feelings that demand that we attend to what is important to us on a nervous system level.

The visceral afferents are a significant part of the vagus nerve. They offer us (often inconvenient) truths about our bodies that western culture teaches us to override and ignore. We tune out these *body up* signals at our peril, inviting illness to go untreated, threats to go unnoticed, and oppressive situations to persist.

When heeded, the visceral afferents help us care for our health, avoid burnout, read our communication partners accurately, track fairness, and trust each other to collaborate on complex issues. BCR helps us attend to the information we receive from our visceral afferents and share it, without feeling ashamed or overwhelmed. This can help us feel deeply safe and connected.

Porges' Polyvagal Theory gives us neuroception, the visceral afferents, and the social nervous system. They are essential internal mechanisms for self-regulation, co-regulation, and understanding trauma and healing.

31
THE VISCERAL AFFERENTS

 0:30 min.

QR for
Video

It is the visceral afferents that let us know, from the body up, how we feel.

6) We Are Wired for Co-Regulation

Co-regulation is our birthright as humans. It is good for us and it feels good, so it motivates us to connect and cooperate. It helps us survive and thrive. Co-regulation helps us shift out of unnecessary threat responses, preserving our health and vitality. Co-regulation prevents burnout and generates hope and a can-do attitude. It adjusts our nervous systems quickly and efficiently for the task at hand.

Co-regulation is as fundamental to our health and survival as breathing and language. It is even more fundamental to human cooperation and survival than language, but it is learned and transmitted in a similar way: relationally.

As children, we learn language and to use our words instead of more primitive behavior. If we are lucky, we also learn effective, nuanced habits for regulating ourselves, so we are inclined to cooperate rather than to fight, flee, or freeze.

When our skills and resources for regulation get overwhelmed, we tend to resort to increasingly primitive and problematic behavior. As individuals, we get overly reactive (fight/flight) or go numb (freeze). We lose our capacity to respond well to the demands of our world. This is burnout. At a societal level, it can mean that our leaders lose the capacity to cooperate on complex issues, and the public has trouble assessing reality and grasping the big picture.

Many of us are habituated to solo regulation. It is a core element of New England self-sufficiency and white supremacy culture. Because we are sometimes alone, the capacity for solo regulation is essential. Because we are fundamentally a social species, our capacity for co-regulation is particularly robust, and our need for it is compelling. In a healthy human system (in an individual or a society), co-regulation becomes the preferred way to regulate, whenever it is available.

The Polyvagal Model of the nervous system orients us to our physiological need for safety and co-regulation. It also highlights some of the physiological basis for our capacity to co-regulate, nervous system to nervous system.

> Solo regulation is a core element of New England self-sufficiency and white supremacy culture.

Let's look at two basic neurological mechanisms for co-regulation: The elements of attunement in relational space and mirror neurons. These mechanisms enable us to absorb and respond to the emotional regulation patterns of our close communication partners.

The Neurological Elements of Attunement

The elements of attunement are the basic set of mechanisms that allow one nervous system to relate to another. They are deep channels of self-expression and are the foundation of human connection and BCR.

3J
ELEMENTS OF ATTUNEMENT

 1:05 min.

QR for Video

The Elements of Attunement in Relational Space

Eye Contact

Facial Expression

Tone of Voice

Posture

Gesture

Rhythm/Timing

Intensity

Weight

Distance

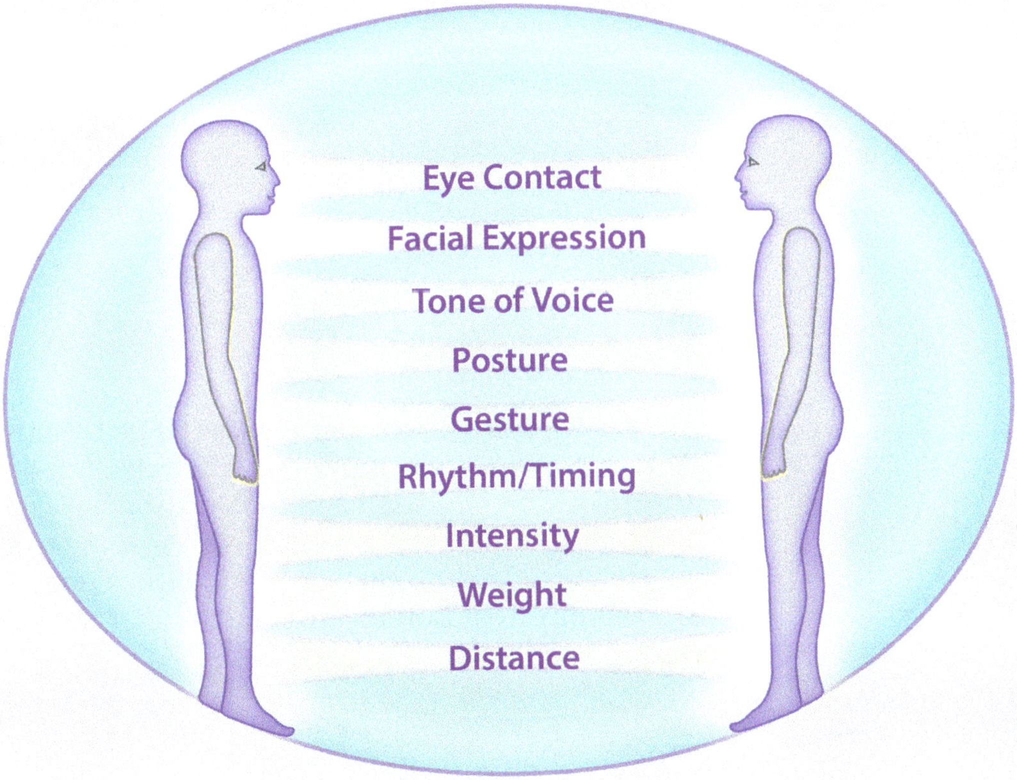

© 2012 Elizabeth Dennison wecoregulate.com

3K

WIRED FOR CO-REGULATION

 0:33 min.

QR for Video

All of the elements of attunement can affect our sense of threat and safety. Eye contact, facial expression, tone of voice, posture, gesture, and rhythm are particularly important when we are connecting online.

Mirror Neurons

Mirror neurons are brain cells that react, both when a particular action is performed and also when it is only observed. In my brain, the same neurons fire when I smile and when I see you smile. When I see you looking relaxed, my body resonates with relaxation (via my mirror neurons). This is a powerful, built-in, evolutionary tool that helps us attune with each other and regulate our emotions and autonomic states together.

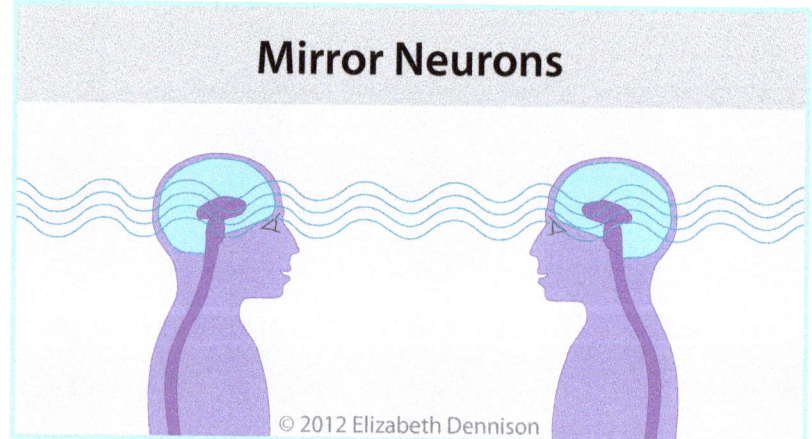

Mirror Neurons

© 2012 Elizabeth Dennison

We are wired to co-regulate! Just the fact that we have mirror neurons tells me that we are designed to work together. Co-regulation and cooperation have given us a huge evolutionary advantage. If we are going to stop oppressing our bodies, each other, and the planet, we need to lean into that cooperative, co-regulatory advantage as a way of being.

4. Chapter Conclusion

For those who are interested, and especially for professionals, understanding the mechanisms of the nervous system can be rich, helpful, and at times necessary.

Please do spend time with this chapter and learn about the autonomic nervous system if you intend to use BCR professionally or with groups. A grasp of the theory gives us a valuable window into ourselves and those around us. It is especially useful to understand how to set practical intentions for shifting out of threat responses and how to adjust the practices to avoid overwhelm in the first place.

The long-term gift of BCR is in training our nervous systems to regulate together. BCR expands our capacity to collaborate and stay steady as we confront complex and contentious problems.

Highlights from this Chapter

- To feel safe we need two green lights, one from our *body up* circuits and one from our social circuits.

- Complexity and intensity can be dangerous and feel dangerous because they are the two things that overwhelm the nervous system.

- We have three different threat responses and three relaxed responses.

- Co-regulation develops in relationships and is essential to healthy individuals and sustainable culture.

CHAPTER IV
Safety in Body Up Co-Regulation

Safety matters! Safe, embodied relationships build trust and cooperation. There is a lovely feedback loop in embodied relating: as we attend to safety, we build our skills for embodied relating, and as we build our skills, safety increases.

I used to walk into our local, social dance thinking: "I am too old and too big and not a good enough dancer, and nobody will want to dance with me." I would start out feeling unsettled and, on a nervous system level, unsafe. Once I got embodied and connected, nervous system to nervous system, I would dance from one end of the room to the other, kicking up my feet and feeling like I owned the place. My curiosity about how this embodied safety emerged brought me to develop BCR.

In BCR, we attend to any perception of threat as significant. Safety from physical threat is important but so is safety from emotional or social threats. Emotional threats include feeling overwhelmed by emotion, feeling shame, or feeling stupid, incompetent, or unwanted. Social threats include fear of being shamed, losing status, and being treated as if we do not belong or matter.

Safety is compromised by any threat, physical, emotional, or social. BCR practice rests on both people feeling safe enough from social, emotional, and physical threats. Connection, regulation, learning, and peer relating all vary directly with our sense of safety.

The two things that overwhelm the nervous system and make us feel unsafe are intensity and complexity. Consequently, we structure our BCR practice to keep intensity and complexity manageable. Otherwise, it is impossible to stay present without going into a threat response.

When two people are relating, it gets complicated. So, it makes sense that we often drop body awareness around other people so that we are less likely to get overwhelmed by the complexity. It also makes sense to learn to include body awareness consciously and carefully.

In BCR, we create safety by tuning in to our nervous system and tending to our needs from the beginning of each BCR practice session. We adjust, or titrate, our practice so that it is engaging but not too intense or too complex. In BCR, talk about your authentic, *body up* experience only as much or as little as you want.

The sections that follow highlight important strategies for social and emotional safety.

1. Safety First

Co-regulators, please empower yourselves. Enter freely into any co-regulation sessions or exercises, and know that you may ask and negotiate for what works for you. Remember that you are free to end the session at any time for any reason, and without explanation. Co-regulation is only co-regulation if it is good for both people, and you are one of those people!

BCR Can Be Therapeutic, But it is Not Therapy

In therapy with a skilled practitioner, BCR can be a powerful tool. For more on Regulatory vs Therapeutic Use of BCR see Chapter IV, p.117 (And our next book The Dance of Co-Regulation in Therapy).

Peer co-regulation is intended for folks who are generally stable and want to build regulation skills and sturdy, embodied, relationships. As a peer practice, BCR is not a substitute for therapy, nor a source of major support in crisis situations or for mental health challenges. In crises, please get professional support.

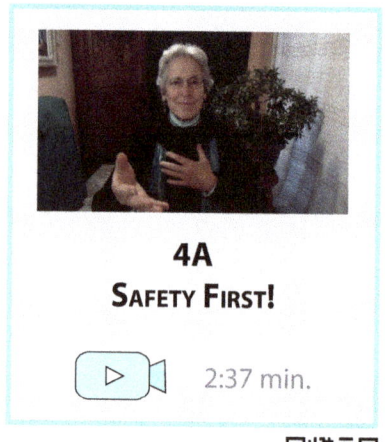

4A
SAFETY FIRST!

 2:37 min.

QR for
Video

The BCR exercises are structured to offer different degrees of safety and challenge. Adjust them to be physically and socially comfortable for you. When we feel safe enough, we can show up to connect authentically and learn. When we feel safe enough, we have the neurological capacity to assess and make conscious choices about taking emotional risks. In BCR, we often take risks to feel more and show more of ourselves and our vulnerability.

When we feel safe enough, like we belong and we matter, then cooperation and creative problem-solving thrive. We become more willing and able to tackle big challenges with a collaborative group.

Threat responses, on the other hand, interfere with safety and learning. Threat responses, including social threat responses, actually deprive the brain of the oxygen it needs to learn. To connect and learn new skills, it is essential that we feel safe enough, not just physically but socially - safe enough from shame, judgment, disrespect, and embarrassment.

2. Co-Regulation is Only Co-Regulation When it is Good for Both People

That might seem simple, but often, it is not. Most of us are predictably unreliable in speaking up for ourselves about what we need to feel safe. Speaking up gives us a much better chance at co-regulation. When both people take responsibility for their own comfort, safety, and needs, the two can create an experience that works for both and regulates both.

When my friend is backlit on zoom, I cannot see her face and cannot fully take in her kindness. She may be feeling very well-regulated as she can see my face. When I ask for what I need and get her to light up her face, voila - there is her smile. I do not have to guess how she is responding to me, I can feel it. Thanks to mirror neurons, my nervous system relaxes and hers does too. Co-regulation goes much better.

3. *Body Up* and *Top Down*

It helps to understand why we avoid giving voice to what we know and feel. The conflict between our *body up* intelligence and our *top down* social agenda happens all the time. When our social agenda prevails, it is common to suppress noticing our needs and avoid showing them.

Our bodies often inform us of things that are legitimate and important, even if they are socially inconvenient. We may not want to admit that we are scared, or tired, that we need a break, that we need to go to the bathroom, or that we don't trust someone. So, our *body up* intelligence is often ignored or overridden.

We humans often do things that feel bad in order to be-long, or to feel like we measure up. We may overextend and deplete ourselves to take care of a friend because we are afraid of not belonging.

We may be so determined to look okay that we do not even know that we do not feel okay. As I age, I assume I can keep up with my younger friends on a hike. The next day, I pay for that assumption, in pain and soreness.

To feel deeply safe, we must validate and attend to our physical awarenesses and neurobiological needs. Our bodies need to know we will not sell them out to our *top down*, social agenda. Don't let your social agenda trump your needs for *body up* safety!

It is important to talk about how you really feel with each practice. Listen to your nervous system. Speak up for yourself. Do not override your own *body up* needs or boundaries.

When we feel safe enough, we can show up to connect authentically and learn.

4. Ten Ways to Cultivate Safety in BCR

1. Pick a partner who wants to practice or learn with you. Choose someone who feels safe enough for you. A colleague or a friend may be a good fit. A competitive boss may not.

2. Tell the truth about what you are comfortable with and what you are not.

3. Start with a Body Up Co-Regulation (BCR) practice that feels safe and cheerful. Then, if you need to, you can return to it if you get triggered.

4. Stop and talk, don't tolerate and pretend.

5. Adjust the exercises for physical comfort and emotional safety right away.

6. Permission - practice asking and hearing what works for yourself and others.

7. Cultivate peer relating by tracking equal time. Fairness matters.

8. Brave sharing - speak about your own experience authentically but only to the degree of risk/vulnerability you choose.

9. Thank your partner for sharing vulnerability.

10. Be human together - notice your judgments and remember that we are all human, fallible, and loveable.

When I feel safe, I want to connect and contribute. I laugh easily and offer suggestions freely. What does feeling safe do for you?

To come back into more body awareness we need to build our capacity to stay present with difficult sensations, emotions, and memories.

5. Safety with Embodiment

Embodiment practice builds our ability to sense and create safety for ourselves. Safer interactions, experiences, and environments allow our embodiment to deepen and our relationships become a more reliable resource. It's another lovely positive feedback loop.

Safety includes safety from shame. Lots of us have shame connected with our bodies. For example, physical size, weight, performance, appearance, pain, and limitations can provoke shame. Because we have such an aversion to shame, we need to deal with it gently and respectfully as we cultivate embodiment.

It is normal to find that being more embodied is challenging. More embodiment means more sensitivity, more information, and more complexity to navigate. Embodiment raises issues that we can avoid when we are ignoring our bodies.

Typically, we dissociate from our bodies when we get overwhelmed. Intensity and complexity can send us over the edge into dissociation. Physical pain, shame, and over-stimulation often trigger dissociation. But sometimes it is just boredom or a habit of prioritizing thinking over feeling.

As a culture, we white westerners are bad at embodiment, which includes feeling our connection to the natural world and living from our hearts. If we have bounced out of connection with our bodies, it is because something got painful, dangerous, intense, or overwhelming. To come back into more body awareness we need to build our capacity to stay present with difficult sensations, emotions, and memories. Co-regulation can help us build that capacity, but only if we stay safe enough.

In BCR, we do our best to practice in a way that does not overwhelm our nervous systems with complexity or with physical or social threats. Do not dismiss or push past shame or anything that is a physical or social threat. A threat may be real and present or triggered from past experience. Either way, it will still pull us out of embodied presence. Titrate! Start slowly with BCR practices so that challenges with embodiment are more manageable.

Stop and talk, don't tolerate and pretend.

QR for Video

4B EMBODIMENT AND DISOCIATION

▷ 🎥 1:20 min.

6. Titration

A pinch or two of salt on our food can be perfect, a handful is unbearable. Titration is about moving into embodiment and self-expression at the right pace for you in that moment, with opportunities to digest challenging issues in bite-size pieces.

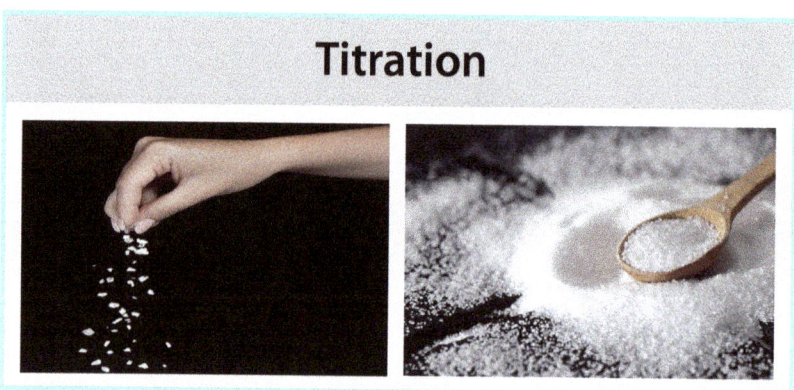

Titration

Titrating the exercises means adapting them to be less intense and more comfortable for the Leader, the Mirror, or both. (Specific exercises have specific suggestions for titration. See List of Practices, P. 157.)

Here are some general titration suggestions to explore:

- Slow down
- Make smaller movements
- Shorten practice time
- Reduce eye contact
- Sitting may be easier than standing
- Also: Witnessing may be more comfortable than mirroring. Watching the video for an exercise by yourself may be more comfortable than practice with a partner.
- It is OK to choose to challenge yourself, and if an exercise makes you too uncomfortable, don't do it!

7. Shame and Suggestions For Reducing Shame

Shame is easy to trigger, especially around body issues. It is also a powerfully limiting and aversive experience. DO NOT skip over it. Learn to face it and talk about it. Shame seldom survives in the light of compassionate, shared attention. URL for an article on Disolving Shame: https://wecoregulate.com/print-library/#

Suggestions for Reducing Shame:

- Belonging and Mattering are important antidotes to shame.

- Listen well. Respond with curiosity.

- Say how your partner makes a difference for you when it is true. Simple presence can make a difference and so do specific behaviors and reflections.

- Track and remember: We feel like we matter when others show that they see us and remember our preferences.

- Be honest when you do not know or do not remember something.

- Normalize things that seem edgy: Eg. "It is OK to cry." Or, "It makes total sense to me that you react that way."

- Appreciate when people raise difficult issues. "Thank you for saying what you did not like. It helps me trust you."

- Track time and check-in about equal time.

- Labels matter: Use the terminology and pronouns that the person uses about themself: "vision got bad" vs. "blind", "they, them" vs. "he, him," or "she, her".

- Inclusive language can help: Use inclusive pronouns like "we" and "us." Eg. "Let's try a practice", or, "If you like, we could ..."

- Use permissive language: "Would you be interested in ...?" "If you are willing..." "If you like, let's..." "Does

QR for Video

4C SHAME, CONNECTION, AND ANTIDOTES TO SHAME

▷ 🎥 2:55 min.

that work for you?" Or, "Would you like to do Sitz Bones Rock?"

- When others attune to our rhythm and timing, it cuts shame and helps us feel like we matter. So, as best you can, do not rush your partner, or talk over them, or make them wait. Especially when it is their turn to lead and set the pace, mirror their rhythm.

Connection, belonging, and mattering are antidotes to shame.

Safe Connection Reduces Shame.

Shame can stop us cold, leaving us stuck in disconnection. BCR offers connection and antidotes to shame. It helps us feel like we belong and we matter. This work is about embodied learning. We need to get it on a sensory level. Before you read on, watch or join in with Connected 8s. (7 minutes).

As you watch, mirror if you like, and take the time to feel your heart. Afterward you might want to journal, reflecting on what you noticed during and after the practice.

How is your breathing? Did you like the rhythms? How is your heart?

Notice any sensation in your body or changes in your nervous system from watching the demo.

If you like, invite someone to do the practice with you, online or in person. This is a good one to do with someone you want to be more connected with.

Practicing with others (online on in-person) wires our system to expect that co-regulation is possible, even online.

Connected 8s

 7:05 min.

- **For Cultivating Connection Heart to Heart**
- **For Cultivating Presence**

 Video QR

Before You Start: Move your hand in a figure 8 in front of you. Let yourself feel the gesture

To Start: Take a breath or two, eyes closed, with hands on your heart. Feel your intention to connect with your own heart and with your world or your partner.

Gesture a figure eight, with an open, relaxed hand. Bring your hand up along your torso, extend out and down the middle, up as you gesture toward your partner's torso or the screen, down the middle, and repeat, with or without eye contact. (See demo video.) You can also try it with two hands.

Find a rhythm and do five to seven rounds.

To End: Bring a hand flat on the chest and take a couple of breaths, eyes closed or open. Feel your connection with the ground and your body.

If practicing with a partner, TALK about what you each noticed.

8. Trauma Triggers

If you suspect that you or your practice partner is triggered, please stop and check in. To help people return to a grounded sense of self and reregulate, consider practices for Finding Home in Your Core and for Exploring Boundaries. In addition, any rhythmic movement can be helpful. Try Sitz Bones Rock, Back Stack, Prayer Push, or Strong Twist. It can also be useful to stop your practice and go for a walk, or talk about something unrelated.

In general, BCR is intended to be a peer practice among capable adults. It is not therapy or a source of major support in crisis situations or for people with major mental health challenges. It can offer highly relevant tools in the hands of a skilled therapist.

9. General Cautions and Contraindications

These are especially important for practitioners.

Embodiment can be challenging, triggering, and complex for people. Go slow and get feedback from your body and your partner or client.

BCR can go deep quickly. Intense memories and trauma triggers can arise unexpectedly, without any digging for them. Unless you are a qualified therapist, focus on regulation and skill-building rather than working emotional edges. Use practices for Finding Home in Your Core. Go slow and get feedback from your body and your partner.

As possible, avoid causing shame and do not push past it. Shame can prompt us to do things that we are not comfortable with, to fit in, to learn, or even to prove ourselves to ourselves. When we shut down to perform, we compromise our capacity for embodiment and connection. Welcome and support your partner's needs, desires, and limitations, and also respect your own boundaries. (See Explore Boundaries.)

Tread gently around power issues. Peer relating can be very vulnerable. When we rely on control or one-up roles to feel safe, we will tend to avoid the vulnerability of peer relating. (Most of us do this at least some of the time.) BCR is likely to seem threatening to those who maintain safety by maintaining hierarchical roles.

When people do not want to do BCR, be curious and respectful about their discomfort. Do not push them.

Some may be empaths who feel overwhelmed by the complexity of owning their own bodily experience and noticing that of another. Others may be on the numb side. They may feel uncomfortable or inadequate when asked to notice and share how they feel, because they do not know how they feel.

There is a lot of pain in life. We can get habituated to not feeling as a way to navigate the world. Please respect what people in your life are willing to do and where they draw lines. Let people take the control they need and take care of yourself. Co-regulation is only co-regulation if it is good for both people.

Beware of triggering addictive behavior. We often engage in addictive behavior to remove ourselves from overwhelming emotional pain. By honoring resistance, we allow ourselves to digest our experience in manageable doses and avoid triggering addictive behavior. This work is biologically based and goes deep very fast. Consider any resistance to be information about important boundaries. What looks like resistance is just the nervous system showing us what feels like a threat. Respect and honor your own edges and capacity. Practitioners take note that protector parts and defenses need to be invited forward, addressed directly, and cooperated with. Do not push. Pause, inquire, adjust, and titrate.

For Clinicians, proceed very carefully in using BCR in therapy with deeply disturbed folk who have attachment issues. They may start to get the connection that they desperately need, and then get angry that an hour a week is not enough and cannot be enough. This can create a difficult catch-22: The therapist is the best hope the client has ever seen. Yet, the client is so angry about the limitations in the therapeutic relationship they can not engage without attacking and thus compromise the relationship. Avoid building deep connection until there

> Consider any resistance to be information about important boundaries.

is a therapeutic team in place, so there is room for the anger without the client being afraid to lose all support.

Most of these issues are not crisp contraindications, but important cautions that warn us to slow way down.

Highlights From This Chapter

- Deep change, including healing and building more capacity for life, happens when we have an embodied sense of safety.

- Safety is physical and social, *body up* and *top down*.

- Social/emotional safety depends on feeling like we belong and we matter.

- Physical safety depends on knowing we can protect our boundaries and speak up for ourselves.

- In BCR, we attend to any perception of threat as significant.

- Embodiment can be awfully challenging. Do not push or rush.

- BCR can go very deep very quickly.

- In BCR, you can cultivate safety by tuning in to your body, taking practical actions, asking for what works for you, stopping whenever you want, titrating, and being sensitive to shame.

CHAPTER V
Intention and Skills: How to Decide What to Do

As you probably know, intention influences our experience. I can walk and think about family drama, or I can walk and be present with the birdsong. My intention can create two entirely different experiences. For example, Sitz Bones Rock from the Introduction of this book can work well with an intention to arrive in your body and find home in your core. However, you can also use the exercise to practice staying connected with yourself around another person.

Clear intention around regulation and skill-building is useful. When you are about to begin a co-regulation exercise, set yourself an intention that works for you. It will focus and deepen your experience. Body Up Co-Regulation (BCR) practices can be used with many different intentions: to energize and to calm down, to connect with one's self or with another, to prepare for an activity or for rest, to take in nurturing, to express ourselves. And perhaps most enlivening, BCR helps us show up and be available in the present moment.

In this chapter, we lay out four intentions for co-regulation and four embodiment skills to support those intentions. The Intentions and Skills Map (p.148) provides a framework of intentions and skills for you to think about each time you practice. Please do be inspired to try on many intentions other than those we discuss here. What about "play," "integrity," and "kindness"?

QR for Video

5A
INTENTION

▷ 0:49 min.

1. Start by Exploring

A standard and useful co-regulatory intention is to be present in your body and connected with yourself and your partner.

No intention is required. It is fine to just pick a basic exercise. Do it with your partner and notice how it feels. Just pick a practice that appeals to you, notice what your body likes, and TALK about it at the end.

Do remember to pay attention to physical and social safety. Give yourself permission to stop anytime or adjust a practice to work better for you. As best you can, avoid causing shame. We suggest using a timer to share time equally. Consider starting with exercises designated as gentle. Sitz Bones Rock, Hands Show Breath, or Prayer Push are good online starters for most people.

2. Regulatory Intentions for BCR

The four co-regulation intentions laid out in the Practice Pie (p.149) and below are all mutually supportive. There is no hierarchy of intentions; practice in any category that calls you. Practices for each of the categories are listed on The Practice Pie and in the List of Practices for Co-Regulation (p.122-123) at end of this chapter.

Remember that choosing an intention does not mean that you stay rigidly focused on it as you practice. There is no need to force an experience. Be with what you notice and adjust your practice as you like. Intention does not dictate outcome but it can open a door.

The Four Regulatory Intentions Are: Arriving in Embodied, Relational Presence; Regulation for Connection; Down-Regulation; and Up-Regulation.

Each of these intentions invites us to get present in our bodies and connected with each other and the earth. They are a great way to begin a session, or a meeting, or to begin learning BCR.

Our intention focuses our attention, and what we pay attention to grows.

POPULAR **BCR** PRACTICES
FOR EMBODIED PRESENCE

Sitz Bones Rock
Hands Show Breath
Reach for the Earth

Arriving in Embodied, Relational Presence

For arrival. For comfort. For getting more embodied.

Embodied, relational presence means being alive in your body, sensing your body, and being available to connect with another being.

At times, we all need help arriving in our bodies. I can think I am grounded in my body, but then if I do 30 seconds of Sitz Bones Rock, feeling my weight pour from one side to the other, I notice how much more alive and available I become.

Cautions and Contraindications

Embodiment involves feeling more. For people with a trauma history, this can be overwhelming. In this, there is no such thing as "resistance to be overcome," only the nervous system showing what it can and cannot tolerate. Do not push. Choose what works for you. This can be a therapeutic issue.

Professional Psychotherapeutic Uses

Therapeutic intentions for embodiment might include building a therapeutic alliance or exploring embodiment, dissociation, and trauma stored in the body.

POPULAR **BCR** PRACTICES
FOR SOCIAL ENGAGEMENT

Sitz Bones Rock
Pinky Paws
Proud Duck

Regulate for Social Engagement

For building connection nervous system to nervous system. For attuned relating to others, especially when it is complex or emotionally challenging.

We humans come hardwired with a basic survival need to feel connected and to feel we belong and we matter. Regulating for connection means getting your best relational self engaged. This helps us to connect with friends and family, to teach, to play, and to talk about tricky relational issues. It gives us the bandwidth we need for complex problem-solving or for deep healing.

Fine-tuned social engagement is complex and requires lots of oxygen to power and connect different parts of the brain. BCR practices are designed to adjust the social engagement system for the complex task of communication.

BCR practices build attunement and wire the social engagement system for connection. They offer antidotes to shame, compulsive ranking, and reliance on role hierarchy. BCR supports teams and individuals to cultivate clear thinking and organized cooperation on complex tasks.

Cautions and Contraindications

Being embodied around others can be complicated and overwhelming for people. Empaths may pretend or even think they are fine but feel drained by the effort. Encourage people to stay connected with themselves even in the Mirror role.

Professional Psychotherapeutic Uses

Therapeutic intentions for social engagement might include exploring more connection or the many challenges that arise with embodiment in relational space.

Down-Regulation

For calming down for any purpose. For rest or sleep. For shifting out of hypervigilance, anxiety, or accumulated tension. For settling down after upset or overwhelm. For integrating new capacity.

Down-regulation is about shifting out of focused work modes or threat responses. With practice, engaging this intention lays in wiring to shift out of chronic hypervigilance and chronic anxiety. We can downshift into relaxed or playful states, and for sleep.

Prominent behavioral neuroscientist Stephen Porges's words are worth repeating: "The most significant threat to our health and relationships is staying caught in unnecessary threat responses."

When we are caught in unnecessary fight/flight responses, anxiety, or hypervigilance, down-regulation settles us.

Down-regulation is also an important part of building capacity. (See the 4-Phase Partner Sequence (p.115) for building capacity.) Once we have revved up deliberately with a faster, rhythmic practice, we practice with a gently down regulatory intention to digest, integrate, and stabilize the increased energy in relational space.

> **POPULAR BCR PRACTICES FOR DOWN RREGULATION**
>
> *Back Stack*
> *Hands Show Breath*
> *Partner Stretches*

Cautions and Contraindications

There are times when people cannot afford to let down because they have essential responsibilities and if they let down, they will need to fall apart for a while before they can function well again. Also, people can get caught in "relaxing makes me nervous." They may need help learning to do reality checks about safety that work for them. This is a therapeutic issue.

Professional Psychotherapeutic Uses

Therapeutic intentions for down-regulation might include exploring challenges with anxiety/depression, hypervigilance, anger, PTSD, rest, and sleep.

Sometimes It Helps to Up-Regulate before You Down-Regulate

Sometimes you can not start with downshifting when you want to clear anxiety and hypervigilance. Try sharing an up-regulatory practice first. Roughhousing or strenuous activity can also be useful. This will help you to meet, feel, and share the energy of the anxiety so you can digest it and let it go. To resolve persistent anxiety, we need to sit with feeling it and give the brain time to digest the reality and importance of it. Then, go for down-regulation.

Up-Regulation

For energizing or revving up. For spilling energy or anxiety. For empowerment. For building capacity in the nervous system (capacity to generate, organize, and utilize high energy).

If we never get going, life gets boring, and we never feel empowered, vital, capable, and influential. Up-regulation keeps us engaged and excited about life. It helps us show up to protect ourselves and take on intense or complex projects. It can relieve anxiety by burning off activation leftover from fight or flight responses.

POPULAR BCR PRACTICES FOR UP-REGULATION

Prayer Push

Spinal Flexes

Breath Wings

Up-regulation helps us wake up in the morning, rev up for a sprint, energize and organize for a challenging day, and respond to threats. Caffeine, nicotine, cheerleading, and other stimulants rev us up. Co-regulation can, too.

When we are frozen in shame, fear, or depression, careful up-regulation is a reliable way out. Breathing and moving together rhythmically is a reliable way to up-regulate. The Leader can increase the tempo as they like. Kids on a seesaw sometimes do this naturally.

When we are anxious or speedy and scattered, up-regulating with a partner can be unexpectedly helpful in two ways. It can engage and burn off excess energy. It can organize scattered energy. Both of these make down-regulation much easier.

Building Capacity for Vitality

Building our capacity for vitality is an important aspect of up-regulation. Learning to generate, organize, and utilize and contain high energy is an essential developmental task. An increase in our capacity for vitality allows us to stay steady and present while handling complexity and intensity.

People with a healthy enough nervous system are usually good at up-regulation and will enjoy it and stop before it gets overwhelming. The 4-Phase Partner Sequence (p.115) for building capacity is an efficient way to use up-regulation to build capacity in our nervous systems.

Building Our Capacity to Heal from Trauma

Building our capacity for facing memories and emotions that once overwhelmed us is a valuable process. However, it can be tricky. Up-regulation can be triggering for people with a trauma history.

Cautions and Contraindications

Strong up-regulation can be challenging or disorganizing at times. People often push into too much intensity without grounding and organizing it. Titrate and consider using The 4-Phase Partner Sequence for building capacity.

In BCR, a Leader may choose on their own to use this exercise to push their edges or work on building capacity. It is the Leader's job to assess their own capacity to integrate the intensity this can generate. Only a qualified therapist should suggest or encourage people to push their capacity for up-regulation. It is a therapeutic intervention. It is outside the scope of practice for a BCR Peer Teacher or a BCR Coach.

Professional Psychotherapeutic Uses

Therapeutic intentions for up-regulation might include exploring issues like waking up from sleep, mobilizing for difficult tasks, upper limits issues, and challenges with limited capacity for intensity and vitality. In addition, building the capacity to tolerate what was once overwhelming is the name of the game in trauma therapy and in stepping up to live a bigger life.

Try Some Gentle Up-Regulation

Watch or join in with Piezoelectric Arms (9:06 min). As you watch, feel the stretch in your arms. Does this wake you up? Do you like it?

Notice any sensation in your body or changes in your nervous system from watching or mirroring the demo.

If you like, invite someone to do the practice with you, online or in person. This is a good one to do when you and others are getting bored or sleepy.

Practicing up-regulation with others (online on in-person) wires our system to expect we can shift gears together when we need to.

Piezoelectric Arms

 9:06 min.

- **For Gentle Up-Regulation**
- **For Noticing Sensation in the Body**

 Video QR

To Begin: Sit or stand comfortably, facing your partner. Decide who will lead first. Make sure you can see one another's outstretched arms.

Leader - Eyes can open or close at will. Start with your hands in prayer position at your chest. Extend arms forward at chest height. Palms press forward, fingertips pull back towards your nose. Open the arms to the sides. Feel the sensation on the inside of your elbows.

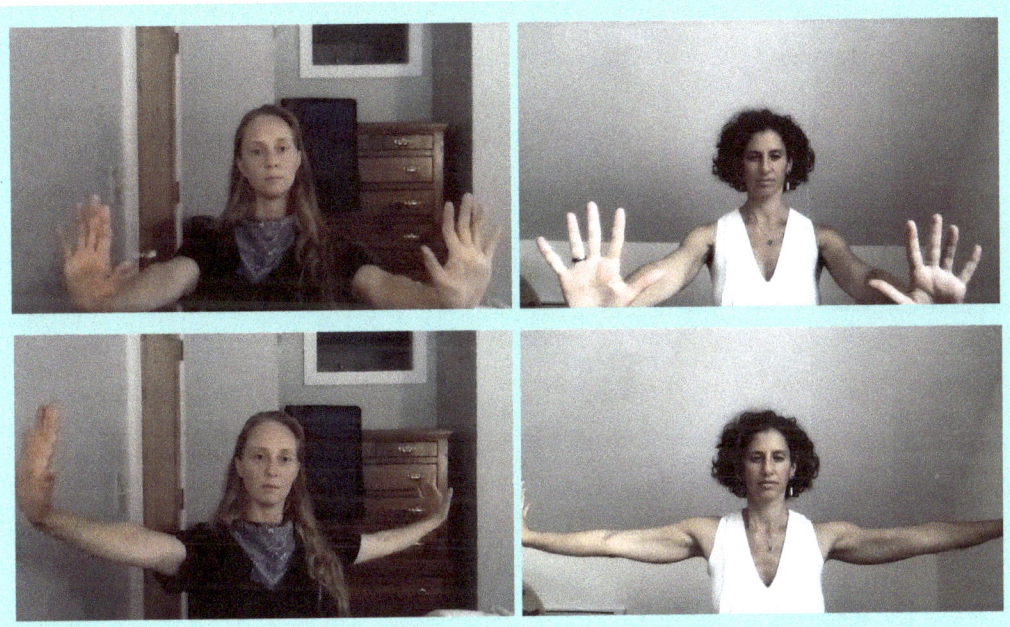

Rotate your wrists forward and feel into your thumbs, then rotate toward the back and feel for the stretch in your pinkies. Bend a little at the elbows and repeat the push outwards in other directions - straight out from shoulders, sides, in-between, upwards. You can imagine pushing against a large, firm beachball. With each push, keep pulling your fingers back towards yourself. Feel the pull in the front of your elbows.

To End: Pause, eyes closed, spine tall, chin slightly tucked, hands flat on your chest. Connect with yourself, sense your feet on the ground and notice your nervous system for a few breaths.

(What is Piezoelectricity? See the Glossary, p.230).

3. Skill Building Intentions for Embodiment and Co-Regulation

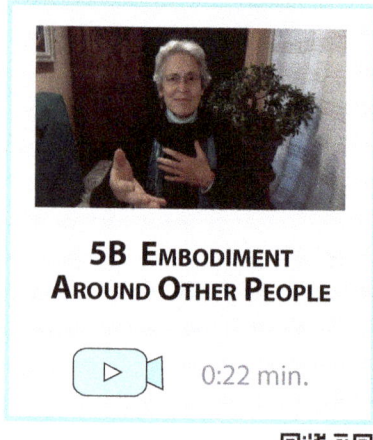

5B EMBODIMENT AROUND OTHER PEOPLE

▶️🎥 0:22 min.

QR for Video

POPULAR BCR PRACTICES TO FIND HOME IN YOUR CORE

Back Stack

Sitz Bones Rock

Spinal Flexes

QR for Video

5C FINDING HOME IN YOUR CORE

▶️🎥 2:38 min.

The four embodiment skills are: Find Home in Your Core, Embodied Boundaries, Give the Body a Voice, and Track Self and Other. They support all the regulatory intentions, especially embodied presence. These skills are fundamental to staying present, embodied, and co-regulatory with others. They all help prevent burnout. They develop with practice, in relational space, in real time.

Each skill has layers to it and supports the next so it can be useful to do them in sequence. You can orient your BCR practice session towards building these skills deliberately. Just set an intention, pick a skill, and pick a practice. The good news is that we are learning and building skills and co-regulating at the same time.

Start gently and build safely. Do not be fooled. These practices seem very simple, but they are neurologically sophisticated and powerful.

Skill 1: Find Home Base in Your Core

For cultivating safety and dignity in a rooted experience of embodiment. For building a solid sense of self. For coming back to ourselves when we get pulled away by social engagement or upsetting triggers.

Safety is key to embodied relating. Because our (most reliable) sense of safety is rooted in our bodies, being grounded in our bodies can help us to be present and find safety in relation to others. Practices for Finding Home in Your Core help us arrive in our bodies and build an embodied sense of self. A solid psychological sense of self is rooted in a solid physical sense of self.

Remember the days of teenage crushes? Wasn't it hard to notice if you were hungry or tired in the throes of infatuation? Did you neglect your favorite music in favor of theirs? Do you still tend to give yourself away in close relationships? Being skilled at Finding Home in Your Core helps us come back to ourselves.

When we can reliably find, or return to, our core, life gets easier. We can stay connected with ourselves, under pressure and around other people. We can reliably come back to ourselves after upset or trauma and avoid burnout.

Cautions and Contraindications

Remember that embodiment can be challenging or triggering for people, so be gentle with yourselves and each other. Embodiment involves feeling more. For people with a trauma history, this can be overwhelming.

Professional Psychotherapeutic Uses

Be sure to welcome and respect resistance to embodiment. Avoid shaming people for resisting embodiment. Resistance is the nervous system showing what it can and cannot tolerate. This is a therapeutic issue.

Finding Home in Your Core gives people a place to stand and start. It helps people develop a physical and psychological sense of self. It is a prerequisite for having agency and getting good at BCR. Knowing how to return to a coherent sense of self after trauma, dissociation, or dysregulation eases the healing process and is fundamental to long-term physical and emotional health.

Skill 2: Explore Boundaries

For feeling safe, finding agency, and getting closer.

Boundaries are for getting more connected! Good boundaries help us get closer to other people and still feel safe. Healthy boundaries allow us to stand our ground when challenged and to feel safe with more closeness when we want it. They let us determine how far and how close we want to be to another person in the moment, and act on it.

What if you had boundaries that work for you? Can you imagine asking a loud friend to speak more quietly? Would it help you relax and feel more connected?

Often our social agenda will trump our *body up* agenda and prevent us from acting to take the space we need. Have you ever wanted to keep your distance from someone but been afraid it would upset them if you moved away?

When we can take action to protect ourselves or adjust what bothers us, we do not have to go for control or distance or cling to hierarchical role boundaries.

> A solid psychological sense of self is rooted in a solid physical sense of self.

POPULAR BCR PRACTICES FOR EXPLORING BOUNDARIES

My Safe Bubble

Prayer Push

My Bubble Now

QR for Video

5D
WANT TO GET CLOSER? GET BOUNDARIES

 2:53 min.

Safety comes with noticing what closeness and distance we want and making it happen. Exploring embodied boundaries helps us notice the degree of closeness we want and builds our capacity to indicate and hold to that boundary in daily life.

Boundary Muscles

We have physical and social boundary muscles that we use to indicate and stick up for our boundaries. Eg. the middle deltoids are social boundary muscles. To feel them, push your elbows out to the sides, as you might in a crowd or on the subway. It is even in our language, "I need elbow room."

5E
BOUNDARY MUSCLES

 1:50 min.

QR for
Video

Cautions and Contraindications

Our social agenda can trump our need for boundaries. Many people feel they will hurt or enrage others if they set boundaries and claim personal space. People who seldom indicate or stand up for their boundaries often have shame about not protecting themselves. Also, attachment issues and entrenched caregiver tendencies often complicate boundary work.

Professional Psychotherapeutic Uses

Exploring Boundaries can be helpful with anxiety and depression. When we do not have sturdy embodied boundaries, social engagement produces anxiety and can be overwhelming. Without comfortable boundaries, we cannot easily use social engagement as an antidote to depression. You can not feel safe in your body if you can not protect yourself with boundaries. The process of setting embodied boundaries develops agency and cultivates our capacity for intimacy.

Good boundaries help us get closer to
other people and still feel safe.

Skill 3: Give the Body a Voice

For listening to our *body up* knowing. For taking agency around expressing ourselves

Our nervous system relaxes when it knows we can and will speak up for ourselves, promptly and effectively in real time.

Giving the Body a Voice is about including *body up* awareness, especially in social spaces. Who feels safe when nobody will speak up for them? The body lets go to a deeper sense of safety when we are willing to notice and advocate for our physical needs.

There are four layers to this skill. Be aware that all of them can stir shame, so go slowly. Practice this only when you feel safe enough to show yourself.

> **First**, be willing to notice your body. Give the body high-priority access to consciousness.
>
> **Second**, act on what you notice. Give your *body up* awareness high priority in decision making, both when you are alone and when you are around other people. That can mean giving body awareness precedence over your social agenda.
>
> **Third**, dare to express your *body up* truth nonverbally, in gestures, posture, and facial expression.
>
> **Fourth**, speak your body's preferences in words. Give voice to your *body up* experience, in relational space.

When we notice and speak up about each little adjustment we need in order to be more comfortable, our nervous systems feel much safer to rest or to connect with others. For example in a BCR session, I might say, "I am not comfortable breathing as fast as you are so I will mirror your movement but breathe at my own pace." This shows how we can prioritize bodily needs and stay connected.

Cautions and Contraindications

Giving the Body a Voice is very challenging for lots of people. Go gently. White supremacy culture gives priority to the mind over the body (and its voice). So, for most of us Giving the Body a Voice is radical, challenging, and important.

POPULAR BCR PRACTICES FOR GIVING THE BODY A VOICE

Prayer Push

The Fan

Up & Down With the Voice

5F
GIVING THE BODY A VOICE AROUND OTHERS

 2:56 min.

QR for Video

Professional Psychotherapeutic Uses

Giving the Body a Voice quickly builds safety into the therapeutic relationship. It supports people to relate authentically in therapy and in their social world. It helps people access and trust body wisdom and emotional expression. Up and Down with the Voice (P. 216) can be transformative. It builds scaffolding that allows clients to touch into dysregulated states without getting lost in them.

Skill 4: Track Self and Other

For connecting with others without giving yourself away or becoming controlling. For learning embodied peer relating and preventing burnout.

Working this intention lays in the circuitry we need for tracking ourselves and others in real time. This is a complex task. Many of us learn a skewed version of this fundamental but much-neglected relationship skill. We may lean towards abandoning ourselves when around others. Or, we may shut others out because relating to them feels too challenging or overwhelming.

> **If we pay too much attention to the other person**, we leave ourselves out and may have trouble knowing or speaking up for what we want. That behavior reads as over-accommodating or codependent.

> **If we pay too much attention to ourselves**, we forget to listen. Others get left out and our behavior reads as selfish or narcissistic.

Either way, it is hard to co-regulate. The trick is to learn to go back and forth between self and other, easily, and by choice. During BCR practice, we rewire the brain at a primitive developmental level. We can learn to let our attention flow back and forth from self to other in a balanced and relaxed way. We can stay comfortably connected with ourselves and respectfully track our communication partners at the same time.

Inner conflicts between our social agenda and our *body up* agenda are very common. We may want peace, quiet, and inward focus at the same time that we want connection. We may know we need to care for ourselves and fear that the other will feel rejected. We may be allergic

---

POPULAR BCR PRACTICES FOR TRACKING SELF AND OTHER

Hands Show Breath

Sitz Bones Rock

Sitting With Self & Other

QR for Video

5G

TRACKING SELF AND OTHER

 2:23 min.

to someone's perfume and worry about looking rude or antisocial. This is a normal but uncomfortable place for our social agenda to be at odds with our *body up* agenda.

Cautions and Contraindications

Our habits of avoiding or over-attending to others often arise out of deep attachment patterns. Do not push or expect big changes too fast.

Professional Psychotherapeutic Uses

It makes sense to build skills for stable, balanced relationships. Becoming conscious of how we attend to self and other helps expose and dismantle codependence and one-up habits of control or domination. And last but not least, learning to Track Self and Other gives us, and our clients, a way to address and reverse burnout.

Track Self and Other:
90/10

Many of us, when we are around other people, give more attention to others than to ourselves. When mirroring in BCR, it can be useful to explore a 90/10 ratio of attention (90% for yourself and 10% for your partner.)

Try doing 90/10 and getting feedback from your partner as to how they liked it. You may be surprised. For some people, it is a relief to notice that you are taking care of yourself. Then they can relax, drop caretaking, and just be present with you and themselves.

---

4. Questions to Find Your Intention

These questions provide an opportunity to get to know yourself and your nervous system even better; they can help you explore what your body and nervous system like, and what helps you co-regulate. As you learn BCR, you can reference these self-reflection questions before or during a practice session if you like

Do you want to get better regulated? If so, ask yourself:

Where am I now?

Am I revved up, shut-down, or wanting to connect more?

Where do I want to be?

Think in terms of the Window of Presence (p.144), or the Mood Map (p. 67). Set an intention for co-regulation practice.

How do I use co-regulation to get there?

Pick from the List of Practices for Co-Regulation (p.122).

Do you want to build skills? If so, ask yourself:

Do I want to get more efficient at coming home to my core self?

Do I want to strengthen my relationships by practicing boundaries?

Do I want to practice giving my body more of a voice in my life?

Do I want more flexibility about when I track myself and when I track the other person?

Pick from the List of Practices for Embodiment Skills (p.123).

5. Do You Want to Feel More or Feel Better?

We can use Body Up Co-Regulation to feel better or to feel more. Both intentions are important and have their moment.

Feel Better: When we are too anxious, traumatized, or dysregulated, feeling more is a bad idea. It is smart to move away from the intensity and overwhelm, and do what helps us get regulated and feel better.

Feel More: When we are a tad numb and want more vitality, BCR can help us feel more alive and authentic, more able to face ourselves and the world.

Navigating your inner landscape involves paying conscious attention to your mood and what your nervous system likes. Once you have explored the practices, you will get a feel for which ones work for you and when. Keep noticing what brings you comfort and what enlivens you.

Here are a few personal examples, not to suggest what should work for you, but to jog your imagination!

When I (Beth) am overwhelmed, I do not want to feel more, I want to feel better. Sitz Bones Rock can be comforting. Proud Duck can cheer me up.

When I want to feel more, I can use Heart Circles to notice tenderness and connection, or Prayer Push to feel more truth and power, or Turn Away and Come Back, to feel more vulnerability.

You get to explore what works for you given your mood of the moment.

Professional Psychotherapeutic Uses

Engaging clients in deciding whether to feel more or feel better at a given time is useful for several reasons.

- Doing so engages them in taking agency.

- It cultivates a relationship between habitual young parts and their adult self.

- It engages the forebrain which is then in a position to calm the amygdala.

- When they do decide to feel more, they are less afraid of getting overwhelmed.

- Considering when to feel more and when to feel better helps people learn what needs to be in place for them to feel more without getting overwhelmed.

6. The 4-Phase Sequence for Accessing and Building Capacity

Let's talk about accessing familiar capacity, building new capacity for vitality, and expanding our capacity for healing.

Accessing Familiar Capacity - Up-regulation helps us access capacity that is familiar to us, but not necessarily available at the moment. Waking up from sleep and revving up for a race are every day examples of up-regulating to access more capacity.

Building New Capacity for Vitality - More vitality means we can handle more intensity and complexity. Building new capacity means organizing our nervous system to thrive in the face of more complex or intense demands than we have managed before. Challenging new situations, sports, or jobs often require us to increase our capacity for handling complexity and intensity.

Building Our Capacity for Healing - Healing from trauma means facing what was too much for our nervous systems in the past. We can expand our capacity to remember, feel, digest, and integrate what once overwhelmed us. We can develop our capacity to stay organized and functional around things that used to trigger us.

Safe sharing makes a huge difference in healing trauma. Yet, high-intensity experience and emotion are often challenging to share. BCR helps. We draw on embodiment and social engagement as fundamental tools to expand our capacity for the therapeutic work of healing trauma.

The 4-Phase Partner Sequence

In BCR, we use this sequence to build our capacity for vitality and healing. This sequence gives us a step-by-step process to include and cultivate high energy states in close connection with others. Start by meeting your nervous system where it is. Then go for gentle enlivenment that includes social engagement, not just raw sympathetic revving up.

In phase one, we cultivate embodied, relational presence. This helps us shift away from defensive or self-conscious performing or pretending and into being present and embodied. Do a practice to Find Home in Our Core: Eg. Sitz Bones Rock, Back Stack, or Spinal Flexes.

In phase two, we invite breath, oxygen, and energy into our system. We expand into organized intensity with an up-regulatory practice: E.g. Chicken Wings, Propellor, Washing Machine, Breath Wings, or Prayer Push. In choosing tempo and intensity for up-regulation, meet your nervous system where it is and push only a little beyond your comfort zone.

In phase three, we notice we can return to being present with ourselves as we digest new energy. We integrate and stabilize alone by walking around for a minute or doing Cross Crawl solo.

In phase four, we integrate and stabilize in attunement with a partner, sharing rhythm and mirroring. This allows us to notice we can bring the new energy into relational space without disrupting our connection with our partner. Do one of these with a partner: Hands Show Breath, Cross Crawl, or Prayer Push.

The 4-Phase Partner Sequence
For Building Capacity

Do this sequence with one leader. TALK at the end, then switch roles.

1. Do a practice to Find Home in Your Core: Eg. *Sitz Bones Rock, Back Stack, or Spinal Flexes.*

2. Expand into organized intensity with a partner. Do any up-regulatory practice: E.g. *Prayer Pussh, Propeller, Washing Machine, Breath Wings,* or *Chicken Wings.*

3. Come back to yourself. Integrate and stabilize solo: Walk around for a minute or, do *Cross Crawl* by yourself.

4. Integrate and stabilize in attunement with a partner: Do any rhythmic practice with mirroring: Eg. *Hands Show Breath, Cross Crawl,* or *Prayer Push.*

7. Regulatory vs. Therapeutic Intention

Body Up Co-Regulation is a sharp tool. It can take us into deep, meaningful territory faster than you might expect.

The good news is that we can access deep layers of our brains and rewire ourselves for healthier relationships and more adaptive regulation habits. The bad news is that BCR can bring us up against challenging defenses, emotions, and memories.

The clearer we are about our intention in doing BCR, the less likely we are to get into deep water that is hard to navigate.

Regulatory Intent

In BCR, regulatory intent means holding an intention to shift our nervous systems into preferred states or lean on each other to stay steady under pressure. Regular practice in shifting our nervous systems will automatically grow our capacity for presence.

Therapeutic Intent

In BCR, therapeutic iintent means using the practices for healing developmental, relational, or physical trauma as well for regulation.

Scope of Practice

In BCR, as in any healing profession, your intentions for your client must line up with your training and scope of practice. Be sure you know your scope of practice and the code of ethics for your field and/or license. If you are not trained in psychotherapy, work with regulatory intent and avoid psychotherapeutic interventions.

Regulatory and Psychotherapeutic Use of BCR

Regulatory Intentions and Uses of BCR

Solo Regulation: To regulate yourself when alone.

Peer Co-Regulation: To regulate yourself and explore your nervous system with another, in present time. No money is exchanged.

Coaches and Practitioners (who are not psychotherapists)**:** To apply BCR exercises in service of regulation and defined goals in the present and future. Do not dig into the past!

As a coach, it is appropriate to offer strategies for resourcing and regulating clients. Unless you are trained to work with trauma, transference, emotional meltdowns, and deep dysregulation, do not go outside your scope of practice. Do not encourage clients to dig into their challenging emotional history.

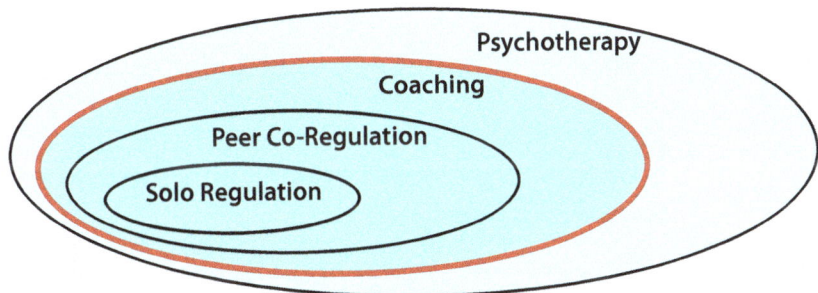

Therapeutic Intentions and Uses of BCR

Psychotherapy: To use BCR practices in service of regulation, exploring dysregulated edges, digesting difficult experiences, and healing developmental and relational trauma.

This does include guiding people to delve into their history and emotional edges, explore trauma triggers, digest traumatic experiences, and rewire their nervous system.

Therapeutic Note/Cautions

When leading, a co-regulator may choose on their own to use BCR to delve into dicey emotions or difficult memories. It is their job to assess their own capacity to return from their emotional edge. Only a qualified therapist should suggest or encourage people to reach for their emotional edges. It is a therapeutic intervention that is outside the scope of practice for a BCR Peer Teacher or a BCR Coach.

©2022 Elizabeth Dennison www.WeCoregulate.com

8. Working Your Emotional Edges with BCR

BCR goes deep very quickly, so proceed carefully and respectfully. When strong feelings arise, it is helpful for both people to stop and make a conscious choice about how they want to proceed. If we always move away from feeling difficult sensations and emotions, we lose vitality and diminish our capacity to engage with life and other people.

However, when we do choose to feel more, there are often challenges. We humans usually turn away from feeling our emotions or our bodies for good reason. So, when we want to reclaim our capacity to feel, we have to find the bandwidth to face and navigate what overwhelmed us in the past.

BCR does tend to expand our bandwidth for staying with intensity and complexity. Up-regulation helps us build capacity at a physical level. Also, tracking self and other expands our attention and presence. As we Track Self and Other consciously, we find that 70% attention for myself and 30% attention for the other can turn to 80% for me and 45% for you. Our capacity for conscious presence expands!

We can use BCR as support to feel more, to go toward the fear, anxiety, shame, anger, etc. When we can stay present with it, we can digest and integrate what was once overwhelming or denied. BCR can offer just the added bandwidth we need if the memory or emotion is not too huge, overwhelming, and traumatic.

Reclaiming our capacity to feel involves finding the bandwidth to face and navigate what overwhelmed us in the past.

Working your emotional eges with BCR?

> **As Leader**, stay within your partner's comfort zone and go toward feeling more in manageable doses.

> **As Mirror**, stay present when you are comfortable with what your partner is doing and stop or change the exercise if you are not.

Working at our emotional edges is important. When the roots of the issue are deep, old, hidden, and habitual, it is profound therapeutic work. Please do so with professional support and within your capacity to stay present.

9. Preventing Burnout with BCR

NOTE: Peer BCR practice is not a substitute for therapy and trauma healing.

Whether you are already in burnout or striving to ward it off, you can practice BCR with the intention to address burnout and build your capacity to meet life with vigor.

Burnout depletes us. Our window of presence shrinks. We lose our capacity for taking on big, important issues. We lose bandwidth for coping with complexity and intensity. We can get too overwhelmed to care about anything beyond our immediate situation. Dysregulation from burnout can keep us frazzled, anxious, reactive, and wearing ourselves out in our hot zone (p.144). Or it can shrink us into our cold zone, where we tend to go numb, hopeless, foggy, and disconnected, with little hope of resting and restoring ourselves.

The pandemic, climate crises, and economic and political upheaval are seriously stressful and breed burnout. Our relationships may be suffering. Our bandwidth for constructive action socially and politically can drop very low. We may be going through the motions because we "have to." We may get reactive on every front. The good news is we do not have to stay in burnout; we can avoid going more deeply into depletion.

For many of us, the pandemic has decreased our opportunities for social engagement. Without the enlivening and regulating influence of social connection, it is easy to lose both embodied presence and our hope and passion for making the world a better place. BCR counters this.

Body Up Co-Regulation prevents and remedies burnout in three big ways:

It Helps Us Learn Nourishing Relationship Habits:
First, BCR teaches us to get better at connecting and caretaking without sacrificing ourselves. When we can tend to our own needs as we nourish others, we do not burn out in the first place. Use any practice from The Practice Pie (p.149).

BCR Helps Us Reregulate Fast:

Second, BCR gives us practices to reregulate efficiently when we need them. We learn how we can shift out of unnecessary anxiety, depression, and depleting threat responses. Getting stuck in threat responses that are no longer necessary is what burns us out! Down-regulation practices allow us to get the rest we need. Up-regulation practices give us the energy we need to feel competent and ready to take on the task at hand. Practices that regulate us for connection help us function cooperatively, get the connection we need, and cultivate a culture of collaboration.

BCR Helps Us Notice Our *Body Up* Needs:

Third, burnout is an embodiment issue as well as a regulation issue. We burn out when we stop taking good care of ourselves. We stop taking good care of ourselves when we forget to come back to our bodies and notice what we need. The four skills for embodiment around other people mitigate burnout because they keep us coming back to our embodied selves. Burnout diminishes when we practice the Four Skills that support embodied, relational presence: 1. Keep coming back to home in our core, 2. Protect ourselves with appropriate, embodied boundaries, 3. Give our body a voice, and 4. Track ourselves and others at the same time.

You can practice BCR with the intention to address burnout and build your capacity to meet life with vigor and enthusiasm.

Practicing the four skills empowers us to take care of ourselves promptly. The better we are at staying present with our own bodies while connecting with other people, the more efficient we can be at noticing dysregulation and re-regulating when we need to. When we build enlivening relationships and turn towards others for connection and co-regulation, burnout goes up in smoke!

Co-regulation is our birthright, but many of us grow up in environments where co-regulation is inhibited by systemic trauma. So, to hold onto this birthright, it helps to be intentional about it. After reading this chapter, you probably have a better understanding of why this work is important for you and how to best use BCR to meet your own needs for co-regulation. You can use the Guidelines for a Basic Sesson (p.136) in Chapter 6 to explore the intentions you identified in this chapter.

Highlights from this Chapter

- You can practice any BCR exercise with a broad intention to explore and see what arises, or articulate a specific intention, holding it lightly in mind or letting it go.

- To dig deeper, explore the eight categories of intention described in this chapter, and in The Skills and Intention Map. Explore, and learn what works and does not work for your body and your nervous system. It is not about doing it right. It is about finding your own authenticity.

- Be clear about your role in BCR. In each session, are you co-regulating as a peer or as a practitioner?

- Practitioners: be familiar with the common Cautions and Contraindications, and be sure you know how to reregulate after triggers.

- With BCR you can choose. Do you want to feel more or feel better? Do you want to work at your emotional edge? Address burnout? Get centered and grounded before a challenging event?

10. List of Practices For Co-Regulation

G - Gentle, **M** - Moderate, **C** - Challenging

Arrival in Embodied, Relational Presence

G - The Fan - p. 172

G - Hands Show Breath - p. 176

G - Sitz Bones Rock - p. 208

G - Pinky Paws - p. 192

G - Prayer Push - p. 196

G - Reach for the Earth - p. 204

G-M-C- Sitting with Self and Other - p. 206

M - Back Stack - p. 158

M - Partner Stretches - p. 186

M - Piezoelectric Arms - p. 190

Social Engagement

G - The Fan - p. 172

G - Hands Show Breath - p. 176

G - Pick Me Up and Hug - p. 188

G - Pinky Paws - p. 192

G - Sitz Bones Rock - p. 208

M - Connected 8s - p. 168

M - Cross Crawl - p. 170

M - Heart Circles - p. 178

M - My Safe Bubble - p. 184

M - Partner Stretches - p. 186

M - Prayer Sweep - p. 198

M - Proud Duck - p. 202

M - Sitting with Self and Other - p. 206

C - Turn Away and Come Back - p. 214

Down-Regulation

G - Hands Show Breath - p. 176

G - Pinky Paws - p. 192

G - Prayer Push - p. 196

G - Reach for the Earth -p. 204

G - Sitz Bones Rock - p. 208

G - Spinal Flexes - slow - p. 210

M - Back Stack - p. 158

M - Connected 8s - p. 168

M - I Stand Guard while You Rest - p. 180

M - Partner Stretches - p. 186

Up-Regulation

G - Piezoelectric Arms - p. 190

G - Prayer Push - p. 196

G - Proud Duck - p. 202

M - Breath Wings - p. 164

M - Chicken Wings - p. 166

M - Cross Crawl - p. 170

M - Good and Grumpy and Good - p. 174

M - Partner Stretches - p. 186

M - Playful Twist - P. 194

M - Propeller - p. 200

M - Spinal Flexes - p. 210

M - Strong Twist - p. 212

C - Up and Down with the Voice - p. 216

C - Washing Machine - p. 218

11. List of Practices for Embodiment Around Others

G - Gentle, **M** - Moderate, **C** - Challenging

Find Home in Our Core

G - The Fan - p. 172

G - Reach for the Earth - p. 204

G - Sitz Bones Rock - p. 208

G - Hands Show Breath - p. 176

M - Partner stretches - p. 186

M - Strong Twist - p. 212

C - Belly Circles - p. 160

C - Spinal Flexes - p. 210

Explore Boundaries

G - The Fan - p. 172

G - Hands Show Breath - p. 176

G - Prayer Push - p. 196

G - My Bubble Now - p. 182

G-M-C - My Safe Bubble - p. 184

M - Breath Wings - p. 164

M - Piezoelectric Arms - p. 190

C - Boundaried 8s - p. 162

Give the Body a Voice in Relational Space

G-M-C - TALK! Each time we share what we notice about and exercise we are giving the body a voice. - p. 15

G - Hands Show Breath - p. 176

G - Prayer Push - p. 196

G - My Bubble Now - p. 182

M - My Safe Bubble - p. 184

M - Chicken Wings - p. 166

M - The Fan - p. 172

C - Good and Grumpy and Good - p. 174

C - Up and Down with the Voice - p. 216

Track Self and Other

G - Hands Show Breath - p. 176

G - Reach for the Earth - p. 204

G - Sitz Bones Rock - p. 208

M - Connected 8s - p. 168

M - Sitting with Self and Other - p. 206

C - Chicken Wings - p. 166

C - Propeller - p. 200

C - Turn Away and Come Back - p. 214

CHAPTER VI
How To Co-Regulate Online or In Person

"I took this training to learn new techniques to help clients regulate themselves, especially while living in a state of perceived threat.

"What I didn't expect is to want to use these techniques with my loved ones, to help me feel more connected. In this time of feeling alone and isolated, these practices provided space to acknowledge that feeling and to be vulnerable with the other person. It allowed me to invite that other person in. It allowed me to be fully present."

- Rebekah Ehrlich, LMSW

Co-regulation practice offers a way to feel present and connected in just a few minutes, in our personal and professional lives.

We can feel and be more available to ourselves and one another with simple, accessible, and easily adaptable practices.

We can get more related without going to vulnerable depths or taking a great deal of time or energy. We can choose and shift to the state we want to be in. See Chapter V on Intention.

This chapter covers practical tips and guidance for co-regulating in your life.

1. What is Body Up Co-Regulation Good for Online?

Body Up Co-Regulation (BCR) practices are great for beginning meetings, for ending with a sense of connection, for building sturdy embodied relationships, and for working deliberately with feelings and moods. Practicing BCR can expand your capacity to handle complexity, to organize your priorities, and to focus or re-focus after disruption or getting stuck or spaced out. Two minutes of practice can make a huge shift in our nervous systems.

6A
GETTING STARTED WITH BCR

 1:20 min.

QR for
Video

Therapists, coaches, teachers, and other practitioners can use these exercises online or in person. Enliven sessions. Deepen connection. Build relationship skills.

You can quickly teach and do these practices with friends, family members, clients, and colleagues.

Whether you are retired, working, a student, a practitioner, or a stay-at-home parent, you can put these skills to use with the people in your life. Moment to moment and day to day, you can ask yourself:

Am I hungry for more authentic connection?

Am I tired of online connections feeling emotionally flat?

Do I want to energize, relax, or connect right now?

Mirroring, sharing rhythm, self-expression, embodied listening, and reflection all have a potent impact on how present we feel with ourselves and others. The good news is that even online we CAN share ourselves via rhythm, mirroring, embodied listening, and verbal reflection.

2. Remember Safety and Intention

Safety is essential. We only drop into embodied, co-regulatory connection if the relationship feels safe enough. Remember to minimize shame (p.91) as best you can. Feel free to adjust the exercises for comfort. Titrate (p.90) if and as needed.

Get clear about your intention (p.112), or just play. Do you want to build skills, get connected, get going, or calm down?

Therapists and BCR Coaches, be sure to understand and remember your role and your scope of practice. (See Regulatory vs. Therapeutic Intent p.117.)

Both people take turns in each role with roughly equal time. Using a timer can be helpful.

3. How to Lead and Mirror in BCR

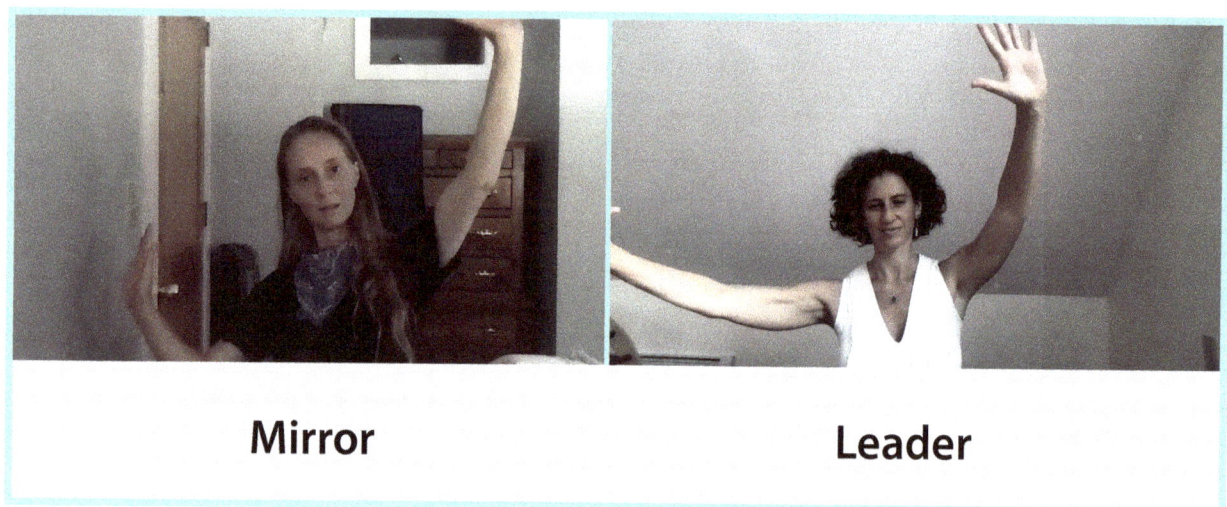

Mirror **Leader**

Leader/Explorer

Take your time as Leader to feel yourself and your nervous system. This is your opportunity to explore what works for you in relationship with another: your rhythm and timing, your internal and external experience. The focus is on you.

Your eyes can be open or closed. You can make eye contact or not. You can talk about your experience in the moment a little if you like, but keep your language in the here and now. (E.g. "I am noticing my breath deepen.") Adapt the exercise to work for you.

Ask for the type of mirroring you want: gestures only, gestures with sound, gestures with words, witnessing without movement, etc.

As Leader, it is not your job to take care of your co-regulation partner. However, if they do not seem to feel safe with you or what you are doing, ask them about it. Remind them that either person can stop at any time. Co-regulation is only co-regulation if it is good for both people.

At the end of the exercise, TALK about what you noticed in your body, your feelings, and your thoughts. Talk especially about how it affected your body and nervous system. Did it calm you down, did it energize you? Do you feel more or less present? Do you feel more or less connected?

There is often a time delay on Zoom, Skype, etc. It will look fine to the Mirror, but the Leader may see a big delay. Laugh and forgive. Going slow or setting a steady rhythm can help. See if you can hold a baseline of trust that your mirror is with you, mirroring you in good faith despite the time delay.

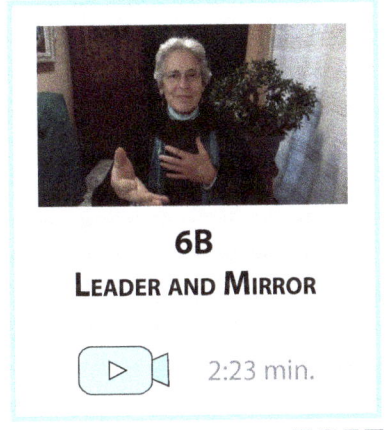

6B
LEADER AND MIRROR

▷ 2:23 min.

QR for Video

The Leader/Explorer Role - in brief

- Take this time to feel yourself.

- Your eyes can open and close. Make eye contact as you like.

- Adapt the exercise to work for you.

- Ask for the mirroring you want.

- Drop caretaking your partner.

- At the end, TALK! about what you noticed.

Mirror/Witness

You are holding space, being a warm witness, offering connection, and mirroring rhythm and movement. Offer your verbal reflections and responses in the TALK time.

Your first job as Mirror is to take care of yourself so that your Leader does not feel that they have to take care of you. Speak up about any adjustments you need. Stop when you need to.

After that, your job is to be present and available - to mirror, to be a witness, companion, receiver, or coach.

Your Leader can ask for the kind of mirroring or witnessing they want. Discuss if needed, so that the mirroring works for both people.

It can be helpful to say things like: "I am here for you." "You can close your eyes." "I will be here when you open your eyes." "You do not have to take care of me."

You will need to keep your eyes open in order to mirror. Mirroring is an opportunity to show up for someone else, and to benefit at the same time. It can be very simple and soothing to mirror someone. Trust that your presence matters. However, do not push your own limits.

You can keep 90% of your attention for you!

Trust that your presence matters.

Radiating presence is often more effective than the kind of caretaking that over-focuses on the other. Co-regulation is only co-regulation if it works for both people, so adapt this role to work for you. Offer a smile when it is authentic.

Be sure to TALK at the end of each turn, the Leader starts. (This is not necessary with young children.) Share what you noticed, your reflection, and your response. You can prompt your partner by asking, "What did you notice?"

The Mirror/Witness Role - in brief

- Match your partner's movements, gestures, and timing.
- Keep your eyes open so you can track your partner.
- Adapt your mirroring to work for you.
- Avoid giving yourself away as Mirror. You can keep 90% of your attention for you!
- Be available to offer a smile.
- At the end, TALK about what you noticed. Leader shares first.

The Surprising Gifts of Mirroring

Mirroring can be a relief: simple, enjoyable, and a path to regulation.

> By being available for someone else, we can feel useful and needed.

> Mirroring can affirm our capacity to show up and be reliable. And, it is possible to relax into following - not needing to make decisions, lead, be in charge, or take care of the other person.

> The nervous system can relax into sharing another person's rhythm and expression. We can feel easy, safe, and connected.

> Mirroring can also invite us to try on new ways of being, if we want to.

Mostly, mirroring is simple. Keep your eyes open, relax, and follow what your Leader is doing, in a way that works for you. If you are not comfortable doing their movement, do a mere shadow of it, but mirror their rhythm.

4. How to Invite More Co-Regulation into Your Life Right Now

Yes, it can feel awkward or risky to invite someone to practice with you or teach them what you have learned. And ... people are often hungry for an opportunity to connect!

Shaking hands is great, but it does not work online.

You can invite a little informal co-regulation before beginning an activity with other people, or anytime you want to drop in and connect.

Try asking, "Would you like to try something with me to get us more present or get us more connected?"

Or, "I could use a little settling down, would you be willing to try something with me that could be good for both of us?"

To ground after a stretch of cognitive work, you could say, "I am getting a little fuzzy and heady, would you do this simple rocking exercise that helps me refocus?"

If they say OK, then say, "Just rock back and forth with me. Watch me so you can mirror my rhythm while I lead. Then, we can share what we noticed, and you can lead and I will follow."

Mirroring for a Dose of Cheerfulness

Proud Duck (5:48 min.) is a short, simple, silly way to tune up our social nervous system and get a quick pick me up.

- Watch and then try it by yourself. What is your rhythm?

- How do you feel after this practice?

- Who in your life could you do this with?

- Would they laugh and be glad of it?

Proud Duck

 5:48 min.  Video QR

- **For Up-Regulation, Self Respect and Playful Attunement**
- **For a Dose of Cheerfulness**
- **For Feeling Good About Ourselves while Connected With Another**

To Begin: Sit or stand comfortably, facing your partner. This can be a mirroring exercise, or you can just practice together. Sit or stand tall. Make eye contact.

Leader or Both: Lift your chest and your chin, and waggle your shoulders forward and back like a duck, in a proud, rapid motion for two or three whole breaths. Notice the expression on your own face, and on your partner's face. Let yourself look pleased with yourself. It is OK to laugh!

Mirror - Eyes open. Mirror your partner's gestures and pacing. When they make eye contact, offer a smile.

Timing - This is a very short pick-me-up, 2-3 breaths.

To End: Close your eyes and press your palms together over your heart for a long slow breath or two.

TALK! 1-2 min. Leader shares first.

Switch roles, and repeat.

CHAPTER VI: HOW TO CO-REGULATE ONLINE OR IN PERSON

5. How to Find Co-Regulation Buddies

6C

FINDING A BUDDY

 1:37 min.

QR for Video

The core benefit of this work comes in your practice sessions with one or more buddies. You cannot build social embodiment skills by yourself, but you can do it online with another person.

Pick someone/s you are comfortable with. You can take turns leading and mirroring and then talking about what you notice. Or you can just start by stretching together with Partner Stretches (p.186).

You might approach finding a buddy from various angles. You could say:

"I want to learn this, will you help me?"

"I think it could be a great way for us to spend time together and get more connected."

"I am studying this book/work and I would love to share my learning with you."

Then, you could continue by saying:

"The time commitment could be a half hour to try an exercise or two."

Sharing why you think this is valuable can be a good way to engage people. You might say:

"I am tired of feeling alone. I want to learn how to feel more connected on Zoom. Will you do this with me?"

"I am doing this to learn to stay more connected with myself around other people. Want to join me?"

"Being good at embodied, peer relationships is core to ending oppression. Will you do this buddy practice with me?"

If it is hard to reach out, make yourself a list of possible people and send each one an email.

I wish you good luck finding one or more great BCR buddies!

132

6. Tips For Finding Nourishing Connection Online

Physical Considerations

6D
PHYSICAL TIPS FOR CONNECTING ONLINE

   2:26 min.

QR for Video

SAFETY
Feeling safe and present is essential to feeling connected and getting regulated. Turn off demanding notifications and phone noises. Be in a private space without background noise or distractions. See Chapter 3 for theory and Chapter 4 for practical considerations around safety.

LIGHT YOUR FACE
We read important safety cues in the face, so make sure your face is well-lit. This makes it easier for others to feel safe and connect with you.

LIFESIZE
We read others as real when they are lifesize, so use your biggest monitor. This helps you feel more connected with others. Adjust your camera so others can see more of your body when you are moving and more of your face when you are talking. This helps others feel more connected.

EYE CONTACT
We feel acknowledged when people look directly at us. Center the window with your Zoom partner in it, as close under your camera as you can, so it looks more like you are making eye contact.

RHYTHM AND TIME LAG
When others attune to our rhythm, we tend to feel like we matter. The time lag on Zoom disrupts this. So, either go slow enough that your partner has time to catch up, or use a steady rhythm so you can sync up. Pay close attention to this. Misattuned rhythm can disrupt our sense of connection and safety.

Principles for Online BCR

PRESENCE
Connection varies with presence. The more present and engaged we are, the more connection is possible. Movement and novelty engage the brain. When we first see someone and make eye contact, it tends to kindle a smile

or at least engage our presence. The exercises that have us look away and look back, or turn away and turn back, create movement and novelty and bring us more present. This is why peek-a-boo is so engaging for young ones.

MIRRORING
Attunement to our rhythm signals that we matter. A smile, especially watching a smile kindle, signals that we belong. It is easy to lose connection with our bodies and our emotions when we go online. Learning to shift back and forth, between attending to self and attending to others, is essential to feeling a satisfying sense of connection, and essential for BCR.

TALK!
Putting words to our *body up* experience allows us to share, digest, and make sense of it. This is essential if we are to stay connected to ourselves and communicate our *body up* truth.

UP-REGULATION
In healthy, in-person social life, our social engagement system (part of our autonomic nervous system) keeps us feeling safe and engaged. Without social engagement, our bodies tend to go freezy. T ight muscles and emotional numbness can creep in. Relating online can easily feel flat. There may or may not be underlying anxiety as well. Up-regulation combats both emotional numbness and anxiety. It is especially helpful to rev up your energy with others, and you can also do it alone. So, breathe and move, and be playful together online.

NEUROCEPTION
Our nervous system can go into threat response even when our conscious self thinks we are safe. When we forget about our bodies we don't notice how we feel. This interferes with our ability to take care of ourselves and feel any deep sense of safety and connection. So, keep coming back to sensing your body and your core: seat, feet, heart, and gut are helpful. (See practices for Finding Home in Our Core p. 123)

PLAY WITH IT
Adjust it to work for you. There is no wrong way!

7. A Basic Online Session Outline

Now, you have an opportunity to practice the physical exercises online or in person, and TALK! about them. Talking about your nervous system is an essential aspect of co-regulation.

It is perfectly fine to practice one BCR exercise and then move on with your day. This Basic Session Outline offers a template for a longer practice session when you want it.

Here is a structure for a basic co-regulation session:

1) Safety: Remind yourselves that you can not do this wrong. It is fine to adapt the exercises to work for you or to stop in the middle.

2) Start with a verbal contract that addresses these time and safety points:

Timeframe - E.G. 15 minutes, or 3 exercises, or whatever works for you both.

Confidentiality - Agree to keep it all confidential if you want to.

Touch or no touch - decide which, if you are in person.

Begin your co-regulation session.

3) Do Sitz Bones Rock to connect with your core. Focus on feeling your body and finding your center. Let your weight pour from one side to the other. Leader's eyes open and close at will, as they explore connecting inward with themself, and outward with the Mirror.

If you cannot feel your sitz bones, it does not matter. You can focus on sensing when your weight is centered, left/right, and front/back. Mirror follows the movement and stays available to make eye contact and offer a smile. TALK! (p.15) after each person's turn leading.

4) Do Hands Show Breath to connect with your breath and your partner. Again, the Leader's eyes open and close at will. If you like, track your connection with self and other. Mirror follows the Leader's movement and stays available to make eye contact and offer a smile. TALK! after each person's turn.

5) Do Partner Stretches to practice listening to your body while you are connected with someone else. Do exactly what feels good to you. Look to your partner for company and inspiration. Be embodied together. No need to mirror movement or rhythm. TALK! during and/or after co-stretching.

6) End your session with a highlight: a gratitude for yourself and/or your partner, a moment when you felt connected, or what was useful. You might notice and share how you feel now as different from how you felt at the beginning.

THANK YOUR PARTNER

8. Guidelines for a Basic Session

Co-regulation depends on:

Expression: To do BCR, we need to show ourselves, to the extent that is safe and appropriate. We can express how we are, our nervous system state, our feelings, and our vulnerability. Showing motion with our body is a good place to start.

Reflection: We need to know that we are seen as we are.

Response: Then, we need to know how our self-expression affects our communication partner.

It can be helpful to make a clear distinction between reflecting and responding. Reflection (verbal or nonverbal) describes what we notice the other doing. Response is how we are touched or affected by their expression. We need to receive both but at different times.

As the Leader/Explorer you are exploring yourself and what works for you to connect to your body. Explore staying connected with yourself while connecting with your partner.

When Mirroring, you might use simple phrases, as seems fitting: "I am here (for you)," "Do exactly what feels good to you," "It's ok to feel/cry/laugh," or "It's ok to close your eyes, I'll be right here when you get back."

When you TALK!, stay with sharing or attending to your physical and emotional awareness. Talk about what you are doing or feeling or liking. Putting words to our experience allows us to share, digest, and make sense of it. This is essential. Feeling safe and talking about emotional edges releases stuckness and shame.

- Be in a private space without background noise.

- Be sure your face is well-lit.

- Be able to get close to your camera, so you can be more life-sized for others.

- Be able to move far enough away to show large movements.

- A tilt screen is helpful, as is a rolling chair.

- Put your partner's image directly under or over your camera.

- Make yourself comfortable sitting upright.

- The time lag on the internet makes the Leader think the Mirror is slow even when the Mirror sees themself in perfect synch. Laugh and forgive!

9. Using BCR with Children

Children, especially very young children, tend to spontaneously regulate their nervous systems all the time, and good caregivers help them regulate. This can be as simple as guiding quiet songs before rest time, and knowing that recess before another bout of academic work is prudent. BCR practices can be useful and fun with children - consider adding a few to your toolbox as a caregiver, therapist, or teacher.

Children who feel safe and comfortable in their bodies tend to take to BCR readily. As always with BCR, avoid shaming anyone and do not force BCR practice on anyone, no matter their age.

Initiating BCR: With children, instruction can quickly become over-explanation. Use simple words and phrases. Show with your body. Do more and talk less. Keep each person's turn brief, no more than one minute.

Power Dynamics: Ideally, BCR is practiced as peers. Consider: how can you show and share your experience authentically in a BCR practice, while remaining age-appropriate. At the very least, respect every boundary a child sets in BCR and accommodate their preferences as much as possible. Consider building a solid BCR peer practice with adults in your life. Children will sense your regulatory capacity.

Mirroring and Being Mirrored: Children do tend to enjoy mirroring and being mirrored. Sometimes they get very demanding and want all the attention to be on them. Eventually it will be important to help them take turns in a balanced way.

Self-Consciousness: If they get self-conscious about doing it "right" as Leader, encourage them to explore how they want to do it. If they get self-conscious as *Mirror*, reassure them that simply paying attention is what imatters. Ask if they want to lead or mirror first. Remind them not to work too hard to be a perfect *Mirror*. You can even encourage them to mirror wrong - which may lead to very co-regulatory laughter!

Changing the Exercise: Like some adults, children may want to change an exercise to work better for them. That is usually great! It can be useful to name what they are doing that is different, and perhaps, to ask about why they like doing it that way. No need to try and make them do it "right," according to the instructions.

TALK!: The TALK! part of the exercise may not interest children. It can be useful to encourage them to learn to talk about what they notice in their body, or simply what they liked. There is no need to push it, especially in the beginning or with very young ones. When it is your turn to TALK, be brief and sincere.

Getting Competitive: Like many games and activities, BCR can spark competition. Depending on their age, it can be useful to describe the competitive behavior, and ask the child what they like about it or why they are doing it.

Shyness: As with adults, some young ones can be very uncomfortable focusing on their bodies in relational space. Invite, model and titrate, but do not push.

Safety - Control or Rules to Follow?: Some children relax when they are given control and can call the shots. For others, that is too much responsibility and they will be much more comfortable knowing there are rules to follow and that they are doing it right. See if these habits change over time?

Language: The bottom line in working with children is to help them pay attention to what they like and what helps them feel safe. "Safe" may not be a relatable word for most children. Try language about sensation and feelings they like, such as, "I felt warm in my heart", "I smiled when …", "I like it when …", "Flapping my arms was fun!", "First I didn't want to open my eyes, and then I did."

Highlights from this Chapter

- Co-regulation works extraordinarily well online! Authentic connection, mutual regulation, and embodied peer relationships are entirely (and easily!) possible.

- You can build sturdy peer relationships with BCR by leaning on the safety of clear and explicit roles for the Leader and Mirror!

- Most people want more connection - your finding the courage to suggest BCR, however awkward, offers a generous gift to those you ask.

- Find a Buddy! Agree to try out the BCR structure for a **Basic Session**. It creates safety and connection even online!

- Lighting matters. If you want your partner to feel connected, do not make them guess what your face is saying because they are struggling to see it.

- Connection might seem like an ephemeral thing. Yet, very concrete and practical choices contribute, from lighting and camera angle to willingness to TALK, and willingness to stop and adjust the practice at any time.

- Use BCR! Try it next time you get grumpy with a friend, stuck on a cognitive task, or caught in burnout.

CHAPTER VII
Navigation Tools for Your Nervous System

Body Up Co-regulation (BCR) is experiential, and the benefits are compounded with regular practice and familiarity.

You can learn to rely on these simple exercises to shift your nervous system and your mood quickly. Expect to get engaged, connected, and more present, online or in person!

1. Reminders

In this chapter, you will find instructions for each exercise. Here are some points to keep in mind as you proceed and practice:

- Do what works for you.
- Navigate using The Practice Pie (p. 149), if you like.
- Choose a specific intention or just explore what appeals to you.
- Be willing to notice your *body up* experience even when it is different from your intention.
- Experiment, and respect safety and boundaries.
- Stop or pause anytime for any reason or no given reason.

- Be familiar with the general contraindications (p. 94) and contraindications for each exercise, and respect them.

- Know and respect the delineations between regulatory and therapeutic use (p. 117).

- Enjoy, play, and nurture good connections with the people in your life.

For each practice we list purposes, suggestions, intentions, likes, and challenges. These are common possibilities for that practice based on our experience.

Staying with an intention from any category of The Practice Pie (p. 149) need not interfere with attending to our moment to moment *body up* experience.

We might, for example, set an intention for connection with the other person, and also find as we lead that our eyes want to remain closed much of the time. How interesting!

Allow what is happening in the body to be in your awareness. Remain in relationship with your body. Share about your intention and your *body up* experience in your TALK time as Leader and Mirror. Remember that TALK is an essential part of BCR (less so with children).

2. Guidelines, Not Rules

BCR practices are platforms to give structure and support for exploring relationships and your nervous system, rather than exercises to be performed correctly.

The instructions offer useful structure and guidelines, especially at first. Once you understand the point of the exercise, adapt it to work for you and for learning about yourself. Adjust the practices to meet your needs in the moment and your chosen intentions.

It's not about "doing it right" or perfecting anything. It is about learning to share, trust and tell the truth in the present moment.

Perusing The Practice Pie is a great way to start thinking about what you want out of a BCR session or practice.

3. The Window of Presence

In BCR, we cultivate presence and embodiment. The Window of Presence (p. 144) helps us notice what pulls us away from being present. Then, we can choose to come back, before we get too lost in distress, dysregulation, and mental distractions.

Once we are deep in a freeze response, we have very little capacity to take action, or think much at all, never mind formulating and taking new action. Once we are revved up in fight or flight our responses will be knee-jerk and defensive.

In a strong social threat response, we can strategize, but it will be about how to placate a scary person in power, or how to improve our status on the ladder. It will seldom be about how we can make the situation work better for everyone.

The Window of Presence/Window of Tolerance

The concept of The Window of Presence comes from Dan Siegel, M.D. He calls it the Window of Tolerance. He describes The Window of Tolerance as the river of awareness where we are able to play, learn and stay organized to navigate our world and our relationships.

When we reach the limit of our tolerance, we get overwhelmed or shut-down. Parts of our brains get disorganized.

It is all about how much intensity and complexity can we tolerate before we stop functioning well. I call it The Window of Presence because presence is appealing to me and tolerating things is not.

The Window of Presence is a map for tracking your regulation and dysregulation.

You can use it to identify what your dysregulated states look and feel like, and how you know when you are well-regulated.

We practice getting a clear sense of the dysregulated states we get stuck in, and finding words to name them.

Then, we can identify our early indicators for when we are starting to get revved up, tense, or stressed, and when we are starting to get freezy, numb, or disengaged. Early indicators might be a twitchy eye or nodding into sleep.

Our early indicators help us notice what is going on while we still have enough oxygen in our brains to think, and consciously choose a healthy response to our situation.

When we get dysregulated, our brains get disorganized and our thinking goes primitive.

The classic example is the person who yells, "I am not yelling." Everyone else knows they are yelling, but they do not. Their brain gets disorganized. The part of their brain that hears is no longer connected to the part that monitors their sound level.

Primitive needs for power or safety often trump any need to be connected, polite, or respectful.

Co-regulation can bring our best self forward, and quickly!

Use The Window of Presence to find your early indicators and help you catch the dysregulation early, when you still have the bandwidth to notice and choose something different. This is worth taking some time with.

Just a minute or two of co-regulation can shift us out of overwhelm and freeze states, out of anxious or combative states, and out of compulsive status and power oriented states.

You can use The Practice Pie (p. 149), in the next section, to explore which exercises work well for you, to shift into states that work for you in the moment.

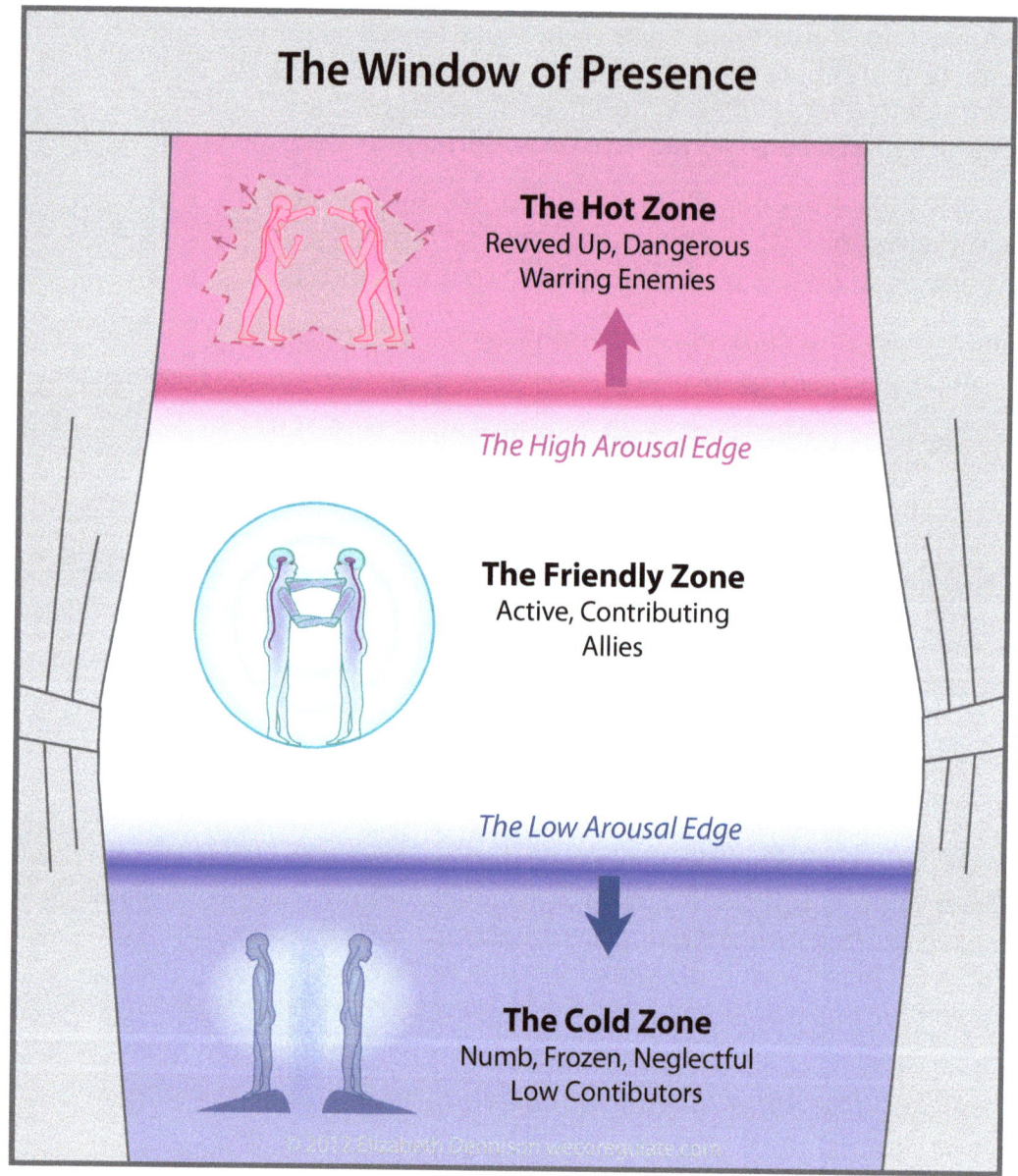

Staying In Your Window

What is it like for you when you are in your window?
What is it like for you when you are at your edges?
Identify your early indicators in the chart on the right.

The more intensity and complexity we are trying to manage, the more we need to be in our window, and the harder it can be to stay there. When do you have trouble staying present and relational?

IDENTIFY YOUR EARLY INDICATORS

Revved Up   In High Arousal? What is it like for you?

Emotional Signs: Anxious, scared, panicky, distracted, defensive, "flipped out", angry, irrational. Feelings hijack thinking: the feelings make us act first and think later.

Physical Signs: Heart and breath rates rev up; Hard to stay still, jittery, twitchy, shaky. Feeling split off from the body; heat, adrenaline rushes; Unable to sleep.

Mental Signs: Thoughts go too fast, confused, jumbled, judging, blaming, planning vengeance.

Your Early Indicator? _____

In Your Window   How do you know?

Emotional Signs: Oriented to present time situations and relationships. Able to think and feel at the same time. Emotions are available, but expressing them is a choice.

Physical Signs: Heart and breath rates are comfortable; Easy to move or hold still. Connected with comfortable or tolerable energy and sensation in the body. Emotions and physical responses may be intense, but remain tolerable.

Mental Signs: Can listen well. Can track complicated communication, collaborate, think.

Your Indicator? _____

Frozen, Shut Down   In Low Arousal? What is it like for you?

Emotional Signs: Numb, hopeless/helpless; Frozen in fear or shame. Depressed, confused, spaced out. Hard to think, feel, or talk. No initiative.

Physical Signs: Heart and breath rates go down; Drowsy, shutdown, rigid, cold, immobilized; Feeling split off from the body.

Mental Signs: Confused, slow, can't think. World shrinks down. Nothing to say. Cannot make decisions.

Your early indicator? _____

145

"The greatest thing then, in all education, is to make our nervous system our ally as opposed to our enemy."

- William James

4. The Intentions and Skills Map and The Practice Pie

The Skills and Intention Map (on the next page) describes each category. The Practice Pie (p. 149) organizes the exercises by intention, to help you choose a practice that suits you in the moment.

The bolded exercises at the top of each section are suggested for starters. When you try an exercise, do the basic exercise for a minute, or for a few breaths before you adjust it to suit you.

Be curious about your personal appetite for each exercise. How long do you want to do it? How fast? How deeply do you want to breathe? How much do you want to stay with yourself or connect with your partner? What would you want to change to like it better?

Using the links in The Practice Pie

Each link leads to the page for that practice.

- Written instructions for the practice
- Pictures and a link to a demo video
- Useful intentions for the practice
- Suggestions for variations and hints about what people like and find challenging
- Tips for focusing on specific intentions

Pick a practice at random, or pick a category and read about it.

Therapeutic Note/Cautions

These explorations can go deep very quickly. A Leader may choose on their own to use any exercise to delve into dicey emotions or difficult memories. It is the Leader's job to assess their own capacity to dive deep and return.

Only a qualified therapist should suggest or encourage people to dig into their emotional edges. It is a therapeutic intervention and outside the scope of practice for a BCR Peer Teacher or a BCR Coach.

The Intentions and Skills Map

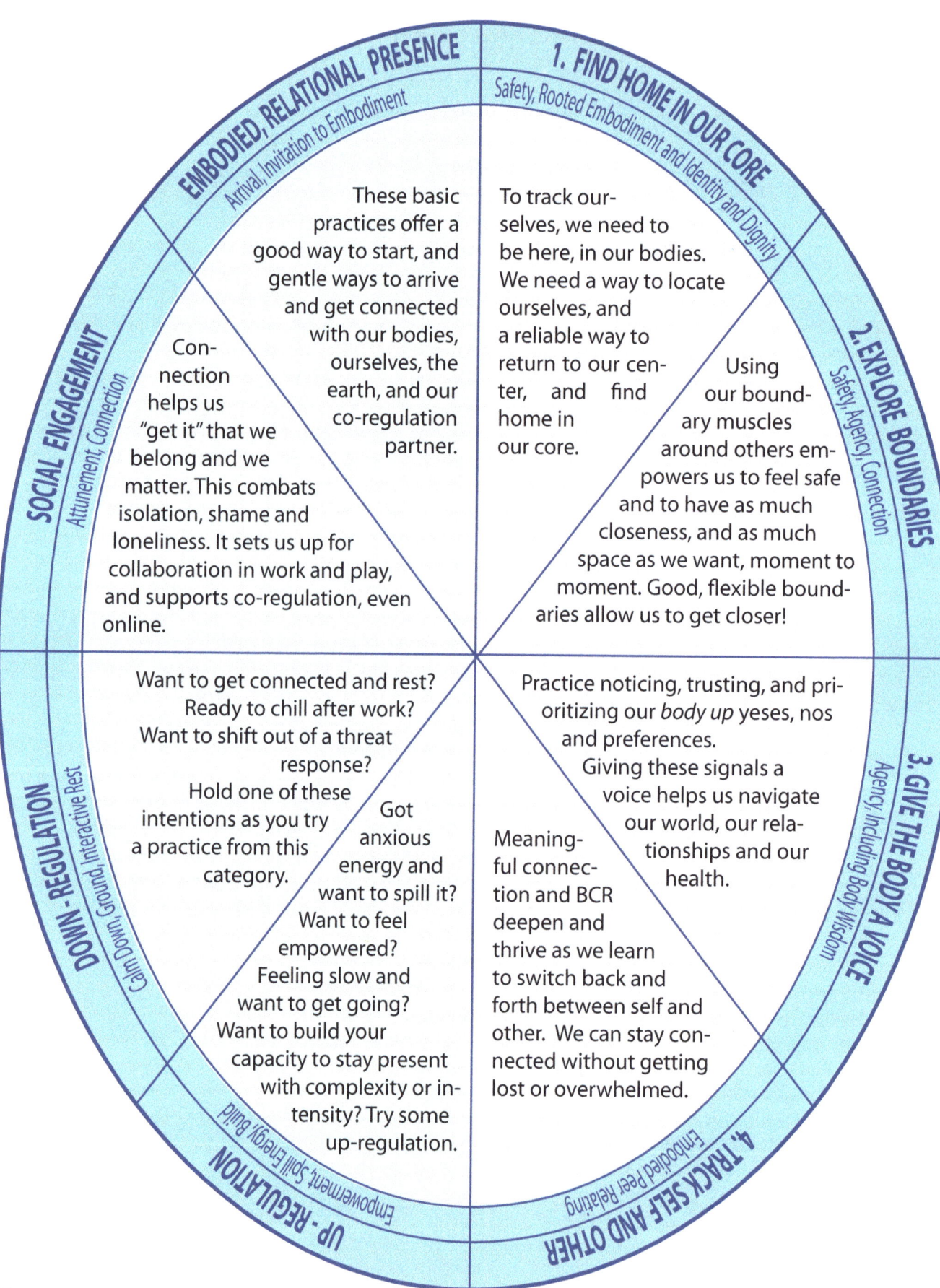

EMBODIED, RELATIONAL PRESENCE
Arrival, Invitation to Embodiment

1. FIND HOME IN OUR CORE
Safety, Rooted Embodiment and Identity and Dignity

SOCIAL ENGAGEMENT
Attunement, Connection

2. EXPLORE BOUNDARIES
Safety, Agency, Connection

DOWN - REGULATION
Calm Down, Ground, Interactive Rest

3. GIVE THE BODY A VOICE
Agency, Including Body Wisdom

UP - REGULATION
Empowerment, Spill Energy, Build

4. TRACK SELF AND OTHER
Embodied Peer Relating

These basic practices offer a good way to start, and gentle ways to arrive and get connected with our bodies, ourselves, the earth, and our co-regulation partner.

To track ourselves, we need to be here, in our bodies. We need a way to locate ourselves, and a reliable way to return to our center, and find home in our core.

Connection helps us "get it" that we belong and we matter. This combats isolation, shame and loneliness. It sets us up for collaboration in work and play, and supports co-regulation, even online.

Using our boundary muscles around others empowers us to feel safe and to have as much closeness, and as much space as we want, moment to moment. Good, flexible boundaries allow us to get closer!

Want to get connected and rest? Ready to chill after work? Want to shift out of a threat response? Hold one of these intentions as you try a practice from this category.

Got anxious energy and want to spill it? Want to feel empowered? Feeling slow and want to get going? Want to build your capacity to stay present with complexity or intensity? Try some up-regulation.

Practice noticing, trusting, and prioritizing our *body up* yeses, nos and preferences. Giving these signals a voice helps us navigate our world, our relationships and our health.

Meaningful connection and BCR deepen and thrive as we learn to switch back and forth between self and other. We can stay connected without getting lost or overwhelmed.

148

The Practice Pie

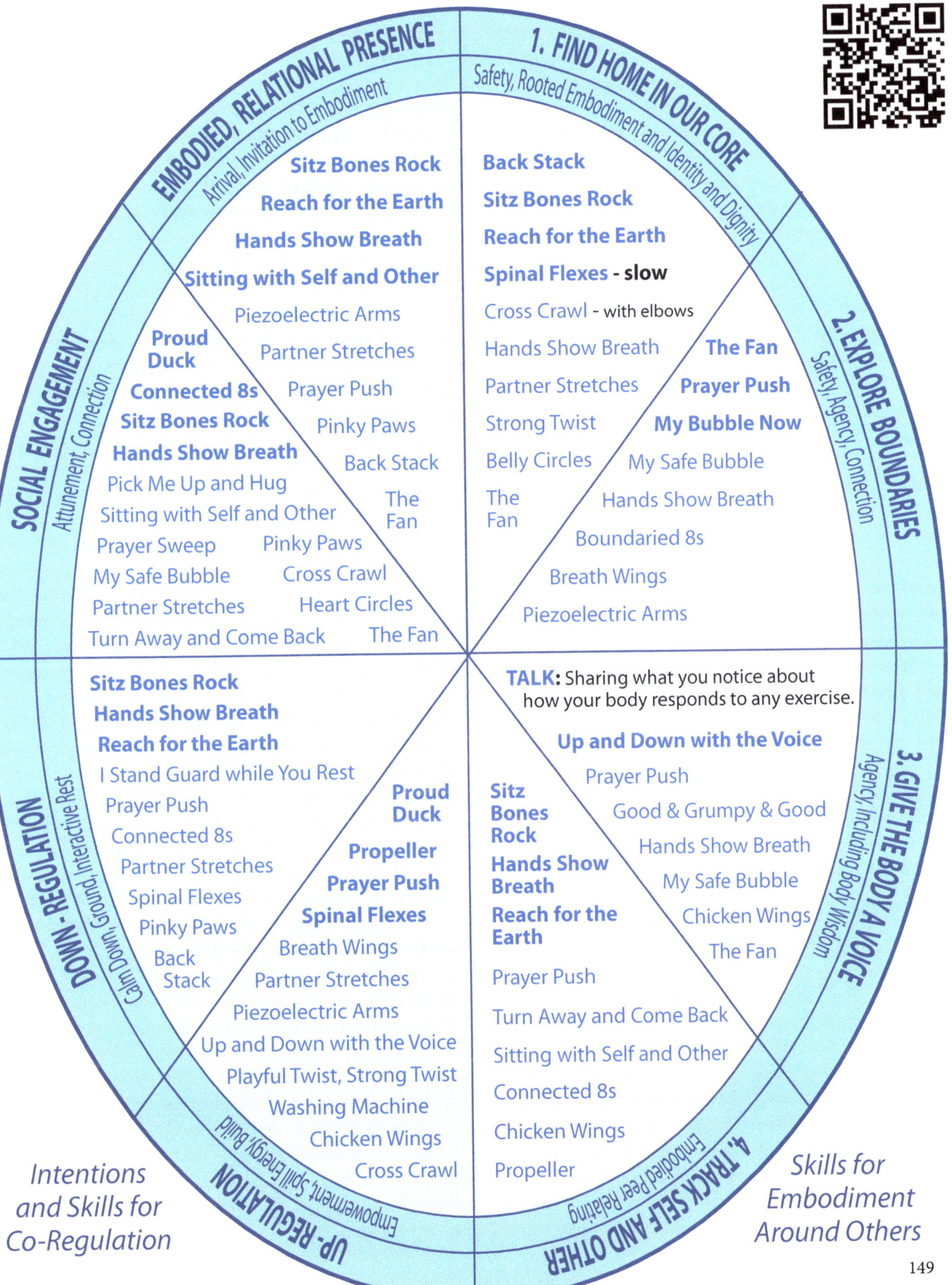

EMBODIED, RELATIONAL PRESENCE
Arrival, Invitation to Embodiment

Sitz Bones Rock
Reach for the Earth
Hands Show Breath
Sitting with Self and Other
Piezoelectric Arms
Partner Stretches
Prayer Push
Pinky Paws
Back Stack
The Fan

1. FIND HOME IN OUR CORE
Safety, Rooted Embodiment and Identity and Dignity

Back Stack
Sitz Bones Rock
Reach for the Earth
Spinal Flexes - **slow**
Cross Crawl - with elbows
Hands Show Breath
Partner Stretches
Strong Twist
Belly Circles
The Fan

SOCIAL ENGAGEMENT
Attunement, Connection

Proud Duck
Connected 8s
Sitz Bones Rock
Hands Show Breath
Pick Me Up and Hug
Sitting with Self and Other
Prayer Sweep
My Safe Bubble
Partner Stretches
Turn Away and Come Back
Pinky Paws
Cross Crawl
Heart Circles
The Fan

2. EXPLORE BOUNDARIES
Safety, Agency, Connection

The Fan
Prayer Push
My Bubble Now
My Safe Bubble
Hands Show Breath
Boundaried 8s
Breath Wings
Piezoelectric Arms

DOWN - REGULATION
Calm Down, Ground, Interactive Rest

Sitz Bones Rock
Hands Show Breath
Reach for the Earth
I Stand Guard while You Rest
Prayer Push
Connected 8s
Partner Stretches
Spinal Flexes
Pinky Paws
Back Stack

Proud Duck
Propeller
Prayer Push
Spinal Flexes
Breath Wings
Partner Stretches
Piezoelectric Arms
Up and Down with the Voice
Playful Twist, Strong Twist
Washing Machine
Chicken Wings
Cross Crawl

TALK: Sharing what you notice about how your body responds to any exercise.

Up and Down with the Voice
Prayer Push
Good & Grumpy & Good
Hands Show Breath
My Safe Bubble
Chicken Wings
The Fan

Sitz Bones Rock
Hands Show Breath
Reach for the Earth
Prayer Push
Turn Away and Come Back
Sitting with Self and Other
Connected 8s
Chicken Wings
Propeller

3. GIVE THE BODY A VOICE
Agency, Including Body Wisdom

UP - REGULATION
Empowerment, Spill Energy, Build

4. TRACK SELF AND OTHER
Embodied Peer Relating

Intentions and Skills for Co-Regulation

Skills for Embodiment Around Others

149

© 2022 Elizabeth Dennison wecoregulate.com

5. BCR Practices Can Make a Big Difference, Fast

The BCR practices are powerful tools for shifting your mood by shifting the nervous system state underneath it. BCR is not the only way to regulate our nervous systems but it is the fastest and most efficient approach I know.

USE THESE PRACTICES!!

You can create a life where you easily and intentionally shift into states that are adaptable for the situation at hand. You can shift out of threat responses when they are no longer needed. You can create more of a sense of connection with others when you want it. You can get yourself going when you are overwhelmed or stuck. You can engage deeply without getting burnt out.

You can play with children as you help them shift states.

You can help a group shift gears and get focused on a task or get more connected and in tune with each other.

You can use BCR to support others to shift out of numb, stuck, or frozen states. You can help another to spill unproductive anger or anxiety so they can drop their rigid defensive behaviors and engage cooperatively.

When we can reregulate fast, it is much easier to relate productively across differences. We can disagree and stay friendly, connected, and collaborative. This is the foundation of a friendly revolution.

If you want to feel better and be more capable,
co-regulate more.

Highlights from this Chapter

- We all have moments of being fully available and present, and times when we are less so. Use **The Window of Presence** (p. 144) to get familiar with your edges and your early warning signs of dysregulation.

- You can use **The Practice Pie** (p. 149) to pick intentions and practices. Or not!

- BCR is for you! – Adjust the practices to work for you, and welcome what is true for you from moment to moment. As long as it works well for both people, there is no wrong way to do it!!

AFTERWORD
The Co-Regulation Revolution, Personal and Collective

"A calm, settled body is the foundation for health, for healing, for helping others, and for changing the world."

-Resmaa Menakem, *My Grandmother's Hands*

Life is hard. I come back to co-regulation over and over. Because I have built up enough trust that co-regulation works, I quickly get connected, embodied, and present.

We all want to feel better and be better at navigating life. We want to savor the good moments and have more of them. At a core level, we also want to know that we belong and that we matter.

I need co-regulation because it is more efficient than solo regulation. I believe in deep embodied connection as a powerful tool in healing trauma. So, as a trauma therapist, I need to reregulate fast and often. I deal with hard things all the time and I am committed to staying steady and present with my clients who have very difficult experiences to share and digest.

Embodied connection with my clients means I feel those hard things in a visceral way. Doing my job well demands I be able to reregulate after resonating with my clients wherever they need to go in a session.

The will and invitation to co-regulate is a blessing. White supremacy culture negates need and self-care and assumes that asking represents weakness and is an unwelcome burden for the other person. Yet, we now know that our nervous systems evolved to be interdependent; our natural inclinations to relate, connect and ask for help make perfect sense.

Take heart with your needs. Be courageous in your asking for co-regulation - chances are very, very good that the people you trust enough to ask will be delighted. Chances are they need co-regulation as much as you and I do. It works because it is good for both people - we simply need to practice.

I hope you see the shades here of "the personal is political" and vice versa. White supremacy culture and any oppressive paradigms begin to lose their power when we humans get embodied. Oppression wilts when we care for ourselves and eachother, and when we build our capacity for collaboration.

We need each other now more than ever. We need to be collaborating to cope with oppression, climate change, war, authoritarianism, economic disruption, and political divides. Because our world is increasingly challenging, we need the most efficient regulation skills we can muster. That means co-regulation. And we need to be able to do it online. The more efficient we are at reregulating our nervous systems for the task at hand, the better our personal and collective lives will go.

If we do not want to be controlled by autocrats, we need to be able to collaborate. We can come to the table to confront charged and urgent topics with a regulated nervous system. Further, with practice, it is possible to expect to reregulate when we get thrown off. This gives our collective undertakings a much better chance of success.

Want to beat burnout and hang on to our humanity in the face of increasingly primitive behavior and autocratic

Co-regulation is not a magic bullet or a quick fix. Yes, it can shift one's state in a moment or two and, it is a practice to engage with over time. Luckily, it is enjoyable!

politics around us? I sincerely do. The more we co-regulate, the more deeply we will trust co-regulation. And, the more likely we are to create co-regulatory experiences for ourselves and others.

The work is cumulative and expands our trust in ourselves and each other. This means we reach out more often and sooner, and we can stay better regulated in the face of challenges, personal and political.

Hope

I want to talk about hope. When we get overwhelmed and discouraged, we get stuck. We stop digesting our experience. We give up on making sense of our world and start reacting from more primitive levels of our brain.

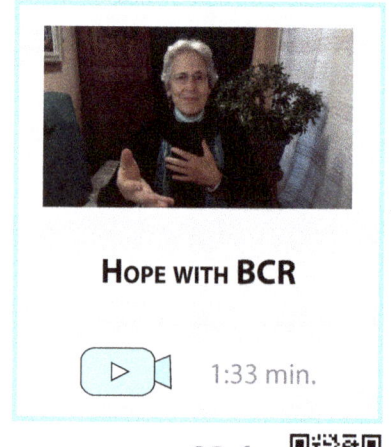

HOPE WITH BCR

 1:33 min.

QR for Video

Body Up Co-Regulation can restore our trust in ourselves to make sense of our world. This embodied practice can give us support and a reality check when we are overwhelmed or triggered or feel that we cannot handle things alone.

Skills for embodiment around others set us up to regulate together and reduce stress quickly. That restores hope. We all carry scars from living in an oppressive system. Oppression is bad for us all, oppressors and oppressed.

Oppression is rooted in the misuse of power - in hierarchical relationships. It robs us all of our trust in humanity. BCR is an important antidote to hierarchy and oppressive dynamics. The practices wire in collaborative, non-hierarchical relationships and mutual empowerment. BCR cultivates the best in us and restores our hope in each other and in humanity.

THE EXERCISES
Instructions for 30 Online BCR Practices

Welcome to the instructions for thirty online Body Up Co-Regulation practices.

You can explore BCR with any of these practices right away. Sitz Bones Rock and Hands Show Breath are good starter exercises for those new to BCR.

You can consider your intentions for a practice with the Skills and Intentions Map (p. 148), or choose a practice based on your need in the moment with The Practice Pie.

To reference the practices in terms of gentle, moderate and challenging check the lists on pp 122-123.

Check P. 126 for reminders of the Leader and Mirror roles.

For important notes on Safety, or Titration or navigating Shame, see Chapter IV.

The Window of Presence (p. 144) is a great tool for getting to know your nervous system and identifying what your regulated and dysregulated states look and feel like.

Remember: Co-regulation is only co-regulation
when it is good for both people!

The Online BCR Exercises List

PRACTICING BCR

 0.50 min.

QR for Video

Back Stack

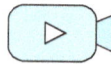 6:32 min.

- **For Arriving in Your Body**
- **For Feeling a Sense of Identity/Dignity**
- **For Finding Home in Our Core**
- **For Finding Readiness to Connect**

 Video QR

To Begin: Sit with feet flat on the floor, palms on thighs. Decide who will lead first. If practicing online, be sure you can see one another's torso, hands, and face. Check in about physical contraindications (below).

Leader - Follow your own timing. Sitting straight, make a few seconds of steady eye contact. Then, curl down toward the ground, taking some of the weight through your arms to your thighs, if you like. Be sure to curl down only as far as is comfortable. Hang there as long as it feels good. Your arms can hang down if you like. Wait until your body wants to come up. Then, slowly, (assisting with your arms if you like), curl up again, stacking your vertebrae until you sit tall. Meet your partner's eyes when you are ready.

Mirror - Eyes open. Be a warm witness. Breathe and feel the length of your own spine as you sit and observe. When they make eye contact, allow a smile to kindle. You can stretch with them as long as you are also there to meet their gaze as they curl up.

Timing: First Leader: 1-2 minutes. Curl down and up at least 2X.

To End: Pause, eyes closed, spine tall. Sense your feet on the ground. Take a few breaths, open your eyes, and TALK.

TALK! 1-2 min. Leader shares first.

Switch Roles, and Repeat.

_____

Suggestions: Simple is good and feel free to vary the movement or stretch backward. Chairs work better than the floor but seated on the floor is OK. Hang down until you feel a _body up_ impulse to come up again.

People Like: "The feeling of letting go to the ground." "A grounded sense of self." "Being greeted/welcomed when I came back up."

Challenges: Be gentle with any limitations. Curl only in ways you can without hurting. Do not override physical pain or discomfort to look good!

PHYSICAL CONTRAINDICATIONS: If you have dizziness, glaucoma, or unmedicated high blood pressure, curl forward only with the neck and head.

To Work with Specific Intentions (optional)

The prompts below can focus your exploration. MIRROR - Sit or move as a warm, responsive witness with any of the intentions.

Arrival in Embodied, Relational Presence:
LEADER - Feel into your body and breath as you curl down. How is it to wait until your body wants to come up? How is it to take in your partner at the beginning and the end? Do you feel your back muscles?

Find Home in Our Core:
LEADER - Where does the movement originate? What does your core feel like before, during, and after?

Track Self and Other:
LEADER - What is it like to take time to be with yourself? How do you know when you are ready to come into connection with your partner?

Down-Regulation:
LEADER - What is it like to go very slow, really, as slow as you like? And only come up when you are good and ready?

Connection:
LEADER - What is it like to take time to be with yourself? How do you know when you are ready for more connection?

Belly Circles

No video

- **For Grounding in Relational Space**
- **For Awakening the Lower Torso**
- **For Laying a Foundation for Building Capacity**
- **For Presence and Grounded Vitality**

To Begin: Sit or stand comfortably facing your partner. Rest a hand on your chest and a hand over your belly. If practicing online, be sure you can see one another's torso, hands, and face.

Leader - Eyes open or closed, start by breathing in and letting your chest expand. Then, continue breathing feeling your belly. Begin circling your belly over your hips. You can put your hands on your knees for leverage and stability if you like. Continue breathing deeply. Find a rhythm and do five to ten slow rounds, then reverse direction.

Mirror - Eyes open, so you can track your partner. Mirror their motion and rhythm. When they make eye contact, offer a smile.

Timing: Do 8 -10 circles in each direction.

To End: Close your eyes and drop into your core for a few breaths.

TALK! 1-2 min. Leader shares first.

Switch Roles, and Repeat.

Suggestions: It can be helpful to keep a hand on your belly and move it a little to keep the sensation alive in the present. Also, eye contact tends to increase the intensity.

People Like: "Getting more grounded and present." "Noticing myself and my core while with another person."

Challenges: It can feel too demanding to be seen showing up as embodied in relational space. Can be triggering. Can feel very intimate.

To Work with Specific Intentions (optional)

The prompts below can focus your exploration.
MIRROR - Move as a warm, responsive witness with any of the intentions.

Find Home in Our Core:

LEADER - Where does the movement originate? What does your core feel like? What is it like to look at someone while you feel your belly or your pelvic floor?
MIRROR - Move as a warm, responsive witness, holding space, available for eye contact and attending to your core.

Track Self and Other:

LEADER - What is it like to have company while you feel your belly and pelvic bowl? Does it make it easier or harder?

Therapeutic Note/Cautions

Including the belly and lower body in our awareness and in relational space can sometimes be triggering. A Leader may choose on their own to use this exercise to delve into dicey emotions or difficult memories. It is the Leader's job to assess their own capacity to return from their emotional edge. Only a qualified therapist should suggest or encourage people to reach for their emotional edges. It is a therapeutic intervention. It is outside the scope of practice for a BCR Peer Teacher or a BCR Coach.

Boundaried 8s

Video for *Connected 8s*

 7:05 min.

• **For Cultivating Connection with Protection**

Video QR

This exercise is a simple variation on Connected 8s with an important added boundary gesture. Follow the indication for *Connected 8s* and add the boundary gesture shown below.

As you gesture the 8 with one hand hold the other hand up in a boundary gesture.

Leader - Begin with *Connected 8s* and feel any sense of connection or discomfort that comes with it. Then, add the protective gesture, and notice how that feels. Which one do you like better? Do you find that you feel more or less available when you add the boundary gesture?

Mirror - Eyes open. Follow your partner's gestures and pacing. When they make eye contact, offer a smile. Notice how you feel with and without the boundary gesture. Talk about it in the talk time.

Timing: First Leader: 1-2 minutes.

To End: Pause, eyes closed, spine tall. Sense your feet on the ground. Take a few breaths, open your eyes, and TALK.

TALK! 1-2 min. Leader shares first.

Switch Roles, and Repeat.

Suggestions: In person, you can hold the boundary gesture with one hand and touch fingertips with your partner as you gesture the 8 with the other hand.

People Like: "Feeling connected and protected."

Challenges: Self-consciousness about doing it right or connecting. Discomfort with emotion coming up.

To Work with Specific Intentions (optional)

The prompts below can focus your exploration.

Track Self and Other:
LEADER - How does adding the boundary gesture affect your focus? Are you more interested in your partner with the boundary gesture in place? Do you feel freer to ignore them?
MIRROR - Notice how your experience changes with and without the boundary gesture.

Connection/Social Engagement:
LEADER - Does your interest in connecting change when you can add the boundary gesture?
MIRROR - Give feedback about how the boundary gesture affects you.

Down-Regulation:
LEADER - Do you breathe easier if you add the boundary gesture and slow it down too?

Breath Wings

 5:44 min.

- **For Arriving, Heart Opening, Expanding Breath**
- **For Building Capacity in Relational Space**

 Video QR

To Begin: Sit comfortably upright, in front of your co-regulation partner. If online, be sure they can see your arms and head.

Leader - Inhale and open your chest, raise your chin towards the sky. Take your head back only as far as is comfortable. Exhale, curling your head and arms inwards towards your chest. Repeat the gesture, breath, and stretch in a comfortable rhythm. Eyes can open or close at will.

Mirror - Match your partner's gestures and pacing, eyes open. Be available to offer a smile when they make eye contact.

Timing: Continue fast or slow for 1-3 minutes, or as much as you like.

To End: Pause, eyes closed, spine tall, chin slightly tucked, hands flat on your chest.

Next, to integrate expanded bandwidth, sense your feet on the ground, gently feeling your heels reach forward and down for connection to mother earth.

Then, stand and do 10 rounds of *Cross Crawl,* or just walk and feel the rhythm of your step and your arms swinging.

Both TALK! 1 or 2 min. Share about your experience. Leader starts.

Switch Roles, and Repeat.

Suggestions: You can do this quickly or slowly. Slower with eyes closed may be easier. Play with intentionally making eye contact as your head goes up.

People Like: "Connection at the end." "Feeling energized." "Tuning in to my breath."

Challenges: It is hard for the Mirror to stretch into the movement and mirror accurately. The connection can suffer. Done fast, for up-regulation, this is not a beginner practice. It can start a lot of energy moving in a short time. Try Prayer Push for a less intense wake-up practice.

To Work with Specific Intentions (optional)

Use the prompts below to focus your exploration of the following intentions.

Exploring Boundaries:
LEADER - Can you let the gestures be expansive and empowering so you feel like you own the space? What rhythm works for you?
MIRROR - Witness or mirror as the Leader requests. Notice your experience of taking up space.

Down-Regulation:
LEADER - What is it like to stretch more and more slowly into the movement?
MIRROR - Witness or mirror as the Leader requests. Notice your response to the slow stretch and movement.

Up-Regulation:
LEADER - What is it like to start with a brisk, steady rhythm and increase it? To integrate expanded bandwidth, be sure to stand and end with 10 rounds of *Cross Crawl*, or just walk and feel the rhythm of your step and arm swing. Then, come back into some connecting practice like *Sitz Bones Rock* or *Hands Show Breath*. (See P.115 for the 4-Phase Partner Sequence for building capacity.)
MIRROR - Witness or mirror as the Leader requests. Notice your response to the movement.

Therapeutic Note/Cautions

Strong up-regulation can be challenging or disorganizing at times. A Leader may choose on their own to use this exercise to push their edges, or work on building capacity. It is the Leader's job to assess their own capacity to integrate the intensity this can generate. Only a qualified therapist should suggest or encourage people to push their capacity for up-regulation. It is a therapeutic intervention. It is outside the scope of practice for a BCR Peer Teacher or a BCR Coach.

Chicken Wings

 3:33 min.

- **For Strong Up-Regulation**
- **For Down-Regulation**
- **For Building Our Capacity to Organize and Contain Intensity Around Others**
- **For Giving the Body a Voice**

 Video QR

To Begin: Stand, facing your screen/partner, with enough distance that they can see your head and torso. Decide who will lead first.

Leader and Mirror - Put your thumbs in your own armpits to make wings. Flap your wings up as you breathe in expanding the lungs, and down as you breathe out. Maintain eye contact, and smile. Let your spine flex with the movement. Increase the speed a bit and then maintain it.

(If your intention is *Giving the Body a Voice* or *Down-Regulation*, use the same movements but go slow and follow the **Specific Intentions** on the next page. End by sitting quietly with your hands on your chest.)

Mirror: Honor what is comfortable for you. Offer attention and eye contact without the arm motion, if need be.

Timing: Leader sets the pace and duration: Build to a strong rhythm for 15-60 breaths.

To End: Hold your breath in a little longer than is comfortable, pulling up on your pelvic floor and in at the navel, chin tucked gently. Breathe out and in slowly for 4 or 5 breaths, but keep pulling the lower muscles in and up. Then, breathe out and relax the lower muscles. Stand and do 10 rounds of *Cross Crawl* or just walk and feel the rhythm of your step and arm swings to integrate expanded bandwidth.

TALK! 1-2 min. Share about your experience.

Switch Roles, and Repeat.

Suggestions: May be easier if you go slower for a shorter time, and/or eliminate eye contact.

People Like: "Running energy through my system." "Playing and laughing together."

Challenges: Intensity in relational space can feel scary and demanding. The Mirror may feel a sense of pressure to "keep up."

To Work with Specific Intentions (optional)

Use the prompts below to focus your exploration of the following intentions. MIRROR, move with the Leader as best you can or witness, with any of the Leader's intentions. Stay at least 50% with yourself.

Give the Body a Voice:
LEADER - What speed feels just right to your system at this moment?

Track Self and Other:
LEADER - Do you stay more with yourself or focus more on your partner? What happens to your ability to focus on yourself and your partner as you increase the speed?

Up-Regulation:
LEADER - What is it like to start with a brisk, steady rhythm and increase it? Be sure to end with 10 rounds of *Cross Crawl* or something to integrate the expanded energy.

Down-Regulation:
LEADER - Start with a medium pace and slow it down. How slowly can you move? Let the exhale be longer than the inhale.

Therapeutic Note/Cautions

Strong up-regulation can be challenging or disorganizing at times. A Leader may choose on their own to use this exercise to push their edges, or work on building capacity. It is the Leader's job to assess their own capacity to integrate the intensity this can generate. Only a qualified therapist should suggest or encourage people to push their capacity for up-regulation. It is a therapeutic intervention. It is outside the scope of practice for a BCR Peer Teacher or a BCR Coach.

Connected 8s

 7:05 min.

- **For Cultivating Connection Heart to Heart**
- **For Cultivating Presence**

 Video QR

Before You Start: Move your hand in a figure 8 in front of you to get a feel for the gesture.

To Begin: Sit comfortably facing your partner. If practicing online, be sure you can see one another's torso and face.

Leader - To start, take a breath or two, eyes closed, with hands on your heart. Feel your intention to connect with your own heart and with your partner. Gesture a figure eight, with an open, relaxed hand. Bring your hand up along your torso, extend out and down the middle, up as you gesture toward your partner's torso, down the middle, and repeat, with or without eye contact. (See the image above and the demo video.)

Find a rhythm and do five to seven rounds, or what the Leader wants. Leader ends by bringing a hand flat on the chest and taking a couple of breaths, eyes closed or open. Feel your connection with the ground. Connect with yourself, then open your eyes and connect with your partner.

Mirror - Eyes open. Follow your partner's gestures and pacing. When they make eye contact, offer a smile.   (See the video to get a sense of a synchronous tandem gesture, which can be nicer than just mirroring.)

Timing: First Leader, 1-2 minutes.

To End: Pause, eyes closed, spine tall. Sense your feet on the ground. Take a few breaths, open your eyes, and TALK.

TALK! 1-2 min. Leader shares first.

Switch Roles, and Repeat.

_____

Suggestions: You can also do this with two hands. Be curious about how you know when you feel connected. How does your body tell you? Some people hate this one, try _Heart Circles_ or _The Fan_. In person you can do the gesture with your fingertips touching your partner's fingertips. If you are an empath or habitual caretaker, try doing this with 90% of your attention on yourself and 10% on your partner, even when you are mirroring.

People Like: "Feeling connected." "A reassuring sense of connection, mattering, and belonging." "The complexity of the gesture engages my attention and brings me more present."

Challenges: Self-consciousness about timing, doing it right or connecting. Discomfort with emotion coming up.

To Work with Specific Intentions (optional)

The prompts below can focus your exploration.

Track Self and Other:
LEADER - When is your focus on yourself, when on your partner? Does your heart like this movement? What expression comes to your face?
MIRROR - Once you are comfortable with the movement, feel how it affects you.

Connection/Social Engagement:
LEADER - How is your sense of connection before, during, and after practicing? How does your body tell you like it or not? Do you feel more connected with your eyes open or closed?
MIRROR - Get comfortable with the movement, then notice your sense of connection.

Down-Regulation:
LEADER - What is it like to slow it down, bit by bit? What do you notice in your breathing and body tensions (jaw, shoulders, etc.)? Do you feel more connected with your eyes open or closed?
MIRROR - Get comfortable with the movement, then notice your breath.

Cross Crawl

 6:29 min.

 Video QR

- **For Up or Down-Regulation, Depending on the Speed**
- **For Integrating Complexity and New Experience**
- **A Good Warm-Up For Team Activities and Cooperative Group Projects**

To Begin: Stand or sit comfortably, facing your partner. Decide who will lead first. Make sure you can see one another's knees when they are raised.

Leader - Stand or sit tall, eyes open with or without eye contact. Start by touching your right hand to your left knee as you raise your knee. If sitting, touch your elbow to your knee. Then, switch sides and repeat, finding an easy rhythm. To add complexity, do it with your eyes closed, or do it faster.

Mirror - Eyes open. Mirror your partner's gestures and pacing. Keep a steady eye on them so you can mirror them and be available for eye contact. When they make eye contact, allow a smile to kindle.

Timing: First Leader 1- 2 minutes, or only as much as you like.

To End: Pause, eyes closed, spine tall. Connect with yourself, sense your feet on the ground and notice your nervous system for a few breaths. Then, open your eyes, and reconnect with your partner.

TALK! 1- 2 min. Leader shares first.

Switch Roles, and Repeat.

Suggestions: Find easy rhythms. Build complexity slowly. In both roles, balance a sense of feeling your own rhythm and movement with attending to your partner.

Can be done as a partner exercise, with no Leader and no Mirror.

People Like: "Feeling present, awake, coordinated and ready." "Energized and focused." "Nice to simply follow and mirror."

Challenges: A sense of pressure to "do it right." Can feel complicated and frustrating, and cause shame.

To Work with Specific Intentions (optional)

The prompts below can focus your exploration.
MIRROR - Sit or move as a warm, responsive witness with any of the intentions.

Connection/Social Engagement:

LEADER - What does it feel like to do it with eye contact? Does practicing with a partner make a difference? How? Can you feel them even with your eyes closed?

Up-Regulation:

BOTH PARTNERS - What happens if you increase the speed and breathe vigorously into your movement?

Down-Regulation:

BOTH PARTNERS - How slow can you go and still enjoy it?

The Fan

 1:21 min.  Video QR

- **For Tracking and Deepening Embodiment and Connection**
- **For Exploring Boundaries and Closeness**
- **For Noticing Your *Body Up* Signals of Attunement and Alarm**

To Begin: Sit or stand comfortably, facing your partner. Standing is more intense. Decide who will lead first. If practicing online, be sure you can see one another's torso, head, face, and arms.

Leader - *First get connected:* Arms resting alongside the torso, move them outwards and upwards to meet above your head, then down again. Find your rhythm. Notice your Mirror and tell them how your body lets you know when you feel connected. If you like, you can just make the first few inches of the fan gesture.

Once you have a sense of connection, use words or gestures to direct your partner to move closer to you, and farther away, several times. Be specific with how close and how far and how fast. Notice how your body feels when the Mirror changes position. (You may or may not want to continue the rhythm of the fan gesture, but come back to it if you lose your sense of being connected with your partner.)

Alternatively, ask the Mirror to decide when and how to move closer and farther, and as Leader, notice your responses.

Mirror - Eyes open. Mirror the motion and pacing of the Leader. When they make eye contact, offer a smile. Move closer and farther away as they direct you. Track what is comfortable or uncomfortable for you as Mirror. Also, notice changes in your partner, so you can reflect them back in the TALK time.

Timing: First Leader 2 - 5 minutes.

TALK! 1- 2 min. Leader shares first.

Switch Roles, and Repeat.

_____

Suggestions: Rolling chairs are helpful when working seated. Also, the movements and distances can be very small. With more time you can explore moving in and out from the side.

LEADER - Notice if it is easier for you to be directive, or if you prefer to just notice your responses.

People Like: "Slowing down and connecting." "Finding, feeling, and seeing my rhythm." "Permission to be in control of distance."

Challenges: Too hard to be directive, or hard to feel any connection.

To Work with Specific Intentions (optional)

The prompts below can focus your exploration.

MIRROR - Move as a warm, responsive witness as the Leader directs.

Arrival in Embodied, Relational Presence:
LEADER - How do you know when you feel a sense of connection? What is it like to take up physical space and connect through shared rhythm? No need to explore changing distances.

Exploring Boundaries:
LEADER - How is it to have your partner come in close or move away? What distance do you prefer and how does it feel to ask for it? Does it change? You can ask your Mirror to try different speeds, postures, and facial expressions to see how they affect you.

Give the Body a Voice:
LEADER - Ask yourself: How does your body tell you what distance you prefer? How is it to ask your partner to move and accommodate your preferences?

Connection/Social Engagement:
LEADER - How does the mirrored movement affect your sense of connection? How is it to know that your Mirror is there for you? Explore different rhythms. No need to explore changing distances.

Good and Grumpy and Good

Video QR

- For Practice Witnessing Our Own Emotional Expression
- For Giving the Body a Voice in Relational Space
- For Wiring in the Capacity to Shift In and Out of Difficult States

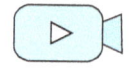

8:09 min.

The important thing is to keep the sound coming!

To Begin: Sit or stand comfortably, facing your partner. Decide who will lead first. If practicing online, be sure you can see one another's torso, head, face, and arms.

Leader - Eyes open or closed, start with happy or cheerful sounds (and gestures). Shift into grumpy/sad/angry/scared sounds (and gestures) - stay with it for 5 - 30 seconds. Then, shift back to cheerful/happy sounds until you can really feel it, stay and enjoy it a bit. Continue back and forth between grumpy and good, for 3 - 5 loops into grumpy. Let your face be expressive. End with good.

CAUTION - Go easy with this one. Do not go longer or deeper than you are ready for. Keep the grumpy phase short.

Mirror - Eyes open. By the Leader's request, just watch, or join the Leader's gestures and sounds, or play cheerleader and encourage them. Do not outdo your Leader, or get lost in emotion. When they make eye contact, offer a smile.

Timing: First Leader 1- 5 minutes. Shorter is less intense.

To End: Pause, eyes closed, spine tall. Connect with yourself, sense your feet on the ground and notice your nervous system for a few breaths. Then, open your eyes, and reconnect with your partner.

TALK! 1- 2 min. Leader shares first.

Switch Roles, and Repeat.

Suggestions: Start with mild, nonverbal expressions of grumpy and good. You may want to think of recent, cheerful and mildly grumpy experiences to put sound to - or not. Be sure you really let yourself enjoy the embodied experience of putting sound to good feelings. Once you get good at going in and out of grumpy, you can explore remembering more intense and upsetting experiences while making sounds.

People Like: "Feeling safe or playful about showing grumpy." "Getting good at shifting out of grumpy." "Having choice and company to share both grumpy and good."

Challenges: Difficulty/shame about making sounds or expressing the negative. Challenging to shift both in and out of grumpy or good. Feeling misattunement when asked to express the good.

To Work with Specific Intentions (optional)

Use the prompts below to focus your exploration of the following intentions. MIRROR - Witness, mirror, or play cheerleader, at the Leader's request.

Give the Body a Voice:
LEADER - How does it feel to notice your face and voice being expressive? What is it like to allow the body to show how it feels? What is it like to be witnessed? What is it like to find and shift states? Which sounds are easier and which are harder, cheerful or grumpy?

Up-Regulation:
LEADER - Can you touch into some enlivening feelings like excitement, anger, fear, or joy? Try exaggerating the sound and gestures, laughter may surface and that's fine.

Hands Show Breath

 6:14 min.

- **For Getting Connected with Self, Other, and Breath**

Video
QR

To Begin: Sit or stand comfortably facing your partner.
If online, be sure you can see each other's torso, hands, and face.

Leader - Elbows bent so hands are near shoulder/chest height yet relaxed.
Palms on your chest or in relaxed, gentle fists in front of your chest.
Open your hands wide as you inhale. Eyes open and close at will.
Return your hands and fingers to the original position as you exhale.
You set the pace and rhythm. Do what feels good to you.

Mirror - Eyes open, so you can track your partner. Mirror their motion and rhythm. When they make eye contact, offer a smile.

Timing: First Leader 1- 2 minutes.
TALK! 1- 2 min. Leader starts.
Switch Roles, and Repeat.

Suggestions: Explore different hand motions:
a) Palms face each other, open and close like a flower with each breath.
b) Palms on your chest, then extend down and open towards your partner.
c) Palms open and close facing your partner.
People Like: "Getting connected." "Noticing myself and another."

Challenges: Fear of being seen. Inability to feel the breath, feeling frozen.

To Work with Specific Intentions (optional)

The prompts below can focus your exploration.
MIRROR - Move as a warm, responsive witness with any of the intentions.

Arrival in Embodied, Relational Presence:
LEADER and MIRROR - How does your breath feel in your lungs?
MIRROR - Track your own comfort as you mirror.

Find Home in Our Core:
LEADER - What is it like to wait for the breath, feel it start, and feel it expand?
MIRROR - Feel for your own core as you mirror.

Exploring Boundaries:
LEADER - Let your hands show your boundaries or your bubble. (Check with your partner. They may not be comfortable with your palms facing them.) Lift your elbows off of your ribs. How big a space do you want to occupy? Use this to add breath awareness to your experience of boundaries.
MIRROR - Track your own sense of boundaries as you mirror.

Give the Body a Voice:
LEADER - Be guided by the rhythm and gesture that your body likes. How do you know you like it?
MIRROR - Is your Leader's rhythm good for you? How do you know?

Track Self and Other:
LEADER - Explore different ratios of attention - from 90% self/10% other, to 50% self/50% other.
MIRROR - Play with 90% attention to yourself and 10% to your partner.

Connection,/Social Engagement:
LEADER - How does the mirrored movement affect your sense of connection? How is it to know that your Mirror is there for you? Can you take them in? You may like exploring different pacing.
MIRROR - Does mirroring give you a sense of ease and connecion today?

Down-Regulation:
LEADER - Gently slow your breathing down. Let the out-breath be longer than the in-breath.
MIRROR - How do you know if you like or dislike mirroring this rhythm?

Heart Circles

 10:18 min.

- **For Feeling Your Heart**
- **For Exploring Heartfelt Connection With Another**

 Video QR

To Begin: Sit or stand comfortably facing your partner. Rest a hand or two over your heart center in the middle of your chest. If practicing online, be sure you can see one another's torso, hands, and face.

Leader - Eyes open or closed, start by breathing in and letting your chest expand. Begin circling your heart over your hips. Continue breathing deeply. Find a rhythm and do five to ten slow rounds, then reverse direction.

Mirror - Eyes open, so you can track your partner. Mirror their motion and rhythm. When they make eye contact, offer a smile.

Timing: First Leader 1- 2 minutes.

To End: Come back to center, eyes closed. Sense your feet on the ground. Connect with yourself, then open your eyes and connect with the other person.

TALK! 1-2 min. Leader shares first.
Switch Roles, and Repeat.

Suggestions: What is it like for you to feel your heart?
What is it like, as Mirror, to be a steady base for your partner?
People Like: "Feeling heartful and sharing vulnerability." "A reassuring sense of connection, mattering, and belonging."
Challenges: Self-consciousness about timing, doing it right, or about connection. Discomfort with emotion coming up.

To Work with Specific Intentions (optional)

The prompts below can focus your exploration.

MIRROR - move as a warm, responsive witness with any of the intentions.

Self and Other:
LEADER - What balance of attention helps you feel more heart?
MIRROR - You can play with 90% attention for yourself and 10% for your partner as you mirror.

Connection/Social Engagement:
LEADER - What is it like to keep coming back to your heart?
MIRROR - Keep at least 50% of your attention on your own breath and chest or heart energy.

I Stand Guard While You Rest No video

- **For Down-Regulation**
- **For Using Connection to Help Us Settle and Rest**
- **For Learning to Trust that it is Safe to Let Go and Rest**
- **For Taking in Co-Regulation as You Wake Up**

To Begin: Face your co-regulation partner. Decide who will lead first. Get connected with any practice you like, e.g. *Connected 8s, Sitz Bones Rock, Hands Show Breath.*

Leader - Get comfortable resting in any position you like. You might make a nest for yourself. Take time to tell your Mirror how you want them to be with you, what distance, and what posture, what attitude (protective, loving, close in, respectful, non-intrusive, sitting outside and guarding the door).

Tell them how you want to be signaled when it is time to wake up. (E.G. call your name, hum, ring a bell, touch you.) Allow yourself to rest, sleep, day-dream, dissociate or check-out. Breathe deep with a long, relaxed exhale. Open and close your eyes at will. In-person, you may want to ask for touch.

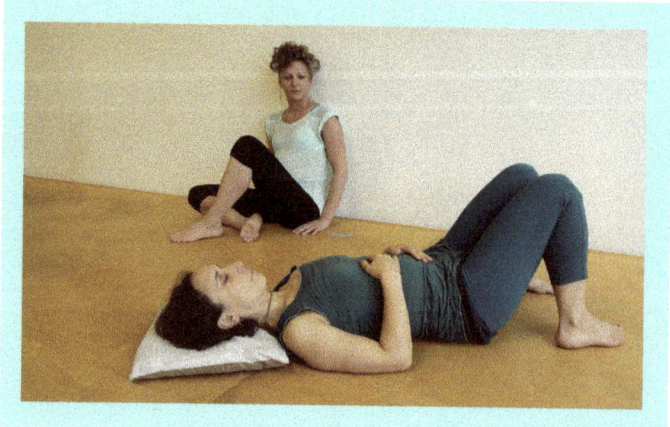

Mirror - Before you start, ask your Leader how they want to be called back to wakefulness. You could say, "How would you like me to wake you? I could sing, I could talk to you, I could say your name like I'm delighted to see you. I could call your name very softly." "This is your time. You don't have to worry about keeping me happy, that's my job."

Then, get comfortable so that you can give your attention to your Leader. Keep your eyes open and offer a smile if they open their eyes. The Mirror is there to help the Leader let go into sleep or rest, and wake up gently. The Mirror may say: "I am here to help you let go and rest," "I'll be standing guard so you are safe," or "I'll make sure that you wake up or come back gently when it is time."

To End: Mirror, prompt your partner as requested.

Timing: First Leader rest/doze for 3 - 6 minutes. Take 1- 3 minutes more to awaken.

TALK! 1- 2 min. Share about your experience. Leader starts.

Switch Roles, and Repeat.

Suggestions: LEADER - Notice how you feel before you begin, during your practice, and afterward. Explore feeling at home in your body, or let go of thoughts and attention completely. Let your Mirror know if you want quiet, or to be spoken or sung to during your rest, or as you awaken.

MIRROR - Notice your nervous system as you watch your partner rest. You may say: "I'm going to manage everything, and stand guard while you rest," and "I'll make sure to wake you gently."

People Like: "Feeling safe and cared for." "Knowing I can just be, and not have to do to get connection ad support." "Learning to expect support as I wake up to face the world."

Challenges: Not trusting the Mirror (or anyone). Shame about dissociating/checking out. Too vulnerable resting and/or "waking up" with someone else.

To Work with Specific Intentions (optional)

Use the prompts below to focus your exploration.

Down-Regulation:
LEADER - What is it like to tell another just what you need to rest, and get it, or not get it? Is it a relief to have someone else to stand guard? Is it hard for you to trust and relax?

MIRROR - What is it like for you to be the guard, to be responsible, to try to stay present while someone else pays no attention to you?

Video for *My Safe Bubble*

My Bubble Now

 13:33 min.  Video QR

- **For Finding Our Safe Space**
- **For Exploring Boundary Muscles and Gestures, in Relational Space**
- **For Feeling Safe in Our Own Skin Around Others**

This exercise has two parts. Do *My Bubble Now* first. Move on to *My Safe Bubble* for more emotional and verbal exploration.

To Begin: Sit or stand comfortably, facing your partner. Decide who will lead first. If practicing online, be sure you can see one another's torso and arms.

Mirror - Eyes open. Ask the Leader what kind of mirror they want: just watch, or mirror the Leader's gesture.

Leader - Eyes open or closed. Start with your hands against your chest. Raise your elbows and embrace your "safe bubble," palms facing inward. (As if holding a beach ball or a small bunny in front of your chest.) Explore what size feels right for now.

Explore again, pushing your palms outward, away from you, protecting your "safe bubble."

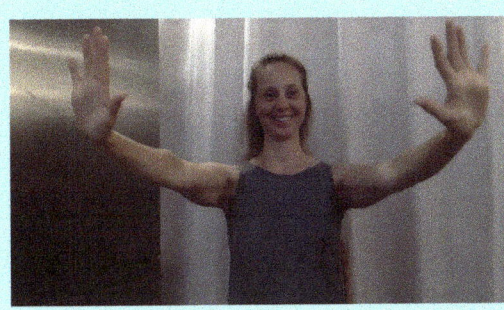 

Bring your hands back and explore whichever gesture you like a few more times.

Timing: First Leader 4 - 10 cycles.

TALK! 1- 2 min. Leader shares first.

Switch Roles, and Repeat.

Suggestions: Can you drop ideas about what size your bubble should be and feel what is comfortable for you in this moment? As you do this, first track just yourself, then yourself and your partner.

People Like: "Feeling my power." "Having boundaries and feeling connected at the same time." "Having boundaries without being shamed or pushing people away."

Challenges: Unable to feel any safe bubble. Fear of pushing people away. The Mirror can get triggered by the boundary gesture.

To Work with Specific Intentions (optional)

Use the prompts below to focus your exploration of the following intentions. MIRROR witness or mirror and reflect as the Leader requests.

Exploring Boundaries:
LEADER - Do you think your bubble should be a certain size? Could you take in how it was for your partner to be with you as you make boundary gestures?
MIRROR - How is it for you to feel your Leader's sense of bubble space?

Give the Body a Voice:
LEADER - Simply explore. Let your body show you what bubble size is comfortable.

My Safe Bubble

 13:33 min.  Video QR

- **For Finding Our Safe Space**
- **For Exploring Boundary Gestures and Words in Relational Space**
- **For Feeling Safe in Our Own Skin Around Others**

My Safe Bubble expands on *My Bubble Now* for more emotional and verbal exploration.

To Begin: Sit or stand comfortably, facing your partner. Decide who will lead first. If practicing online, be sure you can see one another's torso and arms.

Mirror - Eyes open. Ask the Leader what kind of mirror they want: a) just watch, b) mirror the Leader's gestures, c) after each gesture of the bubble, reflect the gesture and words, d) mirror the gestures with the Leader, and then pause and reflect the words and gestures.

Leader - Eyes open or closed. Start with your hands against your chest. Raise your elbows and gesture your "bubble."

Add words: Say, "This is my safe bubble and _____." Then, say whatever comes to mind - no planning ahead. E.g. "...You are not welcome here,. Or "...I like company." Or "...You can come a little closer if you do what I say." Or perhaps, "... I am safe because I am strong and I will protect myself." Let your tone be shy, intense, aggressive ... whatever feels authentic for you. Bring your hands back and explore new words and gestures several times.

Timing: First Leader 4 -10 cycles.

TALK! 1- 2 min. Leader shares first.

Switch Roles, and Repeat.

Suggestions: Notice the fears and enjoyment that come up with different words. Explore fears, strength, protection, and welcoming. As you do this, first track just yourself, then yourself and your partner.

People Like: "Feeling my power." "Having boundaries and feeling connected at the same time." "Having boundaries without being shamed or pushing people away."

Challenges: Unable to feel any safe bubble. Fear of pushing people away. The Mirror can get triggered by the boundary gesture.

To Work with Specific Intentions (optional)

Use the prompts below to focus your exploration of the following intentions. MIRROR witness or mirror and reflect as the Leader requests.

Exploring Boundaries:
LEADER - What attitudes come up for you: angry, timid, closed, lonely, empowered, welcoming, delighted Could you take in how it was for your partner to be with you as you make boundary gestures and statements? MIRROR - How is it for you to witness your Leader's boundary?

Give the Body a Voice:
LEADER - Simply explore. What words and gestures feel authentic right now?

Therapeutic Note/Cautions

Boundaries can be an edgy topic for people. A Leader may choose on their own to use this exercise to delve into dicey emotions or difficult memories. It is the Leader's job to assess their own capacity to return from their emotional edge. Only a qualified therapist should suggest or encourage people to reach for their emotional edges. It is a therapeutic intervention. It is outside the scope of practice for a BCR Peer Teacher or a BCR Coach.

Partner Stretches

 3:33 min.

- **For Stretching and Getting Embodied**
- **For Enjoying Embodiment in Relational Space**
- **For Up or Down-Regulation**

 Video QR

To Begin: Sit or stand, facing your partner. If online, move and position your monitor so your partner can see what you are doing.

This is not a mirroring exercise.

Both Partners - Move, stretch and twist: arms, neck, shoulders, back, or legs. Partners stretch in their own rhythm and sequence. Open and close your eyes as you like. You can look to your partner for inspiration and company being embodied. Once in a while look up at your partner. Smile if you make eye contact.

Timing: Practice for 2 - 4 minutes.

TALK: 1-2 min, each share about your experience.

Suggestions: Twist, bend, reach up/back/out. Use your chair to pull/push on. Notice your thoughts and feelings.

People Like: "Getting into my body." "Feeling less alone." "Shifting my energy."

Challenges: Self-consciousness, not knowing what to do. Fear of doing it "wrong". Mirroring and forgetting to listen to your own body.

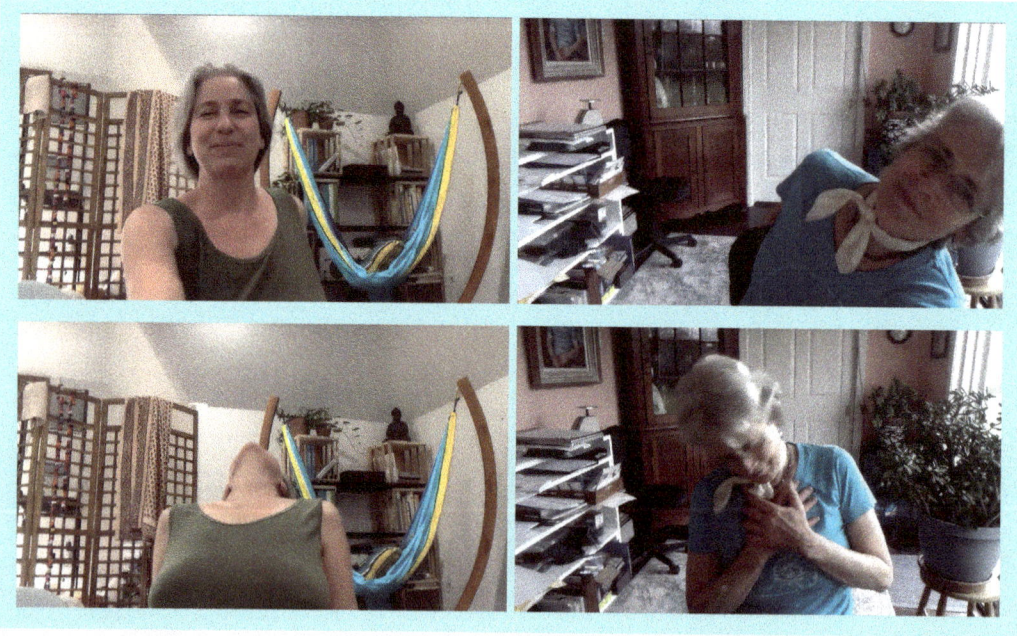

To Work with Specific Intentions (optional)

The prompts below can focus your exploration.

Arrival in Embodied, Relational Presence:

BOTH PARTNERS - How does your body want to stretch? How do you know when you like it?

Connection/Social Engagement:

BOTH PARTNERS - Does practicing with a partner make a difference? How? Can you feel them even when you are not looking? How is it to hold awareness of yourself and your partner as you stretch?

Up-Regulation:

BOTH PARTNERS - What happens if you breathe vigorously into your stretches? Take inspiration from your partner. Can you find back-and-forth stretches from one side to the other, and move briskly?

Down-Regulation:

BOTH PARTNERS - How slowly can you stretch and enjoy it?

Pick Me Up and Hug

 12:51 min.

 Video QR

- **For Getting Connected and Feeling Nourished**
- **For Practice Reaching for Help, Connection, or Intimacy**

To Begin: Sit or stand comfortably, facing your partner. Decide who will lead first. If practicing online, be sure you can see one another's torso, head, face, and arms.

Leader - Arms at your sides. Maintain eye contact and reach towards your partner slowly. Then, bring your hands back to cross over your chest and hold your upper arms, as if welcoming them into your arms for a hug. Let yourself feel as if you are getting the hug you want. Pause, eyes open or closed, and repeat.

Mirror - Eyes open. Mirror their gestures and pacing. Smile at them, when there is eye contact. If it seems right, you might say, "I am here with you."

Timing: First Leader 2 - 5 slow hugs.

TALK! 1- 2 min. Leader shares first.

Switch Roles, and Repeat.

_____

Suggestions: You might want to push against your own chest as if holding someone, or grasp and feel your upper arms holding (your own) real flesh and blood, as both partners are in the third picture.

LEADER - Notice your nervous system and how it responds to the practice.

MIRROR - You might want to say, "I'm right here," or "It's ok to cry/feel/laugh." You can play with 90% attention for yourself and 10% for your partner as you mirror.

People Like: "Feeling connected." "Offering connection to the other." "Knowing that I belong." "Feeling calm and grounded."

Challenges: Fear of intimacy, discomfort with reaching for connection.

To Work with Specific Intentions (optional)

Use the prompts below to focus your exploration.

Connection/Social Engagement:

LEADER - What is it like to reach for connection? What is it like to feel your solid body and be visually connected? Can you use this to take in support and nurturing? Does reaching feel hopeful or vulnerable or something else?

MIRROR - Move as a warm, responsive witness. Can you let this be nourishing for you?

Piezoelectric Arms

 9:06 min.

 Video QR

- **For Arrival and Energizing**
- **For Noticing Sensation in the Body**
- **For Practicing Embodied Boundaries**

To Begin: Sit or stand comfortably, facing your partner. facing your partner. Decide who will lead first. Make sure you can see one another's outstretched arms.

Leader - Eyes can open or close at will. Start with your hands in prayer position at your chest. Extend arms forward at chest height. Palms press forward, fingertips pull back towards your nose. Open the arms to the sides. Feel the sensation on the inside of your elbows.

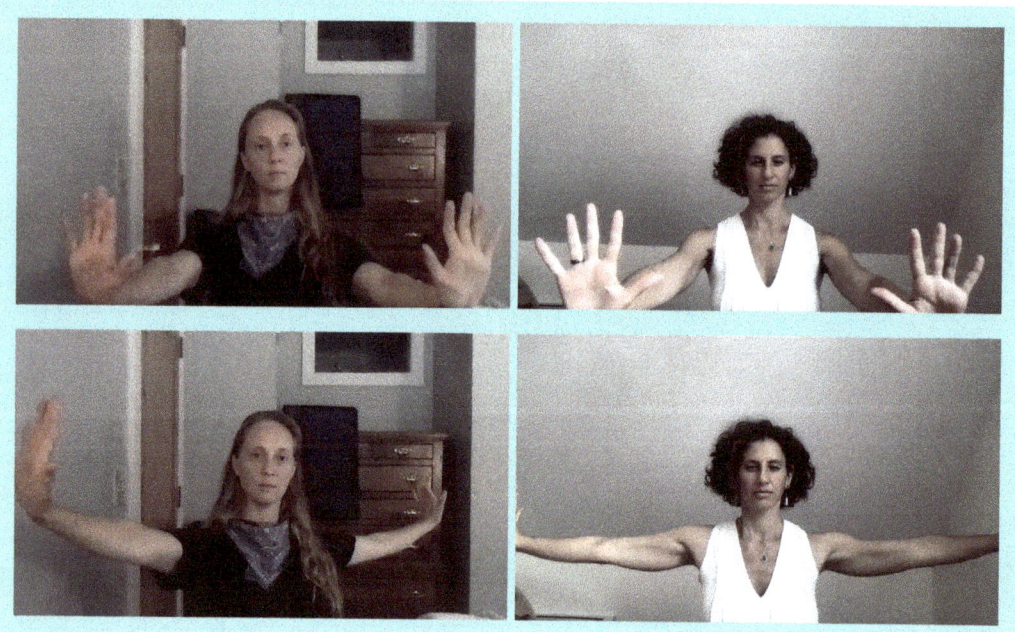

Rotate your wrists forward and feel into your thumbs, then rotate toward the back and feel for the stretch in your pinkies. Bend a little at the elbows and repeat the push outwards in other directions - straight out from shoulders, sides, in-between, upwards. You can imagine pushing against a large, firm beachball. With each push, keep pulling your fingers back towards yourself. Feel the pull in the front of your elbows.

Mirror - Eyes open. Mirror your partner's gestures and pacing. Keep a steady eye on them so you can be available. If they make eye contact, offer a smile.

Timing: First Leader - Explore for 1-2 minutes, or only as much as you like.

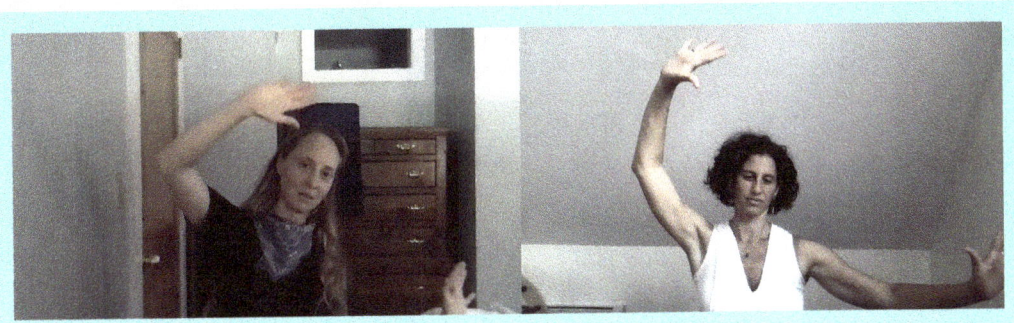

To End: Pause, eyes closed, spine tall, chin slightly tucked, hands flat on your chest. Connect with yourself, sense your feet on the ground and notice your nervous system for a few breaths. Then, open your eyes and reconnect with your partner.

TALK! 1- 2 min. Leader shares first. What did you notice?

Switch Roles, and Repeat

Suggestions: Notice any and all sensations in your arms, palms, and fingers. Observe how the feelings change, fade, or remain. Do you notice changes in your energy level, mood, or state of mind?

People Like: "Feeling energized and engaged." "Practice occupying physical space." "Expansive."

Challenges: Can be an uncomfortable or unusual sensation. This can get a lot of energy moving in the body very quickly. Be sure to take grounding breaths at the end.

To Work with Specific Intentions (optional)

Use the prompt below to focus your exploration.
MIRROR - Witness or mirror as the Leader requests.

Arrival in Embodied, Relational Presence:
LEADER - Does feeling for the enlivening energy in your arms shift you out of your head?

Exploring Boundaries:
LEADER - How does stretching into the hand gesture and the energy affect your sense of physical space around you and your power to protect your physical space?

Up-Regulation:
LEADER - Can you use *Piezoelectric Arms* to wake up the energy in your arms? Does it get the energy moving in the rest of the body, too?

What is Piezoelecticity? See the Glossary P. 230

Pinky Paws

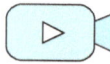 8:05 min.

- **For Taking in Love and Nurturing**
- **For Connecting to Self and Other at the Same Time**

 Video QR

To Begin: Sit or stand comfortably, facing your partner. Decide who will lead first. If practicing online, be sure you can see one another's torso, arms, and face.

Leader - Eyes open and close at will. Begin with hands in loose fists, in front of your chest. As you inhale, unfurl your fingers one by one, beginning with the pinky fingers, while opening your palms towards your partner.

Exhale, reverse the motion: curl fingers and hands inwards again, leading with the pinky fingers. Continue, synching the hand motion with your breath. Find a rhythm you like. Head may curl downwards restfully on the exhale.

Mirror - Eyes open, mirror the motion and pacing of the Leader. If they make eye contact, offer a smile.

Timing: First Leader - 4 -10 cycles.

TALK! 1- 2 min. Leader shares first.

Switch Roles, and Repeat.

_____

Suggestions: LEADER - Notice your body and your nervous system as you begin, and how this changes during and after the exercise.
MIRROR- If the Leader is looking shy, Mirror may want to say, "I'll be right here when you get back," or "There you are, I see you."

People Like: "Slowing down and connecting." "Finding my rhythm." "Dropping into my inner world."

Challenges: Too much feeling and vulnerability, or not feeling any connection.

To Work with Specific Intentions (optional)

Use the prompts below to focus your exploration.
MIRROR - Witness or mirror and reflect as the Leader requests.

Arrival in Embodied, Relational Presence:
LEADER - How does your heart like this movement?

Connection/Social Engagement:
LEADER - Do you get a sense of taking in nourishment from your world and /or from your partner?

Down-Regulation:
LEADER - What is it like to practice more and more slowly, knowing you can open and close your eyes exactly as you like?

Playful Twist

Video for *Strong Twist*

 7:48 min.

- **For Up-Regulation, and Playful Attunement**

 Video QR

To Begin: Sit comfortably, turned 90° from your screen, so that you are shoulder-to-shoulder with your partner. Be sure you can see one another's torso and face.

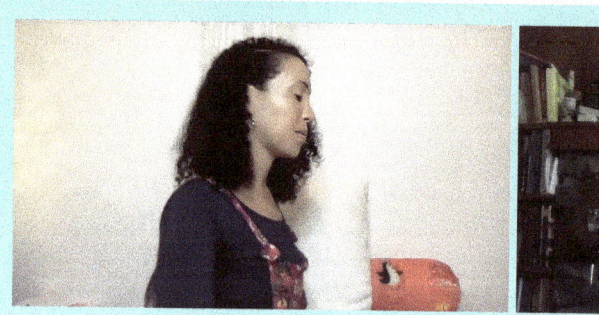 

This is not a mirroring exercise. Practice together.

Inhale as you twist toward your partner for some eye contact.

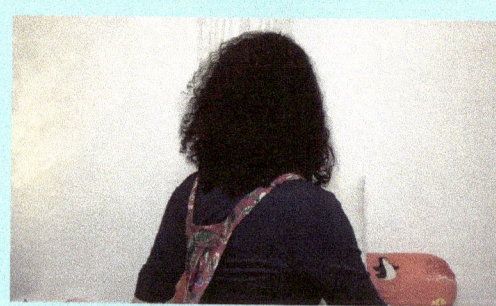 

Exhale as you twist all the way away from your partner.
Continue turning from right to left, breathing deeply.

At first, go slowly so you can make eye contact each time you turn toward each other. Find a steady rhythm together for three or four rounds.

Then, if you like, speed up the pace incrementally, still matching one another. Make eye contact as is possible with the delay on Zoom. If you like, go faster. Push the edges of your capacity to stay in rhythm. Smile when you make eye contact.

Timing: Continue for 1- 3 minutes, or until someone calls stop or you dissolve into laughter.

To End: Pause, press your palms together over your heart for a long slow breath or two.

TALK! 1- 2 min. Leader shares first. What did you notice?

Suggestions: Get into breathing deep and staying connected. Adjust your angle away from your partner to get more of a twist. Be forgiving about any time lag online.

People Like: "Playful, energizing." "Feels good to laugh together."

Challenges: Can get lost in trying to do it right, trying to please or control your partner. Slow internet can make this frustrating. The breathing can be intense and intensity in relational space can feel scary, demanding, or overwhelming.

To Work with Specific Intentions (optional)

Use the prompts below to focus your exploration.

Track Self and Other:
BOTH PARTNERS - Do you stay with yourself or focus more on your partner? What happens to your ability to focus on both yourself and your partner as you increase the speed?

Up-Regulation:
BOTH PARTNERS - What is it like to start with a brisk, steady rhythm and increase it? Be sure to end with 10 rounds of *Cross Crawl* or something to integrate the expanded energy.

Prayer Push

 7:48 min.  Video QR

- **For Exploring Breath, Movement, and Your *Body Up* Preferences**
- **For Embodying Empowerment and Boundaries**
- **For Energizing and Building Capacity**
- **For Expanding to Take in the World**

To Begin: Sit or stand comfortably, facing your partner. Decide who will lead first. Make sure you can see one another's outstretched arms.

Leader - Eyes can open or close at will. Start with your hands in prayer pose, at your heart. Blow out through the mouth and extend arms out straight to the side from the shoulders, palms facing away, and fingertips extending back toward the ears. Inhale, as the hands return to prayer. Repeat 3 - 5 times.

Next, reverse the breath pattern: Inhale as your hands push away. Exhale as you return to prayer hands. Pause and talk about any difference you notice with each breath pattern.

If you like, continue and practice whichever breath pattern you like at your own rhythm.

Mirror - Eyes open. Mirror your partner's gestures and pacing. When they make eye contact, offer a smile.

Timing: First Leader - Explore 3 - 5 repetitions of each breath pattern.

To End: Pause, eyes closed, spine tall, chin slightly tucked, hands flat on your chest. Sense your feet on the ground. Connect with yourself, then open your eyes and connect with the other person.

TALK! 1- 2 min. Leader shares first. What did you notice?

Switch Roles, and Repeat.

_____

Suggestions: As LEADER, you might want to close your eyes as you explore each breath pattern. This is a simple way to explore *Body Up* preferences around breath and movement.
Try a sharp movement with a forceful exhale through puckered lips.

People Like: "Feeling awake and ready for what's next." "A sense of dignity and agency." "A sense of expansion into a larger world."

Challenges: Discomfort with one or the other of the breath or movement patterns.

To Work with Specific Intentions (optional)

Use the prompt below to focus your exploration.
MIRROR - Witness or mirror as the Leader requests.

Arrival in Embodied, Relational Presence:
LEADER - Drop in and feel your body as you occupy physical space.
MIRROR - Simply be present and available to kindle a smile. Enjoy the simple mirroring.

Exploring Boundaries:
LEADER - Let pushing out with the out-breath create a safe space for your embodied presence around another person.
MIRROR - Feel your own safe space as you mirror.

Give the Body a Voice:
LEADER and MIRROR - Focus on which breathing pattern you like better, and how you know.

Up-Regulation:
LEADER - Increase the speed. The gestures can be forceful and empowering.
MIRROR - Enjoy the up-regulation. Do not go beyond your comfort zone.

Down-Regulation:
LEADER - Slow the breath and gestures. If you like reach for a sense of softening into your physical environment.
MIRROR - Notice your own response to slowing down.

Prayer Sweep

 5:20 min.

- **For Inviting Heart Connection and Intimacy**
- **For Down-Regulation**

 Video QR

To Begin: Sit or stand comfortably, facing your partner, hands in prayer position. Decide who will lead first. If online, be sure you can see each other's head, torso, and outstretched arms.

Leader - Eyes open and close at will. Begin with hands folded over the heart. Extend one arm forward. Slide the other palm across the chest and out the outstretched arm until your palms meet. Circle through prayer position, back along the other arm. Pause, with hands on your chest. Make 2 - 6 sweeps and reverse direction.

Mirror - Eyes open. Mirror the motion and pacing of the Leader. When they make eye contact, offer a smile.

Timing: First Leader - 2 - 6 sweeps each way.

To End: Pause, press your palms together over your heart for a long slow breath or two.

TALK! 1- 2 min. Leader shares first. What did you notice?

Switch Roles, and Repeat.

_____

Suggestions: Let yourself soften and be grateful for the chance to feel and connect. Feel your heart and your belly.

People Like: "Slow, shared, delicious movement." "Feeling open-hearted."

Challenges: Can feel too intimate.

To Work with Specific Intentions (optional)

Use the prompts below to focus your exploration. MIRROR - You can play with 90% attention for yourself and 10% for your partner as you mirror.

Connection/Social Engagement:
LEADER - What is it like to tune in to self-touch and sensation that can feel intimate, and be seen feeling your own skin?

Down-Regulation:
LEADER - What happens if you move very slowly and stay more internal?

Caution

This exercise can be quite sensual and inappropriate for some co-regulation partners or situations.

Propeller

No video

- **For Strong Up-Regulation**
- **For Building Capacity**
- **For Regulating Intensity in Relational Space**

To Begin: Sit or stand comfortably, facing your partner. Standing is more intense. Decide who will lead first. If practicing online, be sure you can see one another's torso, face, and arms.

Both Partners - Palms face each other in front of your chest, right palm facing your chest. Link your fingers and pull your elbows apart evenly. As one elbow goes up, the other goes down. Maintain eye contact and smile. Move and breathe together.

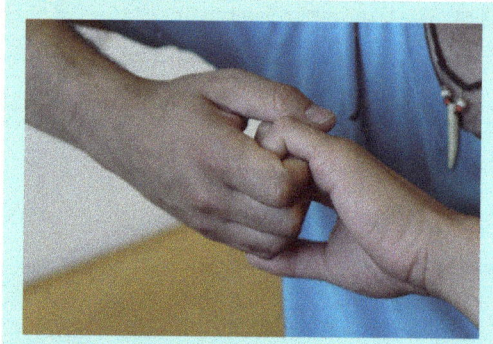

Leader - You set the pace.

Mirror - Eyes open. Mirror the motion and pacing of the Leader. Honor what is comfortable for you. Offering attention and eye contact without the arm motion is fine.

Timing: Leader sets the pace and duration: Build to a brisk rhythm for 1- 2 minutes.

To End:

- Raise the hands over the head. Keep pulling the elbows apart.

- Hold the breath in, for a comfortably long time, while pulling up on the pelvic floor, and in at the navel.

- Keep pulling the lower muscles, and slowly breathe out, then in, then out.

- Relax the arms and lower muscles. Walk around for a minute, then breathe deeply and feel your expanded capacity.

TALK! 1- 2 min. Leader shares first.

Switch Roles, and Repeat.

Suggestions: To make it gentler, go slower for a shorter time, and/or drop eye contact.

People Like: "Fun, connected container for building high energy." "Running energy through my system."

Challenges: Too intense, scary, complex and confusing.

To Work with Specific Intentions (optional)

The prompts below can focus your exploration.
MIRROR - Move with the Leader as best you can, or witness.

Track Self and Other:
LEADER - Do you stay with yourself or focus more on your partner? What happens to your ability to focus on yourself and your partner both as you increase the speed?

Up-Regulation:
LEADER - What is it like to start with a brisk, steady rhythm and increase it? Does steady eye contact stress or stabilize you? Be sure to end with 10 rounds of *Cross Crawl* or *Sitz Bones Rock* or a rhythmic walk around the room to integrate the expanded energy.

Proud Duck

 5:48 min.  Video QR

- **For Up-Regulation, Self Respect, and Playful Attunement**
- **For a Dose of Cheerfulness**
- **For Feeling Good about Ourselves while Connected with Another**

To Begin: Sit or stand comfortably, facing your partner. This can be a mirroring exercise, or you can just practice together. Sit or stand tall. Make eye contact.

Leader or Both - Lift your chest and chin. Waggle your shoulders forward and back in a proud, rapid motion for two or three whole breaths. Notice the expression on your own face, and on your partner's face. Let yourself look pleased with yourself. It is OK to laugh!

Mirror - Eyes open. Mirror your partner's gestures and pacing. When they make eye contact, offer a smile.

Timing: This is a very short pick-me-up, 2 - 3 breaths.

To End: Close your eyes and press your palms together over your heart for a long slow breath or two.

TALK! 1- 2 min. Leader shares first.

Switch roles, and repeat.

Suggestions: Repeat often!

People Like: "Makes me laugh." "Feels good to laugh together."

Challenges: Getting lost in trying to do it right. "Self-conscious about sticking out my chest." "Pride or intensity in relational space can feel scary and demanding.

To Work with Specific Intentions (optional)

Use the prompt below to focus your exploration.
MIRROR - Witness, if asked, or move with the Leader as best you can, or just practice together.

Connection/Social Engagement:
LEADER- Just enjoy each other and yourself!

Up-Regulation:
LEADER - Increase the speed. Note your energy level before and after. Did it change?

Reach For the Earth

 6:08 min.

- **For Arrival and Grounding**
- **For Supporting the Heart**

 Video QR

To Begin: Sit with your feet flat on the floor, palms on thighs. Decide who will lead first, or do it together.

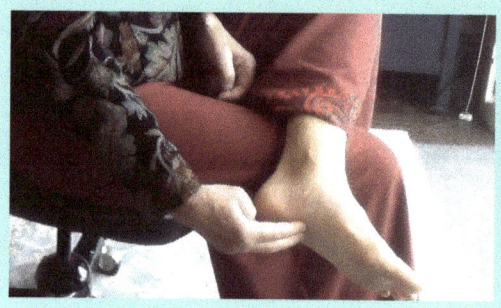

The Front of the Heel

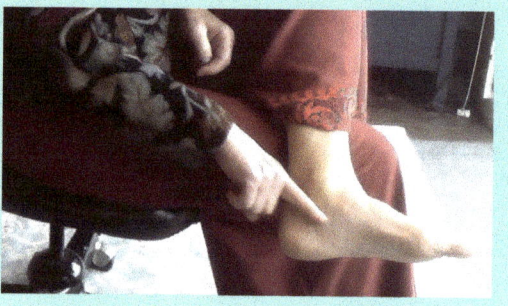

Push Forward and Down

Leader - To begin with, keep your eyes closed. Push forward and down gently with the front of the heel, just enough that you can feel the big muscles in the thigh start to work (quadriceps). Pulse it slowly and gently, for 30 - 60 seconds. Imagine reaching for connection with the floor or ground under your feet. Make sure you are breathing. Try it again with some eye contact. It need not be steady.

If you have back support, go another step: Start with closed eyes, and push from the front of your heels through to your low back. Pulse gently, once each breath, reaching for connection from your heels, through your thighs to your low back support.

For another step, reach for the earth with each breath and feel awareness fill in around and under the heart. Try it with eye contact.

Mirror - Eyes open. As you do the exercise with your partner, keep a steady eye on them so you can be available when they open their eyes. When they make eye contact, allow a smile to kindle.

Timing: Pulse a gentle reach for 30 - 60 seconds, or 10 -15 breaths, or only as much as you like.

To End: Pause, eyes closed, spine tall, chin slightly tucked, hands flat on your chest. Sense your feet on the ground. Take a few breaths and open your eyes.

TALK! 1- 2 min. What did you notice?

Switch Roles, and Repeat.

_____

Suggestions: Can be done as a partner exercise if both people know it.

People Like: "The feeling of gently reaching for the ground." "Feeling grounded, connected with the earth." "Gentle heart connection with the other person."

Challenges: When we are more grounded we feel more, which can be overwhelming for people who use dissociation to feel safe.

To Work with Specific Intentions (optional)

Use the prompts below to focus your exploration.
MIRROR - Act as a warm, responsive witness with any of the Leader's intentions.

Arrival in Embodied, Relational Presence:
LEADER - What happens to your breath and your posture as you reach for the earth?

Find Home In Our Core:
LEADER - Can you draw up support and vitality from the ground to your core with each breath?

Track Self and Other:
LEADER - As you breathe, what is it like to shift the attention slowly back and forth between your connection with the ground, and your connection with your partner?
MIRROR - Can you hold 90% attention for yourself and 10% for your partner as you mirror?

Down-Regulation:
LEADER- What happens if you pulse very slowly and gently, once with each long slow breath?

Sitting With Self and Other

14:21 min.

- **For Developing Your Wiring to Track Self and Other**
- **For Noticing Your Internal Preferences, *and* Your Internal Habits**

To Begin: Sit comfortably, so you can see one another.

PART ONE: No movement or words are required.

Leader - Start eyes closed, focusing inward, and then allow yourself the freedom to focus as you wish. When you want to, open your eyes to focus outward or on your partner, unless you just want to stay in. If so, notice how that feels. Simply sit in silence and track the focus of your attention as it shifts between yourself and your partner. When do you want to focus inward on your own experience, and when do you want to sense the other person?

Mirror - Eyes open. The Mirror is really a warm witness, holding a safe container, and offering a welcoming smile when the Leader makes eye contact.

Timing: Continue for 1- 3 minutes.

TALK! 1-2 min. Leader shares first.

Switch Roles, and Repeat.

PART TWO: Narrated

Leader: Track the focus of your attention as it shifts between yourself and your partner. Narrate what you notice happening as it happens. Do your habits sometimes override your *body up* preferences?

Mirror - Eyes open. Continue as a warm witness, and offer a welcoming smile when the Leader makes eye contact.

Timing: Continue for 1- 3 minutes.

TALK! 1-2 min. Leader shares first.

Switch Roles, and Repeat.

_____

Suggestions: Be curious about different ways of tracking self and other, e.g eyes open for both inward and outward focus, or eyes closed to focus inward or on your connection with your partner. Can you feel them even with your eyes closed?

People Like: "Allowing my nervous system to focus where it wants." "Noticing my subtle preferences."

Challenges: Getting lost in trying to do it right, trying to please or control your partner.

To Work with Specific Intentions (optional)

Use the prompts below to focus your exploration.
MIRROR - Mirror serves as a warm, responsive witness. You can play with 90% attention for yourself and 10% for your partner as you mirror.

Arrival in Embodied, Relational Presence:
LEADER - How often do you want to connect? How long? How much of the time do you want to be inside?

Tracking Self and Other:
LEADER - With the silent version, what pulls you in and out? Explore different ratios of attention for self/other such as 90/10 or 50/50.

With the narrated version - track and report on the social "supposed tos " and what your body or nervous system really wants.

Connection/Social Engagement:
LEADER - Do you have parts that want to connect and parts that do not? We may not always want to share out loud all the ways we do or do not want to connect.

Sitz Bones Rock

 4:13 min.  Video QR

- **For Arriving in your Body**
- **For Comfort**
- **For Finding Home in Our Core**
- **For Tracking and Connecting with Self and Other**

To Begin: Sit comfortably upright, in front of your co-regulation partner. If online, be sure they can see your torso and head as you sway back and forth.

Leader - Allow your torso to sway left and right. Breathe comfortably. Set a steady pace or change pace at will, as you lean side to side. Your eyes can open and close at will. Keep silent or share what you notice in the moment. You can also stretch to each side or feel your weight pour from one side to the other.

Mirror - Eyes open, track your partner. Mirror their motion and rhythm. When they make eye contact, offer a smile.

Timing: First Leader, 1- 2 minutes.

Both TALK! 1 - 2 min. Share about your experience. Leader starts.

Switch Roles, and Repeat.

Suggestions: To find your center, make each sway smaller and smaller. Feel yourself and your partner. LEADER notice what changes as you open or close your eyes. How does it feel to make eye contact? You may choose to shift your focus: internally tracking your weight or stretching or, externally tracking your Mirror and sense of connection. If you have discomfort or dizziness with the movement, do not do it.

MIRROR may offer simple words, "I'm here with you," or "Let yourself breathe." When you are mirroring someone, if you do not want to sway, you can simply move a hand as a stand-in for your spine.

People Like: "Coming home to myself." "Feeling connected."

Challenges: Flooding with emotions when getting embodied. Getting overly chatty or distracted. Discomfort at being seen, wanting to hide or run, getting critical about imperfect mirroring.

To Work with Specific Intentions (optional)

Use the prompts below to focus your exploration of the following intentions. MIRROR - Move as a warm, responsive witness with any of the Leader's intentions.

Embodied, Relational Presence:
For Arriving in Your Body, in the Present, around Others and *For Comfort.*
LEADER- Simply start rocking. Feel into your own comfort, presence, rhythm, and stretch. Notice your partner if you like.
MIRROR - Track your own comfort as you mirror.

Find Home in Our Core:
LEADER - Notice your weight shifting as you rock. Where is your center? Start with obvious rocking and let it get smaller and smaller to help you find your center. How much awareness can you bring to your core?
MIRROR - Feel for your own center as you mirror.

Track Self and Other:
LEADER - Starting with an inward focus, notice when you look for connection, and when you focus inward. Play with the balance for self/other such as 90/10 or 50/50.
MIRROR - Play with 90% attention for yourself and 10% for your partner.

Connection/Social Engagement:
LEADER- How does the mirrored movement affect your sense of connection? How is it to know that your mirror is there for you? Can you take them in? You may like exploring different rhythms. Notice if you want your eyes open or closed.
MIRROR - Be as warm and responsive as is authentic for you.

Down-Regulation:
Both partners can deepen your breathing and relax your face and jaw.
LEADER- Start with a rhythm you like and slow down! Honor every inclination to slow down.
MIRROR - Notice how the intention to slow down lands for you.

Up-Regulation:
LEADER - Focus on enjoying the vitality and the connection. You may want to start swaying briskly and breathing deeply.
MIRROR - Keep up only as much as you want to.

For Building Capacity:
Use *Sitz Bones Rock* after up-regulatory practices like *Chicken Wings*, *Breath Wings*, Propeller, or *Washing Machine* to stabilize and ground high energy in relational space.

Spinal Flexes

No video

- **For Bringing Awareness, Aliveness, and Flow to Our Core**
- **For Tapping into a Sense of Dignity and a Sense of Self**
- **For Up-Regulation or Down-Regulation**

To Begin: Sit facing your partner. Decide who will lead first. If practicing online, be sure you can see one another's torso and face. Decide who will lead first.

Leader - Sit cross-legged, spine erect, holding your shins, facing your partner. (You can also sit in a chair, feet flat on the ground, and hands holding your knees.)

Exhale, letting the low back slump back.

Inhale, stretching upright and forward.

Mirror - Eyes open. Follow your partner's movement and pacing. When they make eye contact, offer a smile.

Timing: Increase the rhythm for 20 - 60 repetitions.

To End: Come back to your center, and inhale. Pull up on the pelvic floor, pull in the belly, and hold your breath in. Hold a tad longer than is comfortable, then exhale.

To Ground and Integrate the Expanded Energy: Do 10 rounds of *Cross Crawl* or *Sitz Bones Rock*, or take a rhythmic walk around the room.

TALK! 1- 2 min. Leader shares first.

Switch Roles, and Repeat.

Suggestions: Slower with fewer repetitions, is easier. Less eye contact may be easier. Sitting side by side, or at an angle to the screen (instead of facing) can be more comfortable. Keeping the head facing forward as the spine bends allows for steady eye contact as you up-regulate.

People Like: "Enlivenment, increased sense of flow." "Sense of presence and dignity."

Challenges: Sore back. Worrying about being too much or not enough. Feeling pressured to keep up with the Leader, when the Mirror is uncomfortable. Intensity in relational space can feel scary and demanding. The time lag online makes it look like the Mirror is behind.

To Work with Specific Intentions (optional)

The prompts below can focus your exploration. Mirror, move as a warm, responsive witness as the Leader directs.

Find Home in Our Core:
LEADER - What does your spine want? How does it feel to close your eyes, listen to your spine and move at a pace your spine likes?
MIRROR - Feel your core as you mirror or witness the Leader.

Down-Regulation
LEADER - Start at a rhythm that fits your current state. Slow to a comfortable steady rhythm, or pause after each flexion and extension. You can let your head flex and extend as well. You may want to pause until your body wants to move. Do not let your head hang back if there is any discomfort.
MIRROR - Feel your spine as you move or witness the Leader.

Up-Regulation:
Consider the *4-Phase Partner Sequence* for building capacity and vitality.
LEADER - Start at a rhythm that fits your current state. What is it like to increase slowly to a brisk, steady rhythm? To integrate the expanded energy, be sure to end with 10 rounds of *Cross Crawl* or *Sitz Bones Rock*, or a rhythmic walk around the room.
MIRROR - Enjoy your breath as you move or witness the Leader.

Strong Twist

 8:13 min.  Video QR

- **For Feeling Our Core and Arriving**
- **For Up-Regulation and Building Our Capacity for Complexity**

To Begin: Sit comfortably, turned 90° from your screen, so that you are shoulder-to-shoulder with your partner. Be sure you can see one another's torso and face.

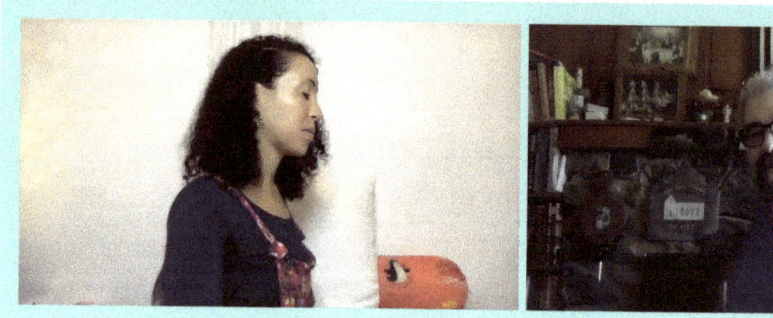

Leader: Inhale, twist towards your Mirror and make eye contact. Exhale, twist away. Take your time. Repeat, getting a strong twist in each direction. To get a deeper twist, push on your knees, your chair, or your desk. Synchronize or slow your rhythm so you can make eye contact. Be sure to smile if you feel like it. A loud exhale can help your Mirror follow you.

Mirror - Follow your Leader and get yourself a good stretch, too. Allow a smile to kindle on eye contact, if it feels real.

To End: Come center, eyes closed, and take 3 deep breaths.

TALK! 1- 2 min. What did you notice?

Switch Roles, and repeat.

Suggestions: Adjust your angle away from your partner to get more of a twist. Be forgiving about the time-lag online.

Shift your awareness between 1) your own body and the sensations of the twist, and 2) your sense of connection with the other person. Explore these two focal points, then try holding both at the same time.

Practice as a partner exercise without Leader and Mirror roles.

People Like: "Feeling connected in a peer/equal way." "Feeling energized and connected with my core and my partner." "Getting grounded and ready for what's next."

Challenges: Getting lost in trying to do it right, trying to please or control your partner.

To Work with Specific Intentions (optional)

Use the prompts below to focus your exploration.

Finding Home in Our Core:
LEADER - Can you feel your core as you twist? How is your sense of your core afterward?

Up-Regulation:
LEADER - What is it like to start with a brisk, steady rhythm and increase it? Be sure to end with 10 rounds of *Cross Crawl* or *Sitz Bones Rock*, or a rhythmic walk around the room to integrate the expanded energy.

Turn Away and Come Back

7:09 min.

- **For Practicing Connecting and Disconnecting with Another**
- **For Playfully Practicing Trust**

To Begin: Sit or stand comfortably, facing your partner. Decide who will lead first. If online, sit as close to your camera as is comfortable for both you and your partner. Check in about it.

Leader - Eyes open and close at will. Start by feeling into a sense of connection with your partner. You might want to do *Connected 8s* first. Then, turn your head and torso to look away from your partner. When you are ready, turn back to your partner and make eye contact for a few seconds. Repeat, turning away to the other side. Notice your nervous system as you practice. Keep silent and feel, or share what you notice in the moment.

Mirror - Eyes open. Be a warm witness and home base. You may mirror some, but keep an eye on them so you can be available when they turn back. When they make eye contact, offer a smile.

TIMING: Leader: 2 - 4 turns to each side

TALK! 1- 2 min. What did you notice?

Switch Roles, and Repeat.

Suggestions: The MIRROR may say, "I'll be right here when you get back," "There you are," and "I see you."

LEADER - Try turning away and back quickly, all of a sudden, and also slowly. How does it feel at different speeds?

People Like: "Knowing my partner will be there for me." "Choosing when I connect." "Feeling more connected with my co-regulation partner." "Playfulness, like peek-a-boo with a kid."

Challenges: It can bring up discomfort about eye contact and being seen and attachment issues like abandonment.

To Work with Specific Intentions (optional)

Use the prompts below to focus your exploration.

Track Self and Other:
LEADER - What is it like to wait until you really want to turn back or turn away? What emotions or images come up for you?
MIRROR - Play with 90% attention for yourself and 10% for your partner.

Connection/Social Engagement:
LEADER- Do you have parts that want to connect and parts that do not? Can you feel your partner when you are not looking?
MIRROR - How do you feel as your partner turns away and comes back?

Therapeutic Note/Cautions

This exercise can bring up powerful attachment issues. A Leader may choose on their own to use this exercise to delve into dicey emotions or difficult memories. It is the Leader's job to assess their own capacity to return from their emotional edge. Only a qualified therapist should suggest or encourage people to reach for their emotional edges. It is a therapeutic intervention. It is outside the scope of practice for a BCR Peer Teacher or a BCR Coach.

Up and Down with the Voice

10:14 min.

- **For Giving the Body a Voice Around Others**
- **For Building a Reliable Ramp In and Out of Difficult Emotions**

The important thing is to keep the sound coming!

To Begin: Sit comfortably, facing your partner. Decide who will lead first.

Leader - First get present and connected with your partner. (E.g. both partners put a hand on your own chest and take a few breaths while making eye contact with your partner.) When you are ready, let your breath out with a sound. If you can, enjoy it, exaggerate it. Go for feeling upbeat, with happy feelings and sounds. Then, curl or contract down. Find some grumpier sounds, while continuing to make some sounds. Then, expand up and out again, continuing to produce some sounds. Repeat the cycle 2 - 4x.

Mirror - Witness, mirror, or play cheerleader - by Leader's request. Your job is to be present and available. Only mirror the Leader's sound and movement, if they ask you to. It is helpful to mirror their moods. Encourage them to keep the sound coming in any way that works for both of you. Be sure you stay with yourself and your own comfort.

TALK! 1-2 min. What did you notice?

Switch Roles, and Repeat.

Suggestions: LEADER let your partner know what level of mirroring and encouragement you want. Give yourself permission to be noisy. If this is hard for you, you could try saying "Yes, Yes, Yes ...", and then "Yuck, Yuck, Yuck ..." with emotion for a few cycles.

MIRROR - Let yourself enjoy being trusted to be there for someone. How is it to be present for another while also being aware of yourself?

People Like: "Following the flow of my partner's moods as I mirror them." "Hearing my partner mirror my sounds helped me know my expressions are ok." "Feeling safe to go into difficult states because I know just how I am going to come out of them."

Challenges: This can highlight trust and shame issues.

To Work with Specific Intentions (optional)

Use the prompts below to focus your exploration.
MIRROR - Witness, mirror, or play cheerleader - by Leader's request.

Give the Body a Voice:
LEADER - What is it like to dare to give voice to various feelings? What is it like to be in charge of how long you stay in difficult feelings? Can you feel the moment you are ready to come out? Go in deep if you like but put the emphasis on wiring your system to go in and out at will.

Up-Regulation:
LEADER - Be curious about finding authentic self-expression for different feeling states. Does your energy level shift?

Therapeutic Note/Cautions

A Leader may choose on their own to use this exercise to delve into dicey emotions or difficult memories. It is the Leader's job to assess their own capacity to return from their emotional edge. Only a qualified therapist should suggest or encourage people to reach for their emotional edges. It is a therapeutic intervention. It is outside the scope of practice for a BCR Peer Teacher or a BCR Coach.

Washing Machine

 6:44 min  Video QR

- **For Up-Regulation, Increasing Energy and Oxygen in the Bloodstream**
- **For Building Our Capacity to be High Energy and Connected With Another, at the Same TimPe**

To Begin: Sit comfortably, turned 90° from your screen so that you are elbow-to-elbow with your partner. If practicing online, be sure you can see one another's arms and faces.

Leader - Eyes open and close at will. Spine straight, hands on your shoulders, elbows up and out at shoulder height. Exhale and twist all the way away from your partner. Inhale and twist toward your partner for a moment of eye contact. Continue turning from right to left, breathing deeply. Aim to make eye contact, if you can, but a comfortable rhythm is more important.

Mirror - Eyes open. Mirror the motion and pacing of the Leader.

Timing - Continue for 30 -100 twists (a minute or so).

To End: Come to center and gently tuck your chin. Breathe out, then breathe in deeply and hold your breath, pulling in at the belly and up on the pelvic floor. Hold until you need to exhale. Rock or wriggle a bit, eyes closed, feeling your energy. Stand and walk around, or do 10 quick rounds of *Cross Crawl* to integrate.

TALK! 1- 2 min. Leader shares first.

Switch Roles, and Repeat.

Suggestions: Adjust your angle away from your partner to get more of a twist. Loud exhales can help your Mirror follow your rhythm.

People Like: "Feeling energized and cheerful." "Getting grounded and ready for what's next."

Challenges: The time lag online often makes it look like the Mirror is behind. The breathing can be intense. Intensity in relational space can feel scary and demanding. Worrying about being too much or not enough.

To Work with Specific Intentions (optional)

Use the prompts below to focus your exploration.
MIRROR - Move with the Leader as best you can, or just witness.

Track Self and Other:
LEADER - Do you stay with yourself or focus more on your partner? What happens to your ability to balance your focus between yourself and your partner as you increase the speed?

Up-Regulation:
LEADER - What is it like to start with a brisk, steady rhythm and increase it? Be sure to end with 10 rounds of *Cross Crawl* or *Sitz Bones Rock*, or a rhythmic walk around the room, to integrate the expanded energy.

Therapeutic Note/Cautions
Strong up-regulation can be challenging or disorganizing at times. A Leader may choose on their own to use this exercise to push their edges, or work on building capacity. It is the Leader's job to assess their own capacity to integrate the intensity this can generate. Only a qualified therapist should suggest or encourage people to push their capacity for up-regulation. It is a therapeutic intervention. It is outside the scope of practice for a BCR Peer Teacher or a BCR Coach.

Appendices

MAKE EMBODIED RELATIONSHIPS PART OF YOUR LIFE

▷ 0:29 min.

QR for Video

Appendix A: Basic Online Session Outline

This Basic Session Outline offers a template for a longer practice session when you want it.

1) Safety: Remind yourselves that you can not do this wrong. It is fine to adapt the exercises to work for you or to stop in the middle.

2) Start with a verbal contract that addresses these time and safety points:

   Timeframe - E.G. 15 minutes, or 3 exercises, or whatever works for you both.

   Confidentiality - Agree to keep it all confidential if you want to.

   Touch or no touch - decide which, if you are in person.

Begin your co-regulation session.

3) Do *Sitz Bones Rock* to connect with your core. Focus on feeling your body and finding your center. Let your weight pour from one side to the other. Leader's eyes open and close at will, as they explore connecting inward with themself, and outward with the Mirror. If you cannot feel your sitz bones, it does not matter. You can focus on sensing when your weight is centered, left/right, and front/back. Mirror follows the movement and stays available to make eye contact and offer a smile. TALK! after each person's turn leading.

4) Do Hands Show Breath to connect with your breath and your partner. Again, the Leader's eyes open and close at will. If you like, track your connection with self and other. Mirror follows the Leader's movement and stays available to make eye contact and offer a smile. TALK! after each person's turn.

5) Do Partner Stretches to practice listening to your body while you are connected with someone else. Do exactly what feels good to you. Look to your partner for company and inspiration. Be embodied together. No need to mirror movement or rhythm. TALK! during and/or after stretching with your partner.

6) End your session with a highlight: a gratitude for yourself and/or your partner, a moment when you felt connected, or what was useful. You might notice and share how you feel now as different from how you felt at the beginning.

THANK YOUR PARTNER

Appendix B: Guidelines for a Basic Session

Co-regulation depends on:

Expression: To do BCR, we need to show ourselves, to the extent that is safe and appropriate. We can express how we are, our nervous system state, our feelings, and our vulnerability. Showing motion with our bodies is a good place to start.

Reflection: We need to know that we are seen as we are.

Response: Then, we need to know how our self-expression affects our communication partner.

It can be helpful to make a clear distinction between reflecting and responding. Reflection (verbal or non-verbal) describes what we notice the other doing. Response is how we are touched or affected by their expression. We need to receive both but at different times.

As the Leader/Explorer, you are exploring yourself and what works for you to connect to your body. Explore staying connected with yourself while connecting with your partner.

When Mirroring, you might use simple phrases, as seems fitting: "I am here (for you)," "Do exactly what feels good to you," "It's ok to feel/cry/laugh," or "It's ok to close your eyes, I'll be right here when you get back."

When you TALK!, stay with sharing or attending to your physical and emotional awareness. Talk about what you are doing or feeling or liking. Putting words to our experience allows us to share, digest, and make sense of it. This is essential. Feeling safe and talking about emotional edges releases stuckness and shame.

- Be in a private space without background noise.

- Be sure your face is well-lit.

- Be able to get close to your camera, so you can be more life-sized for others.

- Be able to move far enough away to show large movements.

- A tilt screen is helpful, as is a rolling chair.

- Put your partner's image directly under or over your camera.

- Make yourself comfortable sitting upright.

- The time lag on the internet makes the Leader think the Mirror is slow even when the Mirror sees themself in perfect synch. Laugh and forgive!

Appendix C: Physical Considerations for BCR Online

SAFETY:

Feeling safe and present is essential to feeling connected and getting regulated. Turn off demanding notifications and phone noises. Be in a private space without background noise or distractions. See Chapter 3 for theory and Chapter 4 for practical considerations around safety.

LIGHT YOUR FACE:

We read important safety cues in the face, so make sure your face is well lit. This makes it easier for others to feel safe and connect with you.

LIFESIZE:

We read others as real when they are lifesize, so use your biggest screen. This helps you feel more connected with others. Adjust your camera so others can see more of your body when you are moving and more of your face when you are talking. This helps others feel more connected to you.

EYE CONTACT:

We feel acknowledged when people look directly at us. Center the window with your zoom partner in it, as close under your camera as you can, so it looks more like you are making eye contact.

RHYTHM AND TIME LAG:

When others attune to our rhythm, we tend to feel like we matter. The time lag on Zoom disrupts this for the Leader, but not the Mirror. So, be forgiving. Also, it can help to go slow enough that your partner has time to catch up, or use a steady rhythm so you can sync up. Pay close attention to this. Misattuned rhythm can disrupt our sense of connection and safety.

Appendix D: Bibliography

Applied Neuroscience and Interpersonal Neurobiology

Cozolino, L. (2002). *The neuroscience of psychotherapy: Building and rebuilding the human brain.* W.W. Norton & Company.

Cozolino, L. (2012). *The neuroscience of human relationships: Attachment and the developing social brain* (2nd edition). W.W. Norton & Company.

Porges, S.W. (2011). *The polyvagal theory: Neurophysiological foundations of emotions, attachment, communication, and self-regulation* (1st ed.). W. W. Norton.

Sapolsky, R. (2017). *Behave: The biology of humans at our best and worst.* Penguin Press.

Schore, A. (2012). *The science of the art of psychotherapy.* Norton Professional Books.

Siegel, D. (1999). *The developing mind: Toward a neurobiology of interpersonal experience.* Guilford Press.

Siegel, D. (2012). *Pocket guide to interpersonal neurobiology: An integrative handbook of the mind.* (Part of: Norton Series on Interpersonal Neurobiology.) WW Norton & Company.

Siegel, D., Foshe, D., & Solomon, M.F. (Eds.) (2009). *The healing power of emotion: Affective neuroscience, development & clinical practice.* WW Norton & Company.

van der Kolk, B. (2014). *The body keeps the score: Brain, mind, and body in the healing of trauma.* Penguin.

Approaches to Healing

Brown, B. (2012). Listening to shame [Video]. Ted Conferences. https://www.ted.com/talks/brene_brown_listening_to_shame?language=en

Heller, L., & LaPierre, A. (2012). *Healing developmental trauma: How early trauma affects self-regulation, self-image, and the capacity for relationship.* North Atlantic Books.

Jackins, H. (1970). *Fundamentals of co-counseling manual.* Rational Island Publishers.

Jackins, H. (1997). *The list.* Rational Island Publishers.

Levine, P.A. (2010). *In an unspoken voice: How the body releases trauma and restores goodness.* North Atlantic Press.

Levine, P.A. & Frederick, A. (1997). *Waking the tiger: Healing trauma.* North Atlantic Books.

Marcher, L. & Fich, S. (2010). *Body encyclopedia: A guide to the psychological functions of the muscular system.* North Atlantic Books.

Maté, G. (2021). *The wisdom of trauma* [Film]. Produced by: Science and Nonduality.

Schwartz, R.C. (1999). "The internal family systems model". In Rowan, J. & Cooper, M. (eds.). *The plural self: Multiplicity in everyday life.* Sage Publications.

On Embodiment and Oppression

Menakem, R. (2017). *My grandmother's hands: Racialized trauma and the pathway to mending our hearts and bodies.* Central Recovery Press.

Reevaluation Co-counseling, *Liberation Journals,* and *Present Time* (1970 - 2022) Rational Island Publishers.
https://www.rc.org/tile/publications

On the Nature of Consciousness and Embodiment

Damasio, A. (1994). *Descartes' error: Emotion, reason and the human brain.* Penguin.

Damasio, A (1999). *The feeling of what happens: Body and emotion in the making of consciousness.* Houghton Mifflin Harcourt.

Damasio, A.(2003). *Looking for Spinoza: Joy, sorrow, and the feeling brain.* Harcourt.

Damasio, A. (2010). *Self comes to mind: Constructing the conscious brain.* Pantheon.

Sapolsky, R. (1994). *Why zebras don't get ulcers: The acclaimed guide to stress, stress-related diseases, and coping.* Holt.

Sapolsky, R. (2017). *Behave: The biology of humans at our best and at their worst.* Penguin.

Solms, M. (2021). *The hidden spring: A journey to the source of consciousness.* W. W. Norton & Company.

Appendix E: Glossary

Activation: Arousal in the nervous system, e.g. excitement of any kind, or a threat response.

Amygdala: The brain's first responder to danger. It records what has been dangerous in the past and reacts fast.

Arriving in Embodied, Relational Presence: Being alive in your body, sensing your body, and being available to connect with another being.

Attunement: Sensing what is going on with oneself and/or another, consciously or unconsciously, often by tracking the neurological Elements of Attunement (p. 81).

Autonomic Nervous System (ANS): Our ANS runs the basic life support systems in our body: digestion, heart and lungs, immune and inflammatory systems, sleep, temperature, and our threat responses. When it wears out, we die. It evolved in three layers:
The Social Nervous System, or Social Engagement System
The Sympathetic Nervous System
The Parasympathetic Nervous System

Bandwidth or **Capacity:** This is a way of talking about how much complexity and intensity we can handle before our nervous system gets overwhelmed. When our internet connection lacks capacity, it slows down and drops or distorts data. When our nervous system is low on capacity, it can get hard to focus, stay organized and remember things. We may avoid confronting difficult problems, people, or social situations. Or, we may be highly reactive, causing inflammatory situations.

Baseline: What you notice in your body before you start a practice, e.g. your breathing, areas of comfort and discomfort in your body, your emotional state, and your energy level.

Body Up and **Top Down:** *Body up* means originating in our bodily experience. *Top down* means originating in our mental experience.

Body Up and **Top Down Agendas:** What the body wants or needs and what the mind wants or needs. Our *body up* agenda trumps our *top down* social agenda when we are triggered into a strong threat response. Otherwise, our *top down* agenda is often a powerful social agenda that overrides our *body up* agenda. For example, we may act like we are comfortable when we are actually cold or scared, or in pain, but we do not want to say so. Working both agendas is complicated and requires added bandwidth.

Body Up Co-Regulation (BCR): Connecting nervous system to nervous system with another person (or mammal), in a way that helps both of you regulate your own nervous systems. It usually depends on embodiment and attunement with yourself and the other.

Body Up Wisdom (AKA Body Wisdom): Wisdom that comes from being awake in our bodies. It is a felt sense. It bypasses reason and brings us feelings. E.g. the heart can sense when someone else is hurting or happy. The gut can often tell who is safe, who is dangerous, and when a business risk will pay off. Body wisdom includes knowing when to listen to the body, and when to avoid letting cravings and primitive reactions take over.

Boundaries: The edges of the physical, emotional, and social space around us (and within us) that we need to feel safe. Sturdy boundaries allow us to get closer to others because we know we can protect our physical, emotional and social space.

Boundary Muscles: The muscles that we develop and use to protect ourselves physically and socially.

Bubble (Personal Bubble): In BCR, this means the space around us we claim as ours to be in charge of.

Building Capacity: Expanding our bandwidth so we can stay organized, present, and effective in the face of increasing complexity and intensity. When we know where to get warm, we worry less about getting cold. When we know how to reregulate fast, we do not get so anxious about getting overwhelmed. We can build our capacity to stay present with intensity and complexity. (BCR helps with this).

Codependence: In codependence, we often depend on someone else to regulate us. Codependence usually means that we are trying to get another person to take care of us or rescue us from our old wounds, our history of neglect, our shame, or our fear of abandonment. In co-regulation, we regulate ourselves with another person.

Complexity and Intensity: These are the two basic challenges that stress, overwhelm and traumatize our nervous systems. They look like: too much, too fast, too emotional, too painful, too complicated.

Connection: In BCR, this means one nervous system recognizing another nervous system via the elements of attunement or other layers of communication. It can be conscious or unconscious.

Core: Our core runs the length of our torso: head, throat, heart, solar plexus, belly, and pelvic floor.

Co-Regulation: See under Regulation.

Dissociation: Consciously or unconsciously shifting our attention away from something, especially the body or present time reality. Dissociation can be normal, or extreme enough to fragment our sense of self, our memory, or our sense of reality.

Down-Regulation: To shift from higher energy states to lower energy states. This can include shifting out of focused work modes or threat responses or downshifting for sleep. It might mean stabilizing into expansive, relaxed, or playful states, shifting out of hypervigilance and chronic anxiety, and going more parasympathetic.

Elements of Attunement: Our nervous systems understand each other and communicate via the neurological elements of attunement, especially eye contact, facial expression, tone of voice, posture, gesture, rhythm, timing, intensity, touch, sharing weight, distance and words.

Embodiment: Being alive, in a body, and sensing that body. This means staying connected to body awareness, allowing even small changes to register in our consciousness. We can cultivate a habit of listening to the subtle cues our body gives us, about our environment, other people, and our felt sense of alignment with our own behavior. See also Dissociation.

Embodiment in Relational Space: Staying aware and attuned with our bodies around other people. In Western culture, this can be complex and demanding, so we do practices that wire our nervous system to Track Self and Other in real time.

Emotional Edges: We are at an emotional edge when we start to get overwhelmed, confused or frozen by emotional intensity.

Empathy: Cognitive empathy involves putting yourself in another person's shoes. Physical and emotional empathy involve resonating with another person, nervous system to nervous system.

Empowerment: Feeling your capacity to take action on your own priorities, and make a difference in the world.

Fawning: A social threat response involving accommodation and subservient behavior.

Fight/Flight: The revved-up, sympathetic threat response.

Find Home in Our Core: Home base in your body can be sensed anywhere along the length of your core: head, throat, heart, solar plexus, belly, pelvic floor. Noticing and naming our core helps us return to it. Any place you find your core in your body is a good place to start tracking your embodied self: head, heart, belly...

Freeze: The very low energy, parasympathetic threat response.

Give the Body a Voice: This means to notice and acknowledge our *body up* awareness, and then give it high priority in decision making.

Intention: A goal or purpose that organizes our thinking and behavior.

Nervous System: The physical system that coordinates our external behavior and our internal functioning by transmitting signals to and from different parts of the body via nerves, hormones, and other signal cells. The nervous system detects changes in the internal and external environment and coordinates a response to those changes. The Voluntary Nervous System produces conscious movement and speech.

Neuroception and **Perception:** Neuroception detects threat before it comes to conscious awareness. It is our fast, more primitive threat response system. Perception registers in our newer, slower, more complex, cortical circuits. The amygdala reacts to a neuroception of threat about half a second before conscious perception notices anything.

Parasympathetic Nervous System: The part of the nervous system that calms us down for rest and digestion, or turns our energy way down in a freeze/hide/dissociate response, where it can be hard to move, talk or even think.

Piezoelectricity: Fascia and tendons are piezoelectric. When we stretch tendons, it compresses their molecular structure and produces a noticeable electrical sensation. In Piezoelectric Arms (P. 191) we use this stretch to wake up sensation in the body. Piezoelectricity is a property of some metals. If you run electricity through them, their molecular structure compresses. Conversely, If you compress their molecular structure, they produce an electrical charge.

Post Traumatic Stress Disorder (PTSD): Dysregulation in the nervous system, left over from trauma. Peter Levine PhD, founder of Somatic Experiencing® says, "Trauma is in the nervous system, not in the event." When there is PTSD, there is always relational trauma because it means our tribe has failed to help us heal.

Relaxed Responses: The autonomic nervous system's responses to a sense of safety. The social nervous system's relaxed response is compassionate and inclusive, "How can we make this work for everyone?" The relaxed but energized sympathetic response is often called, "Play". (I call it, Happy Puppy to give an example of being relaxed but energized.) The relaxed parasympathetic response is, Rest and Digest.

Regulating for Social Engagement: Adjusting the state of our nervous system to supply blood flow to the brain. The complex circuitry of our social brain requires a great deal of oxygen to stay organized and fully functional. With insufficient oxygen, the social brain goes more primitive and disorganized. Co-regulation is a very efficient way to regulate for social engagement.

Regulation: The ongoing process of shifting our bodily systems to be ready and available for the task at hand, be it rest, healing, relating, public speaking, or self-protection.

Co-Regulation: Using our connection with each other to shift emotional gears, or to stay steady in challenging situations. It is cooperative, and two-way. Like cooperation, co-regulation is interactive, by definition. Together, we are each regulating our own nervous system. It is a way we can support another person while benefitting rather than depleting ourselves. Co-regulation means good for you, and good for me too.

Dysregulation: This means our nervous system does not adjust for the situation at hand. We may be revved up when we want to sleep, frozen when we need to take action, or anxious, combative, or misattuned when we want to reach for attuned connection.

Reregulation: Shifting out of dysregulation and into adaptive states. Shifting out of threat responses as soon as they are not needed is the most important form of reregulation. Co-regulation helps us reregulate fast.

Self-Regulation: Regulating ourselves, both in solo space and in relational space. We learn basic self-regulation skills, or lack of them, from our early caregivers.

Solo Regulation: Regulating ourselves, when we are alone. For basic solo regulation, breathe and move in an organized way.

Relational Space: Being with another person (or mammal), and noticing it.

Relational Trauma: Trauma from rape or the death of a loved one is relational trauma. It can make intimacy or any human connection feel dangerous. (Trauma from earthquakes and most traffic accidents is non-relational.) See also PTSD and Trauma.

Rhythm and **Timing in BCR:** Attuning to each others' rhythm and using sensitive timing is an important way we communicate that someone matters to us. It cuts through shame. Insisting on controlling rhythm and timing reads as dominance.

Shame: A powerful emotion and set of physical responses. It can freeze us down or rev us up. It is an extremely aversive relational experience. We may organize our whole reality to avoid it. To survive, we need to belong to a group, and we need to matter to some individuals. Shame warns us that we may stand to lose important relationships. Sharing weight helps us feel we belong. Others attuning to our rhythms helps us feel that we matter.

Sharing Weight: Resting some or all of our weight on another person, or receiving the weight of another. It need not involve touch.

Social Engagement System AKA Social Nervous System: The newest layer of our autonomic nervous system, in terms of evolution (according to Porges' Polyvagal Theory). It adjusts our system for communication, sending blood to the complex, energy-consuming networks in the brain, for coordinating speech, and the Elements of Attunement. The social threat response, (my hypothesis) is "us against them or it." The relaxed response is cooperative, inclusive.

Stabilization: Settling the nervous system in a steadier state, after an overwhelming or intense experience.

Sympathetic Nervous System: The part of the nervous system that revs us up for fight/flight, wakes us up in the morning, and energizes us for work and play.

Threat Responses: Physiological strategies for responding to survival threats. Three threat responses evolved with The Three Layer ANS (p. 64). There is the social threat response (my hypothesis) us or me, against him, her, them, or it. Here we are geared for social engagement and blood flow is directed to the complex oxygen-hungry, social circuitry of the brain. There is the revved-up threat response of fight/flight, where the blood is directed to the muscles for movement. And there is the freezy, shutdown, dissociative threat response, where the metabolism drops and it can be hard to move, talk or even think.

Tracking Self and Other: In BCR, this means noticing our own experience (sensations, emotions, and thoughts) and also paying attention to another person's experience, their likely sensations, emotions, and thoughts.

Trauma: Trauma means we could not protect ourselves and our nervous system got overwhelmed by intensity and/or complexity. Trauma may be relational as in abuse, or non-relational as in an earthquake.

Trauma Triggers: A person, place, date, sensation, or experience that trips re-association with a traumatic memory that may still be overwhelming, or at least upsetting.

Up-Regulation: To shift from lower energy states to higher energy states: getting going, revving up your sympathetic nervous system to wake up from sleep, energize for work or play, or to spill anxiety so you can downshift more easily.

Window of Presence: The range of nervous system states in which we can stay present, organized, and at choice. In our window, we think clearly and do not get carried away by our emotions. When we push the edges of our window too far, getting too revved up or too frozen down, the nervous system gets disorganized. We get more and more uncoordinated in our movement, primitive in our reactions, and black-and-white in our thinking.

Appendix F: List of Figures

Appendix G: List of Teaching Videos

List of Teaching Videos (continued)

QR code for teaching videos webpage
https://wecoregulate.com/
coregulation-revolution-videos/

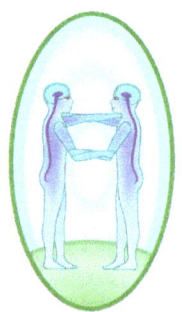

The Center For Body Up Co-Regulation

www.WeCoregulate.com

QR code for all teaching videos webpage
https://wecoregulate.com/coregulation-
revolution-videos/

QR code for all BCR demo videos webpage
https://wecoregulate.com/new-body-up-
coregulation-video-library/

QR code for The Practice Pie webpage
https://wecoregulate.com/practice-pie/

QR code for WeCoregulate.com
https://wecoregulate.com/

Notes

Practice Notes